SCM STUDYGUIDE TO
PHILOSOPHY AND CHRISTIAN FAITH

SCM STUDYGUIDE TO PHILOSOPHY AND CHRISTIAN FAITH

Ben Pugh

scm press

© Ben Pugh 2018

Published in 2018 by SCM Press
Editorial office
3rd Floor, Invicta House,
108–114 Golden Lane,
London EC1Y 0TG, UK
www.scmpress.co.uk

SCM Press is an imprint of Hymns Ancient & Modern Ltd (a registered charity)

Hymns Ancient & Modern® is a registered trademark of Hymns Ancient & Modern Ltd
13A Hellesdon Park Road, Norwich,
Norfolk NR6 5DR, UK

British Library Cataloguing in Publication data

A catalogue record for this book is available
from the British Library

978 0 334 05710 9

Typeset by Regent Typesetting
Printed and bound by
Ashford Colour Press

Contents

To the second year BA Theology students of Cliff College, whose enthusiastic participation in classes on 'Contemporary Issues in Philosophy and Ethics' contributed to the shape of this book.

Also to the staff of Hallward Library at the University of Nottingham.

Introduction

The challenges that Western culture keeps posing to the Christian faith are ever new – and yet maybe never wholly new. What is for sure is that the goalposts keep changing. This study guide will, I hope, equip you to understand the culture-shaping beliefs that are driving the kinds of questions it brings to faith. But the aim in introducing you to the discipline of philosophy is not merely a rearguard action. It is not as though all we need are weapons for our apologetic battles with people who have very different worldviews to our own – perish the thought. I am a very peace-loving sort of person. I have an instinctive distaste for the idea of humiliating atheists in public debate. I see the discipline of philosophy rather as a skill to learn, a language to acquire or as a lens to add. Let's take the last of these first. I believe it is just as necessary to add philosophy to our collection of lenses as it is to have biblical studies, church history, systematic theology and practical theology. I find that the greater the number of different angles from which I am able to view this thing called Christianity, the simpler, the nobler, the more magnificent and worthy of my faith it becomes. By way of contrast, I find that the more I look at Christianity through only one lens the more complicated, less certain, more doubtful it becomes. Philosophy seems to be an especially important lens to use. Philosophers themselves seem to occupy a broad range of estimations of their own importance. Some, such as the rationalists perhaps, seem to see themselves as standing outside of the flux of everyday life like an umpire at a tennis match judging everyone else's wrong moves. Others, such as the early Wittgenstein and Richard Rorty, seem to see themselves as finishing the business of philosophy altogether and making it redundant. I suppose both positions could be seen as equally self-important in different ways. The truth seems to be that, while no philosophical system is perspective-free and no philosophy gives us a complete picture of reality (and some philosophers make a point of not doing so), yet all the philosophies in this book do succeed in elevating us. They lift us up beyond the confines of our particular discipline. They don't quite give us a bird's-eye view of it, but they do give us an elevated perspective which allows us to see our discipline interlacing with other disciplines and with life itself. This is why researchers, in whatever discipline they are working in, will typically invoke the name of a philosopher somewhere in their methodology section. They will say that they are working with this 'epistemology' or assuming that 'ontology'. I have come to love more and more the way philosophy concerns itself with the really big questions of life. There is something about asking those big questions with the philosophers that allows me then to return to my theologizing or my biblical study with fresh confidence. Philosophy makes you feel like you know what you're doing for once, however fleeting that feeling may be!

I mentioned that philosophy is a language to acquire. To help with this, most chapters have a glossary of some sort, some of which will be revision from previous chapters and others will be new terms pertinent to the new chapter. Sometimes I provide a 'Terminology Time-out' when I'm aware that I have been using a lot of technical vocabulary and a pause might be needed so that we can examine each term. At other times, rather like someone teaching a language in class, I will throw in unexplained terminology that is new, but you can tell by the way I'm using it what it means. In all these ways I am catering to the fact that, for most theology students, learning abstract philosophical concepts involves literally learning a new language, a language that the initiated converse in with ease but which leaves the uninitiated completely baffled. Soon, you too will know that language, and I am going to help you converse in it.

I also mentioned that philosophy is a skill to learn. The way skills are learned is through application: you try them out. This is why there are regular pauses for reflection or for discussion with others. You will be asked, for example, to think of a film or book that seems to express elements of existentialism or postmodernism, or to describe how something very like idealism can sometimes show itself in Sunday morning ministry. This is more than light relief; it is an essential part of the learning process, especially important when studying philosophers as they tend to speak in the abstract almost all the time. It is only when we apply philosophy that the lights go on in our thinking and we realize we might be starting to become a bit of a Platonist or an existentialist. We suddenly see the benefit of seeing life from the viewpoint of a philosopher.

Lastly, I will not be guiding you into trying to fit your faith into a philosophy and twisting and distorting it or lopping bits off in the process. In relation to your faith it is only a lens, though a very important one, and it is only a language, not a replacement for the living or written Word, and it is only a skill through which you can learn to express your faith better in the world today.

I sincerely pray that this book will be a great blessing to you, bringing within your reach concepts that you never knew about or which were going right 'over your head' before.

Let's begin straightaway with our first glossary:

Ontology: An aspect of philosophy that seeks to answer the question: What is there?

Epistemology: An aspect of philosophy that seeks to answer the question: How do we know what is there?

Metaphysics: Seeks to answer the question: Why is there anything there at all?

Dualism: The sharp distinction between material things and non-material.

Forms: In Plato, the unseen original versions of the copies we encounter in life.

Scepticism: The admission of non-certainty about the reliability of information received via sense data, and any knowledge purporting to be based on it.

1

Understanding Plato

Chapter Outline

1 Introduction

The safest general characterization of the European philosophical tradition is that it consists of a series of footnotes to Plato.[1]

You may consider yourself entirely unfamiliar with the thought of Plato (c.423/8–c.347 BC), but consider the following words and concepts:

Idea, ideal: 'in an ideal world', theory and practice, absolutes, things 'universally' true, 'the good, the true and the beautiful', essences, substances, a 'particular instance' of something, dialogue, definition.

These concepts are fundamental to the way Westerners have tended to think. Where other cultures think mostly in terms of concrete reality and then tack on to that some religious but unverifiable beliefs about a spiritual realm that is tied up with it, in the West we pride ourselves on being able to think abstractly as well as concretely. This abstract thinking differs from the religious or mythical mindset in that it claims that its particular abstractions are objectively and self-evidently true and real, more real (some Platonists have claimed) than the physical world itself. In other words, we often derive from particular instances of, say, justice, the existence of an ideal or absolute justice that is the perfect version of particular laws that we enact. Where we depart from that way of thinking is in casuistic law: the passing of laws purely on the basis of precedent rather than some overarching principle. But the very fact that we like overarching principles betrays the very long shadow that Plato has cast. The very attachment to ideologies, especially in the political realm, is, in part at least, a legacy of Plato which is likely to persist despite the ravages of the postmodern revolt against him.

Platonic thinking has tended to create a dualistic mindset that places the unseen and the seen in radically different categories. Our education system assumes this division: we sharply differentiate theory from practice, the humanities from the sciences. And, in our politics, we sharply distinguish between the sacred and the secular, and the private and the public, placing religion in the private world and secular thinking in the public. In reasoning, we distinguish between the deductive and the inductive, the rational and the empirical. In leadership we place great value in having a 'vision' and strategize for that vision to become 'reality' via the use of mission statements that attempt to give an abstract vision some concrete and achievable form. In Trinitarian theology, we make a distinction between the divine 'essence' that suffuses the Godhead and the three particular 'subsistences', or 'substances'. We could go on, but, in order to evaluate whether these things are good or bad, we need to go back to their source.

2 Plato's Theory of Forms

Athens had seen much unrest and war and there was a desire to begin the process of building a more civilized and enduring society, hence Plato's interest in politics exhibited in his famous *The Republic*. For Socrates, and his pupil Plato, a big part of the task of rebuilding society involved philosophy. It was hoped that if people could just be shown how to think better, society itself would be better. And this was the chief motive for founding Plato's Academy. The existence of all modern philosophy, and of Western academia itself, begins here. By the way, nearly all the most important writings of Plato are not written in the first person but are reports of dialogues that take place between Plato's mentor Socrates (who left us no writings at all) and some other interlocutor. In the early Dialogues, Plato poses quite successfully as nothing more than the scribe. In the later Dialogues, Plato's own distinct philosophy is seen to emerge, even though this too tends to be put into the mouth of Socrates. Scholars differ on the exact order of the Dialogues but the latest one-volume compilation of all the works of Plato, arranges them in a plausible chronological order.[2]

Many Philosophers prior to Plato (we call them Presocratic) had ideas about what the essential nature of the universe was. For Thales, everything was made of water; for Anaximenes, it was air; while for Xenophanes, all was earth. These became known as the 'elements'. But for Plato's Socrates, the defining of things by reference to other physical things was not enough. The Dialogues aim for an absolute definition of things, usually things such as justice or the good or the beautiful that do not have a physical existence as such but which can be instanced for particular examples. He opposed attempts to only define things by describing particular examples of them. He was in earnest pursuit of the fundamental Idea or ideal Form lying behind them.

> The Many are to be understood, not by seeking their physical constituents, nor even the efficient causes of their motions and changes, but by isolating and understanding the Idea to which we are referring when we use a certain word . . . Plato had grasped the truth that conceptual understanding is different from natural science, and just as important.[3]

In seeking after this, it is clear that there was a conviction about each individual soul's pre-existence in an ideal state in which the perfect versions of everything were literally 'seen' (the Greek *idea* is all to do with sight. From *ideō*, I see). In this life we still possess a dim recollection of these ideal Forms from what we saw before we were born. In *Phaedo*,[4] Socrates is shown arguing for this on the basis of the fact that no two physical things can ever be exactly equal. One will, even if only to a tiny degree and because of the most miniscule imperfection, be slightly bigger or smaller. Therefore, our strong concept of equality cannot have been derived from what we have seen in this life but must be a memory of a previous life:

> Then before we began to see or hear or use the other senses we must somewhere have gained a knowledge of abstract or absolute equality, if we were to compare with it the equals which we perceive by the sense, and see that all such things yearn to be like abstract equality but fall short of it.[5]

Plato wants to know what we really mean, for instance, by a triangle. We do not, in the first place, mean any particular triangle since all triangles differ. We mean the Idea or Form of a triangle that the word or concept 'triangle' reminds us of: quite literally, that is, from a previous life. This is even truer of higher concepts such as beauty. In fact, the higher you go, the harder it becomes to define a thing by reference to particular examples revealed to the senses. We are compelled to make reference to some unseen realm from which all this earth's particulars receive their definition and hence their true meaning and purpose. Hare highlights the shift in thinking we must make today just to be able to appreciate Plato: 'Whereas for us a definition is one kind of analytically or necessarily true proposition, for him it was a description of a mentally visible and eternally true object.'[6]

It may already be clear why this way of doing philosophy (often referred to as metaphysics or ontology) has been so appealing to Christians, Plato having been by far the most useful dialogue partner to Christian theology ever. He posited for us the existence of a realm that is neither internal to us, and hence restricted to our reasoning (though certainly discoverable by it), nor external to us, and hence revealed only to our senses. To employ the language of eighteenth-century scientific method, it entails neither 'rationalism' nor 'empiricism'. Plato thinks there is a third option, a transcendent realm. And not only is this realm no less real than the other two realms, it has a title to be *more* real than them and the true source of their existence. Christians were not slow to identify this transcendent realm as heaven and the ideal Forms as thoughts in the mind of God. They were quick, however, to dispense with the idea of the pre-existence of the soul.

Though discussed quite extensively here and there in the Dialogues, the clearest short statement of Plato's theory of Ideas is actually in one of his letters:

For each thing that there is three things are necessary if we are to come by knowledge: first, the name, second, the definition, and third, the image. Knowledge itself is a fourth thing, and there is a fifth thing that we have to postulate, which is that which is knowable and truly real. To understand this, consider the following example and regard it as typical of everything. There is something called a circle; it has a name, which we have just this minute used. Then there is its definition, a compound of nouns and verbs. We might give 'The figure whose limit is at every point equidistant from its centre' as the definition of whatever is round, circular or a circle. Third, there is what we draw, or rub out, or rotate, or cancel. The circle itself which all these symbolize does not undergo any such change and is a quite different thing. In the fourth place we have knowledge, understanding and true opinion on these matters – these, collectively, are in our minds and not in sounds or bodily shapes, and thus are clearly distinct from the circle itself and from the three entities already mentioned. Of all these items, it is understanding that is closest to the fifth in kinship and likeness; the others are at a greater distance. What is true of round is also true of straight, of colour, of good and beautiful, and just; of natural and manufactured bodies; of fire, water and the other elements; of all living beings and moral characters; of all that we do and undergo. In each case, anyone who totally fails to grasp the first four things will never fully possess knowledge of the fifth.[7]

So then, transcending, the word 'circle', as well as the verbal attempt to define the qualities that a circle always has, and above our attempts to represent circles visually, is our knowledge of what a circle is. It is simply a mental concept. But none of these things is 'the circle itself'.[8] And as far as Plato was concerned, the circle-ness of all circles, the very circle itself, has a real existence. He does not say where. He does not imagine some perfect circle in heaven, but he posits that the realm of absolute definition is real and the source of all lesser realities. And this realm is not subject to change. It is a realm of perfectly static essences.

The whole concept arises out of the desire to define and understand the ultimate meaning of life itself by being able to define everything we come across in life. It is a way of extending the thought that red things have redness in common to the thought beyond this that there must therefore be a singular (and real) thing called redness in order for red things to really have redness in common. Redness hence becomes a real entity that, if taken seriously enough, has a higher status than particular red things.[9]

Reflection

Just for a moment, let's try thinking like Plato. Imagine he is with you in a local park. In the playground there are objects that seem to be almost perfectly circular or square, for example the roundabout or some square panelling on a climbing frame. There are also some magnificent trees: a huge spreading oak, though even this, on closer inspection has a dead branch. Plato would point out that none of the things we see are perfect, ideal examples of their kind. Everything, if you look closely enough, has imperfections, and these mean that there is nothing in this world that is fully in possession of the properties it is supposed to have. Many things, such as a younger oak tree that has recently been planted, seem to be on their way to becoming what they are, while other things, such as the rusty old swings that need replacing are on their way to becoming less than what they are. Yet nothing in this life has ever been perfectly what it is. But the very fact that we are aware of this points to the existence of a perfect version of everything. We can use words to define it, and we might attempt to draw the perfect thing we have in our minds, but, try as we might, the ideal version of everything seems to be a mental concept. Plato would insist it does not stop here, however. The buck cannot be allowed to stop with the mind. After all, how did this notion of the ideal, which is more real, more fully itself, than any particular examples of it, get there? We all have it. Even people who live in non-technocratic cultures, where access to manufactured objects whose geometric qualities seem to approach perfection – even people who live in huts – have a concept of a perfect circle. How is this so, especially seeing as no one has ever physically seen a perfect version of anything whatsoever? Plato would try to convince us that the ultimately real, the *really* real, all that which fully is, cannot be something that is limited to our minds, since then it would not be real at all. Something limited only to our minds could not impart to imperfect objects that reflection or vestige of the fully real that they all have. And as for the things in this life, they are sometimes quite brilliant, sometimes not so brilliant, sometimes on the way up to fullness, sometimes on their way down. Reality, therefore, is primarily transcendent. The fully real transcends our minds, our representations and our world of objects.

This runs in exactly the opposite direction to our culture right now, which is why Plato is starting to sound more and more foreign. In our culture, we have a high regard for 'down-to-earth' people because we think they are *more* not *less* in touch with reality. Our notion of being realistic is tied to an ability to accept this world of change and decay as being entirely definitive. The pursuit of any knowledge of anything beyond this transient world is looked upon as a foolhardy and ultimately doomed quest for the un-knowable.

What would Plato want to say to our culture?

3 The Six Criteria

So, what qualifies as a Form? What qualifies as a category (Aristotle's word) that absolutely defines every particular instance?

1 *Participation.* Every particular instance has this quality in common. And it is the particular instances that participate in the ideal Form, rather than the other way around, hence a kind of a hierarchy is created, hence the next point.
2 *Distinctiveness.* The defining Form or ideal is distinct from particular instances of it. It is not the instances themselves but the Idea. Instances are inferior and imperfect copies of it.
3 *Self-predication.* The Idea of a thing is that thing, the very essence of it, not a pale reflection but the thing itself. It has to be the definitive essence and very being of the quality in question to be able to impart to each instance the quality that it possesses. It is like the concept of 'self-existence' in the Christian theology of the attributes of God. God receives nothing but is the fountain of all other existing things. He is self-sufficient and a source, never a needy receptacle. Forms are likewise.
4 *Purity.* The Idea of the thing is nothing other than the thing. It is not the thing plus something else. To participate in another Idea is to be inferior to it, hence another avenue to a hierarchical view of the metaphysical world, which would later prove theologically rich for Neoplatonists such as Pseudo-

Dionysius, and also for the Gnostics. This concept of purity, especially when applied to God himself, is largely the thing behind the Christological debates of the church fathers: how could a being with an earthly and therefore derived and inferior existence be of the same substance as the one God? He can participate in God but not *be* God.

5 *Uniqueness.* The defining Idea is 'really, truly, altogether'[10] the thing. Nothing else can be that thing to the same degree. Particular instances are thought to be on the way to being more like the ideal or less like the ideal. They are caught between being and non-being. They are becoming. This opens up the idea of process in Plato, which Alfred North Whitehead made full use of in his process theology.

6 *Transcendence.* The Ideas are eternal, unchanging, undivided and not perceptible by the senses. Everything that participates in them is part of the world of change and decay. This became a leading idea in the Eastern fathers and defined their understanding of what we need saving from through participating in the divine nature. What we need saving from on this reckoning is change and decay, rather than sin or sins. For Plato, the most exalted and sublime Idea of all was the Idea of the Good:

> So that what gives truth to the things known and the power to know to the knower is the form of the good. And though it is the cause of knowledge and truth, it is also an object of knowledge. Both knowledge and truth are beautiful things, but the good is other and more beautiful than they.[11]

4 Plato's Ethics

First, I need to introduce the term 'deontology'. This is the word we use for a duty-based system of ethics, as opposed to a 'consequentialist' or 'virtue' based system. We will look at examples of both these other systems in due course. Plato begins to introduce ethical reflection by trying to determine how we decide, in a deontological way, what the standard is. He reflects upon what it looks like to meet the standard using the term 'pious'. Via Socrates, he explores this in his *Euthyphro* dialogue:

Just consider this question: Is that which is holy loved by the gods because it is holy, or is it holy because it is loved by the gods?[12]

This has given rise to what is termed the Euthyphro Dilemma, which is explained very clearly by the early modern philosopher Gottfried Leibniz:

It is generally agreed that whatever God wills is good and just. But there remains the question whether it is good and just because God wills it or whether God wills it because it is good and just; in other words, whether justice and goodness are arbitrary or whether they belong to the necessary and eternal truths about the nature of things.[13]

Is good what God commands or does goodness exist apart from God's standards? If the former, then even murder would be good if God chose to call it such. If the latter, then moral goodness exists by itself independently of God so that even he is accountable to it. What is the relationship between divine commands and ethics? Can we build our ethics on God's command to annihilate the Canaanites, for example? One way of defending theological voluntarism (the preference for the idea that good is what God wills and nothing more) is to liken the morally reprehensible to the logically impossible. We would not say that God's absolute power or sovereignty is threatened by the fact that he cannot do something logically nonsensical such as decide that circles are squares. Likewise, we can balance God's absolute will with the fact that he willed to make a universe that is structured in such a way that certain things will normally be acknowledged as wrong.

Perhaps it was Plato's uncertainty about ethical things that allowed him to become the first eugenicist. Book V of his *The Republic* contains extensive discussion about how to breed more people of the Guardian class, the tone of which becomes more and more outrageous. One wonders whether some of it was intended as humour:

It follows from our previous arrangements, first, that the best men must have sex with the best women as frequently as possible, while the opposite is true of the most inferior men and women, and second, that if our herd is to be of the highest possible quality, the former's offspring must be reared but not the latter's.[14]

> **Reflection**
>
> Consider acts of terror committed in the name of God. What side of the Euthyphro Dilemma do you think the perpetrators fall on?

5 The Platonic Schools

Old, Middle and New Academies

The Academy that Plato founded (mid 380s BC) in Athens lasted for over a thousand years before eventually being shut down by Justinian I, the Eastern Roman Emperor, in AD 529. This was the very first academy as we know it today, the first academic institution. What we call the 'Old Academy' is the one headed up by Plato himself. There was probably no curriculum but instead a method of constant enquiry and dialogue about issues of ultimate significance. He was succeeded by a number of 'scholarchs' until, in c.266 BC, Arcelaus brought a sceptic emphasis to the Academy. This ushered in the period of the Middle Academy. A sceptic approach denies the possibility of ever knowing absolute truth. This mood changed with the New Academy and the shift in Platonist thinking away from Athens itself to the wider Greek world and the beginnings of Middle Platonism. The Academy at Athens was revived during the craze for Neoplatonism before being closed because of its paganism – which, given the extensive borrowing by Christianity of Neoplatonist ideas both at that time and in the centuries that were to follow, was ironic.

Middle Platonism

Just to confuse you, as well as the Old, Middle and New Academies, there are also three phases in Platonic thought: there is Plato himself, then there is Middle Platonism, and then Neoplatonism. All Platonisms since have basically been revivals of one or a combination of these three.

Having already looked at Plato himself, we can skip to Middle Platonism. The Middle Platonists are important to New Testament scholars because by the time they come along we are already emerging into the world of the first century. The two most celebrated names in Middle Platonism are Philo, the first-century Jewish thinker who is thought to have influenced whoever it was that wrote the New Testament book of Hebrews, and Plutarch. Plutarch (AD c.46–c.120) is most famous for his *Lives*, which were the main inspiration behind Shakespeare's Roman plays: *Julius Caesar*, *Anthony and Cleopatra* and *Coriolanus*. But aside from this highly significant historical work, Plutarch also wrote a commentary on Plato's *Timaeus* and a piece of philosophical ethics called *Moralia*, which we will shortly have reason to look at in connection with the apostle Paul.

The beginning of the Middle Platonist period is around 90 BC and ends the sceptic phase of the Middle Academy. Despite the tentative and provisional mood of Plato's Dialogues, which the sceptics of the Middle Academy thought they were emulating, Middle Platonic philosophers recognized the need for greater certainty if any progress in thought is to be possible. To correct this, they seem to have ended up becoming more dogmatic than Plato himself would ever have been. However, this proved to be not all bad as it paved the way for real progress in developing the starting points of Plato into the developed doctrines of Platon*ism*. This new mood pushed back the forces of scepticism and Epicureanism – the two philosophies the Neoplatonist Plotinus would go on to vehemently oppose – and brought Plato (and Aristotle) back onto centre stage, a position they more or less retained until the early modern period.

Besides the greater dogmatism, another defining shift that took place with Middle Platonism was the shift to eclecticism. These thinkers were eclectic enough to bring a wide range of ideas to the light of Platonic thought. The most significant piece of eclecticism was the combining of Plato with Aristotle. Hence, in Philo (who probably was not the first to think of this) there is a combining of Plato's Idea of the Good with Aristotle's idea of the Unmoved Mover. And there is a further combining of Plato's theory of Forms with Aristotle's conception of God as Mind. The result, in Philo, is a picture of God much more conformable to the God of Judaism in which the Forms become thoughts in the mind of God. However, this hybrid of Plato and Aristotle gave us an extremely transcendent and remote being that could only operate via spiritual intermediaries. He could not be directly known.

For the Middle Platonists, matter was mostly understood to be the source of all evil, but they believed that God transformed it by making the world out of it and infusing it with his soul: the World-Soul. However, matter still retained its evil properties.

Middle Platonism forms part of the worldview of New Testament times and also informs the thought of the apologists and of the church fathers of the Alexandrian tradition such as Clement and Origen. In particular, the likening of Christ to the Middle Platonist 'Logos' or intelligence that lies behind all creation seems to be a practice that goes all the way back to John the Evangelist. I did promise we would look at Paul, but before we do that it seems right to complete the picture of the Platonisms and take a look at Neoplatonism.

6 Neoplatonism

Neoplatonism is almost entirely the product of the writings of Plotinus (c.204–70). His massive work, the *Enneads* (Augustine's main source of ideas other than the Bible) has been described as 'once elusive and extraordinarily impressive'.[15] He himself merely thought of himself as an orthodox Platonist and was very opposed to the heretical Platonism of the Gnostics. He was the custodian of Platonic truth. Porphyry is also formative of Neoplatonism, and Iamblichus was not without significance.

Neoplatonism is distinct in that it is entirely a philosophy of religion and does not reflect the more wide-ranging interests of Plato himself. Incidentally, it is also a devoutly pagan religious outlook, despite its wholesale adoption by Christian thinkers. It bases itself on the aspect of Plato's philosophy of religion that had been indebted to the cult of Orpheus. Prominent Orphic ideas included the notion, first, that the soul is imprisoned within the body as a punishment for prior misdemeanours and, second, the notion of the eternal punishment or reward of the disembodied soul after death.

Based on a loose reading of a few of Plato's Dialogues, Neoplatonism espoused the following three principles, all three of which were decisive in the formation of medieval Christian mysticism. The following can be found in Plotinus's *Enneads* V–VI:

The One

This is the one, infinite source of all being and, crucially, beyond being itself. As such, the One is also beyond good, beyond just, beyond any attribute that might be accorded. All other existing things are generated by the One and permeated by the One.

The Mind

Also called *nous*, or intellect, understanding, it has a similar function to the idea of the Logos, which was the Middle Platonists' preferred term. The Neoplatonist concept of Mind can be pictured as a big circle that you could draw around the central circle, which is the One. The Demiurge is an unintended emanation from the Mind and has created all matter. The next circle is as follows:

The World-Soul

Draw a third circle around the Mind circle and call this the World-Soul. This is the intermediary between the Mind and the phenomenal world, the world of matter. The material world is the space still left around the outer circle of the World-Soul. If you think this is starting to look like a trinity, you'd be right, and Plotinus, though remaining a pagan, was aware of the Christian theology that was emerging, as well as Gnosticism, and his philosophy was formed in opposition to and in dialogue with, these two systems.

But there is more to it even than this. Humans, according to Plotinus, live on the very line that marks the outer circle off from the world of matter. We live on the rim. In our natural state, we look outwards to the physical world that keeps stimulating our senses and desires and makes us set our minds on all that it offers.[16] The mystical path is for those who are able to renounce the world and look inwards at the World-Soul which all souls share, and then beyond that to the divine Mind that gives meaning to everything, and then beyond that to the ineffable One that is beyond words to describe. This mystical path is the true original of which all the Christian mystical paths from Pseudo-Dionysius onwards are adaptations. And because the One is solitary, the pursuit of mystical union with the One must involve solitary contemplation, hence Plotinus's most famous phrase: 'the flight of the alone to the Alone'.[17] This solitary quest proves to be a search for the source of one's identity, a 'search for the Beautiful itself and the source of love'.[18] To a great extent it is the solitary quest that gives the word 'Monk' its true meaning. It is derived from the Greek *monachos*, a solitary one, as used by Pseudo-Dionysius.[19] He thus coins the term for Christianity.

7 Preliminary Conclusion

We have now become acquainted with Plato's leading ideas and have already begun to see more and more links between these ideas as they took shape in Middle Platonism and Neoplatonism and Christian thought. We have seen, in particular, that the kinds of Greek thinking that were the most influenced by Middle and Neo- Platonism gave rise to a concept of God that makes him extraordinarily remote from us: a static and unfeeling essence. This may allow you to see the reasons behind the current reaction within Christian thought against this concept of God. We wish to correct this idea by reference to the kind of being that we may more confidently identify as the God of Abraham, Isaac and Jacob, and the God and Father of Jesus Christ: the Living God.

8 Plato and Christianity

Possible traces in Paul

For some time since the emergence in the late 1970s of the New Perspective on Paul, it has not been at all fashionable in academic circles to attribute any Greco-Roman influence to Paul. If it is not Jewish, it is not a Pauline influence. That mood is changing, and a consensus is beginning to emerge that the New Perspective case has been overstated (and overrated). An example of a return to Greco-Roman sources for interpreting Paul has been the work of Emma Wasserman.[20]

While she is keen to point out that she is not saying that Paul is a philosopher, Wasserman affirms that Paul is clearly familiar with the Greek moral traditions that were the product of the Middle Platonism of Plutarch and Philo. But she goes further than this and affirms that in letters such as Romans Paul is borrowing more than the outward forms of expression: he is allowing the doctrines of Middle Platonism to shape his argument.

Plutarch, in his *Moralia*, Philo in his *Legatio ad Gaium* (The Delegation to Gaius) and, later, Galen in his *On the Passions and Errors of the Soul* developed the kinds of ideas that first appear in Plato's *Republic* (Books IV and IX). Here Plato compares the uncontrolled force of appetite in a person's life to a tyrannical ruler who takes over a city. In *Phaedrus* 253c–254e (and *Timaeus* 86b–90a) Plato uses his famous analogy of a chariot rider with two horses. The rider is the *logistikon* or reasoning, the part of human nature that is capable of reasoned objective detachment. It is rational. One of the horses is easier to control than the other. This easier one is the 'spirited' or *thumoeidēs* part of our nature: the part of us that is emotional and expresses deep desires. The more difficult horse is our 'appetitive' or *epithumētikon* side, the part of us that craves food, drink and sex. These too easily become gluttony, drunkenness and lust.

In the Middle Platonists, this tripartite model became simplified into a two-part struggle, a tug of war, if you like, between the reasonable and reasoning side to us and the irrational passions and appetites that forever threaten to upset the balance. Emotions and appetites merge into a single force that pulls against our rationality. In *Delegation to Gaius* 3:116–17, Philo likens these passions and appetites to an evil ruler or monster. These seek to 'make war, enslave, imprison and in some cases even metaphorically kill the mind'.[21]

It looks as though Paul may have simply combined the Hebrew concept of 'sin' with the Middle Platonic ideas about passions and appetites. Like the Middle Platonists, Paul describes sin by personifying it as a power that rules (Romans 6.12), enslaves (6.13, 18, 20; 7.14), makes war (7.23), imprisons (7.23) and kills (7.10, 11, 13). In Middle Platonism, it is reason that must overcome. In Romans 8, it is the Spirit of God that enters in to remedy the situation, though it may be that human reason, now strengthened by the influx of the Holy Spirit is an idea not entirely absent. Similarly, Paul's concept of 'flesh' as the seat of uncontrolled passions and appetites has its nearest precedent conceptually in Plutarch (*Moralia* 101b; 162e; 688d; 734a; 135c; 1087b; 1089e; 1096c).

Taking sin as a representation of the passions illuminates the struggle and conflict in Rom. 6–8 as a specifically Platonic type of struggle between the mind and the passions. Just as Platonists posit fierce, often violent conflict between rational and irrational parts of the soul, so too Paul depicts a war between God and sin in Rom. 6, sin and the mind in Rom. 7, and flesh and spirit in Rom. 8:1–13.[22]

Perhaps a striking thing about Romans 7 is that, despite the obviously conflicted experience portrayed, the mind, the reason, is unswerving in its choice of the right thing. The difficulty lies in carrying it out. This unwavering rightness of reason places the passage within a Middle Platonic cast. Galen, who came later than Paul, did envisage a situation in which the mind gets so accustomed to bad actions having the last word that it begins to follow willingly. This is the condition that we would today describe as 'addiction'.

Gnosticism

Gnosticism first begins to take full shape in a form known as Sethian Gnosticism. This based itself partly on a reading of the early chapters of Genesis and partly on an emerging new form of Platonism: the Neoplatonism that we encountered earlier. They called themselves 'Sethians' because they understood themselves to be descendants of Adam and Eve's third son, Seth, rather than Cain or Abel. And it was Seth that was a carrier of the divine *gnosis* or special knowledge. The Sethians added to the Genesis account an important pre-cosmic back story, but to understand this back story it is worth bearing in mind that their understanding of God was that he cannot be spoken of or comprehended with the unaided intellect. He is, quite literally, the 'Unknown God'. Fortunately, however, this God has a number of emanations (an idea later to dominate Neoplatonism). These come in male and female pairs called aeons. One of these, known as Sophia, decided to create her own set of emanations, without the permission of her fellow aeon colleagues. This upsets the balance of the Pleroma (the fullness, the whole spiritual world) and results in the appearance of the Demiurge (a public worker, a craftsman, artisan), a figure inspired by Plato's *Timaeus*. In Sethian Gnosticism, he takes the form of a serpent with a lion's head. Despite Sophia's efforts to hide this rather hideous and unexpected result of her folly, he escapes with some of her power and goes on to make the physical world that we know today. In this whole system, the spiritual is associated with a light-filled, immediate, intuitive kind of knowing, a first-hand acquaintance with the way things really are, and waking up to it is like Neo in *The Matrix* waking up to the fact that he was not in the real world but a computer simulation. In Gnostic thinking, matter, the opposite of spirit, corresponds to the opposite of knowing: ignorance. So the further down the hierarchy to earth we go, the more ignorance of the real world there is, and the more everything seems to go wrong. So, perhaps rather disturbingly, it is here, with the self-enthroned Demiurge creating the world, that we begin our reading of the Genesis account according to the Sethians. When the Demiurge creates Adam, he unwittingly transmits some of the power he stole from Sophia into Adam – another blunder, though a potentially fortuitous one for anyone among his descendants who wants to recapture this divine spark within themselves. The Demiurge tries to get the power back by extracting a rib, only to find that he has now created Eve. Some of Sophia's spirit then ends up in the Tree of Knowledge, and so the comedy of errors goes on. Seemingly, this divine something or other that keeps jumping about and has a life of its own chose Seth as the person through whom to pass to a certain portion of the human race.

While Gnosticism did not survive, a radically apophatic approach to God did. By apophatic, we mean a way of viewing God as so far beyond words that there is no way of describing what he is, only what he is not or what he is analogous to. This apophaticism was embodied first in the writings of Gregory of Nyssa (c.332–95 BC) and then in the fifth-century Syrian monk whom we call Pseudo-Dionysius. Pseudo-Dionysius was for a long time known as Dionysius the Areopagite in the belief that he was converted when Paul spoke the Mars Hill sermon to the Areopagus in Athens. We will take a closer look at him shortly.

Augustine's Neoplatonism

Augustine of Hippo's (AD 354–430) importance to Christian theology and to Western thought in general is difficult to exaggerate, and plenty has been written of him elsewhere.[23] Here we are interested in the role of Neoplatonic thought in his life. He freely admits to reading the 'books of the Platonists' in Book VII of his Confessions and recalls that their main benefit to him was to disabuse him of his earlier Manichean notions that God was made of matter. His eyes were opened to the fact that God was incorporeal, without any need for a body. His engagement with the Neoplatonists, especially Plotinus and Porphyry, may have been a staging post between his ten-year excursion into the strange religion of the Manichees and his more fully biblical faith of later years. His interest in Neoplatonism flourished at around the same time as his famous conversion in AD 386, which is described in Book VII of *Confessions*. Plotinus was crucial not only via Augustine's own reading of the 'books of the Platonists' but also via the preaching of Ambrose of Milan. Ambrose knew parts of Plotinus's *Enneads*.

The features of Plotinian thought which left an enduring mark upon Augustine's theology are chiefly these:

- The equation is made between Plotinus's divine Mind and the Logos of John's prologue. He is not the first to make this kind of link, and it is highly likely that John is himself using the term in a way that is indebted to both the Jewish ideas about the Word as a semi-personified divine function (Isa. 55.10–11) and a Hellenistic idea already in wide circulation about a universal principle or reason upholding creation called the Logos.
- His belief in the One, derived from Plotinus, leads Augustine to prioritize the oneness of the divine being over his triunity. This sets the stage for a distinctively Western approach to the Trinity, which starts with the question: if God is one how are we to understanding the distinctions? This moves in the opposite direction to the Eastern tradition, which, with the Cappadocians, asks the question: if God is three, how can he also be one? Augustine's answer was that only as we speak of the relations between the three can we preserve a unity of essence and a commonality of action while also being able to describe God as love who can direct his love to a relational 'other' within his own being. Augustine, among many faltering suggestions, came up with the idea that God is Lover (Father), Beloved (Son) and Love (Spirit). It is in this affirmation of relations within the Trinity that Augustine actually departs very definitely from Plotinus, who did not see the One, the Mind and the World-Soul as having any kind of relationship with each other.
- His belief in the importance of the inner self. Augustine is indebted to Plotinus as the philosopher that 'presents the first powerful account of an inner world'.[24] Augustine's move, according to Philip Carey's brilliant little study, is simply to make Plotinus's *shared* inner world made of the faces, as it were, of

all of us turned inwards towards the Mind into an *individual* inner world. He has to make this move because to fail to make it would be to affirm Plotinus's belief that this shared inward turn is possible because of a shared divinity that all souls have. Augustine's doctrine of creation *ex nihilo* – that is, that the created order did not simply emanate from the divine being but was made from nothing and continues to be distinct from him – does not allow this. Creation *ex nihilo* is an especially noteworthy correction of Plotinus. There are about as many of these corrections as there are borrowings. Augustine was a very discerning borrower, which probably explains why his synthesis stood the test of time. The inward turn is still necessary in Augustine's reckoning because of the need, already identified in Plotinus, to turn away from the allurements of the world, but, after this inward turn, there must be an *upward* gaze at the light of the Creator who is above us all. He describes God's light shining over him:

> Under your [God's] guidance I entered into the depths of my soul, and this I was able to do because your aid befriended me. I entered, and with the eye of my soul, such as it was, I saw the Light that never changes casting its rays over the same eye of my soul, over my mind.[25]

Pseudo-Dionysius

Almost nothing certain is known about Pseudo-Dionysius, but one thing that is widely agreed upon is that he is a 'pseudo'. He uses a pseudonym, claiming to be Dionysius the convert of Paul's Mars Hill sermon who is mentioned, alongside a woman called Damaris, as becoming believers (Acts 17:34). The writings of Pseudo-Dionysius have been dated to the fifth or sixth century. However, pseudonymity cannot be allowed to overshadow the power of his writings whose influence upon Western mysticism has been immense. Besides coining the term 'monk' he is also the inventor of the word 'hierarchy'.

Pseudo-Dionysius develops his vision of Christian contemplation in dialogue with Plato's *Symposium*, which says a lot about love, and Plotinus's *Enneads*, which informs his thinking about solitary contemplation. Here is an extract from Pseudo-Dionysius' *Divine Names*:

And, in truth, it must be said too that the very cause of the universe in the beautiful, good superabundance of his benign yearning for all is also carried outside of himself in the loving care he has for everything. He is, as it were, beguiled by goodness, by love, and by yearning and is enticed away from his transcendent dwelling place and comes to abide within all things, and he does so by virtue of his supernatural and ecstatic capacity to remain, nevertheless, within himself.[26]

In dialogue with Plotinus, Pseudo-Dionysius insisted that to be solitary before the One entailed a stripping away, an aloneness that, according to Corrigan, 'signifies primarily that which is without barriers or distinctions which could prevent the most complete union',[27] but it is also an encounter with that which is beyond words and beyond all perception since, by definition, the things that can be perceived and described are precisely the earthly things which need to be turned away from. The Divine is the opposite of all that:

and, Timothy, my friend, my advice to you as you look for a sight of the mysterious things, is to leave behind you everything perceived and understood, everything perceptible and understandable, all that is not and all that is, and, with your understanding laid aside, to strive upward as much as you can toward union with him who is beyond all being and knowledge. By an undivided and absolute abandonment of yourself and everything, shedding all and freed from all, you will be uplifted to the ray of the divine shadow which is above everything that is.[28]

The Cambridge Platonists

The Cambridge Platonists – Henry More, Ralph Cudworth, Benjamin Whichcote, Anne Conway, John Worthington, Jeremy Taylor and others – were a small group of Christian philosophers in seventeenth-century Cambridge who were of the Puritan tradition and were distressed by the growing materialist agendas of new philosophies, especially those of Hobbes and Locke. This was the eve of the Enlightenment when the ideas behind empiricism were just taking shape. The Cambridge Platonists were also opposed to Descartes' notion of an inward thinking self and were keen to reiterate the third option: the transcendent yet imperceptible realm. One of the most provocatively materialist statements had been that of Thomas Hobbes in his *Leviathan*:

> Every part of the Universe, is Body, and that which is not Body, is not part of the Universe: and because the Universe is All, that which is no part of it, is *Nothing*; and consequently *no where*.[29]

In their opposition to such materialism they were joined by the famous Anglo-Irish bishop George Berkeley:

> What Ralph Cudworth, the other Christian Platonists, and Bishop Berkeley all protested was what they conceived to be the naturalizing tendency of the new science and new philosophy, its seemingly inevitable rush to envisage a universe whose reductive explication in terms of material causation was so complete and so exclusive as to render the world entirely opaque and silent about its Maker.[30]

Simone Weil

The French thinker and left-wing political activist Simone Weil (pronounced the French way: 'vale') led a short but remarkable life (1909–43), dying of tuberculosis at the age of 34. The turning point in her life came in 1937 during a visit to Italy when she underwent a powerful conversion. Her faith in Christ was then integrated into her already deep grasp of Plato to transform the latter into a living practical wisdom. Her version of Platonism successfully resisted all the popular caricatures of Platonism as 'otherworldly, dualist, idealist, anticosmic and anti-materialist'.[31] Her brand of mysticism has been branded 'authentic mysticism'[32] because it is resolutely this-worldly, seeking to hold together the paradox of divine perfection and a world full of pain. Even before conversion, Weil had felt the pain of the downtrodden acutely, to the point of having volunteered to serve in the Spanish Civil War.

Weil draws inspiration both from Plato's descriptions of the Good in *The Republic* and his musings about the Beautiful in his *Phaedrus* and *Timaeus*. She sees the beauty in the world as a sacrament which, if attended to puts us in touch with 'absolute Love'.[33] God, according to Weil, 'penetrates the world and envelopes it on all sides'.[34]

She was interested in this ontological participation of the world in God, a kind of reading of Plato which looks at the dependence of all things upon a transcendent reality. This moves in both directions: God gifting things with existence and life, and yet all existence and life continuing to be encompassed by God. This, in fact, seems to be the crucial element that keeps the best Christian Platonisms clearly Christian. The two worlds are neither merged nor separated.

Paul Tyson

A very recent voice in the wilderness is worthy of note. Paul Tyson, formerly of Nottingham University, is clearly influenced by the Radical Orthodoxy (RO) movement and, in finding common cause with RO's disdain for secular modernity, has become one of Plato's very few supporters in theological circles today. He finds in Plato an ally in the quest to assert transcendence in the midst of a culture that has become stultifying in its closed attachment to all that is immanent and earth-bound:

> Modern philosophers will only believe something to be true if it is 'smaller' than our minds, if it fits within what we can, at least in principle, master with our knowledge. Valid knowledge is only that which can be demonstrated in purely rational and empirical terms. This outlook assumes that when it comes to knowledge and meaning, we are at the top of the tree, and whatever we cannot see when we look down does exist . . . we never look above ourselves for knowledge and meaning.[35]

With Plato, Tyson is convinced that, 'the ultimately real is unseen, inherently and eternally meaningful, transcending flux and contingency'.[36]

Reflection

One of the most interesting things about Plato is, as we have seen, the many and wondrous Platonisms that have been developed as people have taken certain trajectories of thought that might be located in only one or two of his Dialogues and followed these through to their logical conclusions.

We have had:

- The scepticism about sensory knowledge of the Middle Academy.
- The synthesis of Plato with Aristotle of Middle Platonism.
- The influence of Middle Platonist morality upon the apostle Paul's concepts of Flesh and Spirit.
- The absurd distortions that resulted from the Gnostic synthesis of Plato's *Timaeus* and *Parmenides* with bits and pieces from Judaism and Christianity.
- The wonders of Neoplatonism with its holy trinity of One, Mind and Soul.
- Augustine's version of Neoplatonism which gives us a new take on the Trinity and the contemplative life of the individual soul.
- The other-worldly Plotinian spirituality of the mysterious Pseudo-Dionysius.
- The Cambridge Platonists and their insistence on the primacy of the transcendent realm over against the materialism of Hobbes.
- Simone Weil's materialistic or sacramental Platonism based on Plato's *Phaedrus* and *Timaeus*.
- Paul Tyson's use of Plato's transcendent realism to bring about the desired release of our culture from its blinkered materialist metaphysic.

What do you think are the most promising ingredients for a genuinely Christian version of Platonism that could be embraced today?

Notes

1 Alfred North Whitehead, *Process and Reality: An Essay in Cosmology*, corrected edition, ed. David Ray Griffin and Donald W. Sherburne, New York: Free Press, 1979, p. 39.

2 John Cooper (ed.), 1997, *Plato: Complete Works*, Indianapolis, IN: Hackett.

3 R. M. Hare, 1982, *Plato*, Oxford: Oxford University Press, p. 70.

4 This is where Plato's theory of Ideas or Forms first appears. It can also be found fully expounded in his *The Republic* and *Symposium*. All three belong to Plato's middle period when his own independent thought is finding its voice and the figure of Socrates is no longer looming so large. *Meno* probably also belongs to this period.

5 *Phaedo* 74b–75b, e.g. 75b in Plato, *Euthyphro. Apology. Crito. Phaedo. Phaedrus*, tr. Harold North Fowler, Loeb Classical Library 36, Cambridge, MA: Harvard University Press, 1914. Also *Meno* 82b–86a.

6 Hare, *Plato*, p. 46.

7 Seventh Letter of Plato 342a–d. Highlighted by Anthony Kenny, 2010, *A New History of Western Philosophy*, Oxford: Oxford University Press, p. 45.

8 Kenny, *History of Western Philosophy*, p. 45.

9 The redness illustration is from Kenny, *History of Western Philosophy*, p. 47.

10 Kenny, *History of Western Philosophy*, p. 47.

11 Plato, *The Republic*, Book VI.508e. Cooper, *Plato*, p. 1129.

12 Plato, *Euthyphro* 10.a. From *Plato in Twelve Volumes*, Vol. 1, tr. Harold North Fowler; introduction by W. R. M. Lamb. Cambridge, MA, Harvard University Press/London, William Heinemann Ltd, 1966.

13 Gottfried Leibniz, 'Reflections on the Common Concept of Justice', in Leibniz, *Philosophical Papers and Letters*, ed. and tr. Leroy Loemker, Dordrecht: Kluwer, 1989, p. 516.

14 Plato, *The Republic*, Book V. 459e. Cooper, *Plato*, p. 1087.

15 L. P. Gerson, 1990, *God and Greek Philosophy: Studies in the Early History of Natural Theology*, London: Routledge, p. 1.

16 See Plotinus, *Enneads* V.8; VI.5.

17 Attributed to Plotinus by W. T. Stace, 1952, *Time and Eternity*, Princeton, NJ: Princeton University Press, p. 91.

18 Kevin Corrigan, 'Mysticism in Plotinus, Proclus, Gregory of Nyssa, and Pseudo-Dionysius', *Journal of Religion* 76:1 (1996), 28–42 [at 34].

19 Pseudo-Dionysius, *Ecclesiastical Hierarchy* 536D. Corrigan, 'Mysticism in Plotinus, Proclus, Gregory of Nyssa, and Pseudo-Dionysius', 40.

20 Here I refer especially to her 'The Death of the Soul in Romans 7: Revisiting Paul's Anthropology in Light of Hellenistic Moral Psychology', *Journal of Biblical Literature* 126:4 (2007), 793–816, and 'Paul Among the Philosophers: The Case of Sin in Romans 6–8', *Journal for the Study of the New Testament* 30:4 (2008), 387–415.

21 Wasserman, 'Paul Among the Philosophers', 388.

22 Wasserman, 'Paul Among the Philosophers', 402.

23 If you are completely new to him, then Jonathan Hill's, 2003, *The History of Christian Thought*, Oxford: Lion, pp. 75–88, is a very interesting and accessible introduction.

24 Philip Carey, 'The Mythic Reality of the Autonomous Individual', *Zygon* 46:1 (March 2011), 121–34 [at 123].

25 Augustine, *Confessions* VII.10, tr. R. S. Pine-Coffin, Harmondsworth: Penguin, 1961, p. 146.

26 Pseudo-Dionysius, *The Divine Names* IV.13, in Colm Luibheid (ed. & tr.), 1987, *Pseudo-Dionysius: The Complete Works*, Mahwah, NY: Paulist Press, p. 82.

27 Corrigan, 'Mysticism in Plotinus, Proclus, Gregory of Nyssa, and Pseudo-Dionysius', 42.

28 Pseudo-Dionysius, *The Mystical Theology* I.1. Luibheid, *Pseudo-Dionysius*, p. 135.

29 J. C. A. Gaskin (ed.), 1996, *Thomas Hobbes, Leviathan*, Oxford University Press, Part 4:15, pp. 446–7, discussed in Mark Allen McIntosh, 'Newman and Christian Platonism in Britain', *Journal of Religion* 91:3 (2011), 344–64 [at 352].

30 McIntosh, 'Newman and Christian Platonism in Britain', 353.

31 Patrick Patterson and Lawrence Schmidt, 'The Christian Materialism of Simone Weil', in E. Jane Doering and Eric Springsted (eds), 2004, *The Christian Platonism of Simone Weil*, Notre Dame, IN: University of Notre Dame Press, pp. 77–93 [at p. 77].

32 Patterson and Schmidt, 'The Christian Materialism of Simone Weil', p. 78.

33 Simone Weil, 1957, *Intimations of Christianity Among the Ancient Greeks*, tr. E. C. Geissbuhler, London: Routledge & Kegan Paul, p. 103.

34 Weil, *Intimations of Christianity*, p. 103.

35 Paul Tyson, 2014, *Return to Reality: Christian Platonism for our Times*, Eugene, OR: Cascade, p. 7.

36 Tyson, *Return to Reality*, p. 25.

2

Aristotle and His Interpreters

Key words revisited
Dualism: The sharp distinction between material things and non-material.
Epistemology: The study of what can be known and how we can know it.
Forms: The unseen original versions of the copies we encounter in life.
Metaphysics: A grand theory about how the whole universe works.
Scepticism: Usually quite extreme uncertainty about knowledge, especially the information received via sense data.
Ontology: The study of existence and being.

New words
Categories: Aristotle's ten ways of describing existence as we know it.
Substance: Aristotle's way of answering the difficult question: What is being?
Syllogism: An 'if, therefore' argument often based on a minor premise, major premise and a conclusion.
Virtue ethic: Good actions based on the cultivation of right thinking.
Universals: Qualities that particulars share.
Nominalism: Universals are names or descriptions only and do not exist as objects.

Chapter Outline

1 Life

As with Plato, you may not consider yourself very well acquainted with Aristotle (384–322 BC) or Aristotelianism, but just consider how commonplace many of the following concepts are, all of which either originate with him or are fully explored for the first time in his writings:

> Syllogism, premise, conclusion, substance, essence, accident, metaphysics, species, genus, potentiality, category, 'begging the question'.

The words listed here also indicate the true genius of Aristotle: his immensely wide-ranging interests. Plato was a hugely original thinker, Aristotle more of an adapter. And, while Plato was himself very wide-ranging, sheer breadth of vision is the most outstanding feature of Aristotle. He later became the inspiration behind the classic 'Renaissance man' such as Da Vinci, who could paint a picture of the Madonna one minute and invent helicopters the next.

The works that Aristotle left us are vast. If they were all published individually in modern book form, they would amount to well over 50 books, holding about a million words,[1] yet the Aristotle corpus is 'more remarkable for its scope and variety than for its quantity'.[2] He had been a student of Plato for 20 years from the age of 17. After he left Plato's Academy he seems to have devoted quite a lot of his thought to countering and correcting (as well as enlarging on) Plato.

Aristotle's breadth may be related to his commitment to teaching. He was convinced that knowledge does not become true knowledge until it is taught to someone else. His experience of teaching ranged from tutoring Alexander the Great to lecturing in his own academy called the Lyceum: to students in the morning and the general public in the evening.

He was twice married and had at least one child with each wife, though he died alone on an island in self-imposed exile. After the collapse of Alexander the Great's empire, Athens had won back its independence, and fresh hostility towards Macedonia (Alexander the Great's home and the region with which Aristotle had strong family and professional ties) meant that Aristotle was in danger of suffering the same fate as Socrates. Hence he fled.

The most important works of Aristotle in recent discussion[3] have been *Metaphysics*; *Physics* (important to theology for its concept of the Unmoved Mover); *Nicomachean Ethics* (the founding document of modern ethics); and his tiny volume called *Categoriae*, where his explanation of the Categories (so important to medieval philosophy) is to be found.

2 Categories and Logic

Categories

Perhaps one of the keys to Aristotle's vast learning was his ability to find the right filing cabinet for everything. This filing cabinet was his concept of universals, a development of Plato's concept of Forms. Aristotle appears to have reasoned in the opposite direction to Plato, however. Where Plato starts with the ideal Form of a thing and then uses that to understand the nature and purpose of each earthly copy, Aristotle began with particulars and tried to decide what basic type each thing fell into, and then to categorize these types into a ten-part grid for understanding all reality and everything we would ever wish to say or to deduce about reality. The ten categories[4] were as follows:

- Substance
- Quantity
- Quality
- Relation
- Place
- Time

- Position
- State
- Action
- Affection

How did Aristotle arrive at these ten concepts as definitive of everything that can be said about anything? Perhaps, as Kant claimed, he merely 'picked them up just as they occurred to him'.[5] One of the strongest theories is that he got there by asking a lot of questions, especially the question: 'what is it?'[6] Then he might also have applied other open questions to the same thing such as how, where, when and why. This theory of the origins of Aristotle's Categories is based on teaching found in *Topics* I.9, where a similar list of ten categories appears but with a slightly clearer explanation of the rationale behind them.

Logic

Aristotle's logical theory, known as the syllogism, is expounded in his *Prior Analytics*, a work which was neglected until the mid twelfth century, from which point the syllogism was repeatedly modified by the likes of Peter Abelard and Boethius and is still often referred to as a way of introducing people to logic.

To Aristotle we owe the idea of 'begging the question'. You may have heard politicians saying things like, 'This frankly begs the question: just how does the Prime Minister intend to finance this policy?' But this is not the true Aristotelian usage. The politician is simply saying, 'This *strongly asks* the question.' For Aristotle the phrase was more about how a question was answered (or not answered), not how it was asked. Here is Aristotle himself:

> whenever a man tries to prove what is not self-evident by means of itself, then he begs the original question.[7]

The phrase dates back to some sort of game that he would play with his students that apparently involved trying to figure out what the original question was when presented with the answer. Some students would give up and beg for the question. Over time, the phrase took on a rather different meaning to refer to a logical fallacy. It is something that we often call 'circular reasoning'. An example that atheists often give today of Christians using this kind of circular reasoning goes something like this:

> Bill: 'God must exist.'
> Jill: 'How do you know?'
> Bill: 'Because the Bible says so.'
> Jill: 'Why should I believe the Bible?'
> Bill: 'Because the Bible was written by God.'[8]

Such an argument is simply a restatement, whether implicitly or explicitly, of the original premise in a slightly different form.

To avoid this kind of faulty reasoning, Aristotle invented the 'syllogism' (Greek: *sun*, together + *logizomai*, reason), which consisted of finding ways to demonstrate the truth of a statement by using a first principle that does not need anything else to support it. Most of Book I of the *Prior Analytics* is taken up with a discussion of the different variants of syllogism there are and what qualifies or does not qualify as such, but the climax of the discussion is in chapter 27, where the categorical syllogism is introduced. This type is deemed to be applicable to all problems. An example would be: 'all humans are animals'. Putting this together with a relevant second order statement that refers to a particular – 'Bill is a human' – we arrive at the conclusion: 'Therefore, Bill is an animal.' One of Aristotle's own examples was: 'All humans are mortal and all poets are human. Therefore, all poets are mortal.' The most famous example is 'Socrates is a man. All men are mortal. Socrates is mortal.'

A negatively stated example is this: 'If no philosophers mind about money and all professors do, then no professors are philosophers.' This example is lacking in evidence from close observation and is based more on ideas about humans, poets, philosophers and professors than on any carefully collected data. In this way, sometimes, the conclusion to a syllogism can be wrong because the minor premise is incorrect. For example, the sailors who set sail with Columbus were genuinely afraid of falling off the edge of the world. They would have reasoned in something like the following way: 'The earth is flat. All flat surfaces have edges. Therefore, if we keep sailing we will fall off the edge.'

The key factor, according to Aristotle, is that 'the syllogism proceeds through universal premises'.[9] Care must be taken that what is said to be universally true of the thing cited as the major premise really is true in every case. The major premise thus starts with the word 'All'. The minor premise, similarly, must genuinely be 'that which follows'.[10] As a key to this, Aristotle states, 'that which something follows receives the mark "every"'. Both premises require the sifting of as much data as we can lay our hands on so that we truly have arrived at a universal 'all' and a particular 'every' upon which to base our conclusions. The near impossibility of ever being able to do this in any final way is the reason why we include 'qualifications' in our essays. These show that, while our logic is well founded and not fallacious, there are certain exceptions to the 'all' and/or the 'every'.

As we will see when we come to look at analytic philosophy, Frege, Russell, More and Wittgenstein took logic beyond the syllogism to present us with a more linguistic approach that aimed at a case-by-case conceptual clarity rather than trying use universals and big philosophical systems that boast of being able to determine what happens in all cases.

Time-out: Logic, critical thinking and your essay writing

While we are on the subject of logic, it is worth noting that the philosophy of logic, one of the major subdisciplines of philosophy today, gives us the ground rules of the all-important skill of critical thinking. This is the thinking that voices 'polite doubt' or healthy scepticism and promotes a spirit of enquiry. Critical engagement with texts is the process whereby we assess the merits of someone else's argument.

Supposing, in your essay feedback you are constantly being told that you are using your sources 'uncritically' but you have no idea what that means. Basically, in critical evaluation, we are looking for logical fallacies (and hoping to avoid them ourselves, of course). Here are some of the most common:

- The straw man argument. This is when an opposing viewpoint is taken on but is presented in a weak way so as to be easily demolished. It relies on misrepresenting the countervailing viewpoint. Seen any of those lately?
- The *reductio absurdum* argument. This is similar to the straw man argument, but here the opposing viewpoint is greatly exaggerated. Instead of being made to look pathetically weak, it is made to look ridiculously overplayed. It is similar to the slippery slope argument but less apocalyptic.

- *Ad hominem* (lit. against the man) evidence, which directs attention at the arguer instead of the argument. This is extremely naughty but in the morally highly-strung world of theology it does happen.
- *Tu Quoque* (pronounced 'tue kwokway') evidence. This is often the kind of evidence used to furnish an *ad hominem* argument. Such evidence diverts an argument by pointing to an inconsistency between the arguer's character and the argument they make, yet this is actually irrelevant to the argument itself.
- The false dilemma. This is a way of rebutting alternative views by only picking the two most strident of them and deliberately missing out of the discussion all the more nuanced options.
- The 'slippery slope' or 'thin end of the wedge' argument. An argument should proceed by way of logical steps of inference, not a great bound from limited evidence to ghastly prognostication.
- *Cum hoc, ergo propter hoc* means 'with this, therefore because of this'. It is the type of inference drawn when two things happen at the same time (i.e. there is either a positive or a negative correlation) and the one is claimed as the ongoing cause of the other.
- *Post hoc, ergo propter hoc* means 'after this, therefore because of this'. This is not an ongoing cause but a cause that lies in the past. It is a claim to historical cause and effect – something notoriously slippery to demonstrate historiographically. So, in addition to the familiar *ad hoc* (for this), you now have *cum hoc* (with this) and *post hoc* (after this) in your Latin vocabulary.[11]
- Appeals to popularity (an apparent majority of support).
- Appeals to pity (where highly emotive evidence is relied on, often selectively).
- Appeals to authority (where the person cited is merely famous but lacking relevant expertise).
- Appeals to history (where precedent alone is cited as the reason for continuing with something).

There is no need, of course, to be obnoxious in your critique of other people's hard work, but here you have some useful ways of being more discriminating in your use of sources.

3 Biology and Metaphysics

Biology

Aristotle's detailed and extensive biological observations, which together make up some 25 per cent of his writings, are another first among so many firsts that we can attribute to Aristotle. Some of these observations involved either himself or a research assistant gathering data that today would only be done with the aid of a microscope. These laid the foundations for the modern sciences of zoology and biology (especially marine biology, a keen interest of his). In contrast to the Presocratics, who preferred to observe the motions of the heavenly bodies (which were thought to be divine and eternal), Aristotle felt that the study of creatures that are much closer to hand was a far more reliable source of useful knowledge, and here too we find an indication of the different angle of approach that so distinguishes Aristotle from Plato:

> in certitude and in completeness our knowledge of terrestrial things has the advantage. Moreover, their greater nearness and affinity to us balances somewhat the loftier interest of the heavenly things that are the objects of the higher philosophy.[12]

He anticipates the empiricists of the seventeenth and eighteenth centuries. In the midst of his discussion about how puzzling bees are, he says the following:

> But the facts have not been sufficiently ascertained; and if at any future time they are ascertained, then credence must be given to the direct evidence of the senses more than to theories, and to theories (*logois*) too provided that the results which they show agree with what is observed (*phainomenois*).[13]

Animal taxonomy, found in his *The History of Animals*, originated with his classification of species into genera in an order of ascent relating to the complexity and capabilities of each organism, a system which, though modified considerably at certain points, is still in existence today. There is even a nascent theory of natural selection in Aristotle,[14] which became one of the inspirations behind Darwin's *On the Origin of Species*.

Metaphysics

The true heart of Aristotle's metaphysics lies in his 'teleology'. Teleology is the study of the ends or purposes that a given thing was intended for. It was Aristotle's insistence that absolutely everything in nature exists for a purpose which caught Thomas Aquinas's eye. This teleological imperative, in the hands of Aquinas, would lead to the 'teleological argument' for the existence of God. Further, Aristotle's concept of motion from potentiality towards actualization of purpose pointed to the necessity of movers that act upon the moved. Such movers must exist in a hierarchy that terminates in the Unmoved Mover, a concept beloved by Aquinas in his discussions of the being of God as the 'First Cause, Himself Uncaused'. Such ideas find their origin in Aristotle's *Physics* Book 8.

Aristotle furnishes us with four answers to the question 'why is this so?' These are his famous four causes, in the last of which the 'final cause' is to be found in his teleology as such. They are to be found in *Physics* II.3 (lines 194a23–35) and in *Metaphysics* V.2 (lines1013a24–35). Aristotle's explanation is helpfully condensed here (mostly reflecting the wording in *Physics*):

- The material cause: 'that out of which', for example, the bronze of a statue.
- The formal cause: 'the Form', 'the account of what-it-is-to-be', for example, the shape of a statue.
- The efficient cause: 'the primary source of the change or rest', for example, the artisan, the art of bronze-casting the statue, the man who gives advice, the father of the child.
- The final cause: 'the end, that for the sake of which a thing is done', for example, health is the end of walking, losing weight, purging, drugs and surgical tools.[15]

It is this strong sense of teleology, that everything must fulfil its purpose, must attain to its ultimate good, which also underpins his ethics and politics.

4 Ethics and Politics

Ethics

Aristotle's ethical system is uniquely balanced compared to other systems. These can tend either towards permissiveness (utilitarianism, Epicureanism) or towards being too prohibitive (Christian asceticism, Pharisaism).

Aristotle was clear that certain types of conduct should be ruled out. There was no such thing as just the right amount of adultery or murder, for instance. But in regard to the appetites – food, drink and sex – he advocated a middle or mean position, known as the Golden Mean, that admits of neither abstinence nor excess. He was also clear that what qualified as the mean position will differ from person to person. Likewise, with virtues such as courage and generosity: too much courage is foolishness, too little is cowardice. It is also possible to be too generous. These issues are explored in his *Nichomachean Ethics* (named after his son).

He was also clear that ethics was bound up with happiness. His *Eudemian Ethics* focus on this happiness (*eudaimonia*) and how it is to be attained. He concludes that a life that is a combination of virtue, wisdom and pleasure will be happy (having eliminated divine favour, good fortune, nature, discipline, honour, reputation, riches and culture as the possible causes of true happiness). These three – virtue, wisdom and pleasure – are ends in themselves and make life worth living. And these he links with three lifestyle options: the political, philosophical and voluptuary:

> The things related to the happy conduct of life being three, the things already mentioned as the greatest possible goods for men – goodness (*aretēs*), wisdom (*phronēseōs*) and pleasure (*hēdonēs*), we see that there are also three ways of life in which those to whom fortune gives opportunity invariably choose to live, the life of politics, the life of philosophy, and the life of enjoyment.[16]

Aristotle's ethics are generally described as part of a class of ethical theories called 'virtue ethics'. By this is meant that 'the virtuous agent is a living norm'.[17] The virtuous agent performs morally good behaviour without the need for any external norms to guide behaviour. It is important to recognize that, while Aristotle was hesitant about defining exactly what moral norms ought to look like, he did not reject the reality of objective moral standards. Instead, he believed that only to the morally virtuous person (a person that has developed habitually virtuous habits of mind, passion and desire) does the morally good become visible. It is only to a virtuous agent that the morally right thing to do is crystal clear and unclouded by evil:

> For each state of character has its own ideas of the noble and the pleasant, and perhaps the good man differs from others by seeing the truth in each class of things, being as it were the norm and measure of them.[18]

There are some profound insights here that have stood the test of time and have been the subject of further reflection by Kant, Mill, McIntyre and others. A lasting insight has been that a virtuous person can clearly see *why* a given action is right or wrong. A persistent criticism has been that a virtue ethic cannot answer the question, 'What ought I to do?'[19]

In Aristotle's thought, the virtues are meant to cause us to feel 'the right things at the right times, on the right grounds, towards the right people for the right motive'. The most widely celebrated virtues that Aristotle listed (and which Aquinas took over) were wisdom or prudence (making realistic plans that will lead to personal growth); courage or fortitude (as opposed to the vices of foolhardiness or cowardice); temperance (as opposed to the vices of deficiency or excess); and justice (the one virtue for which there is no Golden Mean – one is either just or is not). Aquinas later added faith, hope and charity to make seven.

The virtues, according to Aristotle, are developed in concrete situations in which courage, for example, is demanded of us because of a perceived threat. In this way, we discover our virtues in the course of everyday life, and these are developed and embedded as we habitually use them. This system is different to deontology and consequentialism in that it is not dilemma-orientated. It is not reacting to some sudden ethical emergency but is proactive, developing itself, not in the context of dilemma and conflict, but in the context of the ordinary. In Aristotle, the virtues are a kind of habituated moderation. They tell us the reason why we repeatedly discipline children and why legislators repeatedly try to shape the behaviour of citizens. And the goal is happiness.

Politics

To Aristotle we owe the familiar catchphrase: 'Man is a political animal.' His *Politics* serves as the sequel to his *Nicomachean Ethics* and has a similar structure. It was written as the result of collecting together 158 constitutions of city states, including the constitution of Athens. Aristotle tries to tease out of this body of data the things that seem good to have in a constitution and what kind of government is most likely to preserve it. He lists six styles of government, adding to Plato's terminology, and creating a list of political terms still in use today: Monarchy (rule by one), aristocracy (rule by the best) and polity (rule by the majority for the common good) are the three good forms. Tyranny, oligarchy and democracy are corruptions of these:

> Of the above-mentioned forms, the perversions are as follows: – of royalty, tyranny; of aristocracy, oligarchy; of constitutional government, democracy. For tyranny is a kind of monarchy which has in view the interest of the monarch only; oligarchy has in view the interest of the wealthy; democracy, of the needy: none of them the common good of all.[20]

It is surprising to Western readers today that Aristotle had such disdain for democracy. His bone of contention with it was that it too easily becomes mob rule. The voices of the virtuous minority are too easily drowned out by the demands of the self-centred masses who have given no thought to the prosperity of the state as a whole:

> If the poor, for example, because they are more in number, divide among themselves the property of the rich – is not this unjust? No, by heaven (will be the reply), for the supreme authority justly willed it. But if this is not injustice, pray what is? Again, when in the first division all has been taken, and the majority divide anew the property of the minority, is it not evident, if this goes on, that they will ruin the state?[21]

> **Discussion**
>
> Is pure democracy with no monarchy and no aristocracy the very best way to do politics today?
>
> In what ways would you answer Aristotle's fears about mob rule: people who are given the vote but care nothing for the common good?

5 The Aristotelian Renaissances

The Neoplatonic commentators

Aristotle fell out of vogue not long after his death. The Middle Platonists sought to reconcile Aristotle's and Plato's concepts of God, but it wasn't until the Neoplatonists that a serious re-engagement with the Aristotle corpus began. Leading the way were Plotinus and Porphyry, who are reputed to have disagreed with each other about Aristotle's Categories, Plotinus allowing only four – substance, quality, quantity and relation – while Porphyry preserved all ten.

Aquinas and scholasticism

For hundreds of years, Western Christendom remained loosely Neoplatonic in outlook but possessed only one of Plato's works in translation (knowledge of Greek had gone into decline) and the study of Aristotle had fallen on very hard times by the time we get to the mid twelfth century. It was at that point that translations into Latin of Aristotle's works began to trickle into Europe.

From the year AD 711, there had been a Muslim presence in Spain. These were Moroccan Muslims known as the Moors. In Moorish Spain there arose an Aristotelian branch of Islam led first by Avicenna (980–1037) and then by Averroes (1126–98). Also in Spain, the Jewish philosopher Maimonides (1135/8–1204) attempted to pioneer an Aristotelian version of Judaism, upon which Aquinas would later model much of his own work of synthesizing Aristotle with Christianity.

The result of the study of Aristotle in Spain was the existence of a large collection of translations, on European soil, of Aristotle. In the mid 1100s translations from these Arabic texts into Latin began to appear. In the 1220s, Grosseteste's influential commentary on Aristotle's *Posterior Analytics* appeared. Initially, Aristotle's works were banned. The Moorish translations of them had put a particular colouring on Aristotelianism that made it seem heretical to the Roman Catholic Church. However, in the hands first of Albert the Great (1193/1206–80) and then of his pupil Thomas Aquinas (1225–74), Aristotle would for the first time be pressed into the service of Christian theology in a comprehensive and momentous way. William of Ockham's reaction against Thomism created a further decisive twist in medieval thought that would pave the way for modernity.

Aquinas and ethics

Natural law was Aquinas's way of describing our innate moral instincts. It is the kind of instinct that would cause us to protest if, for example, we are at the cinema and vacate our seat, having placed a strategic coat or scarf over it, to go to the toilet and we return to find that someone had moved the coat and taken our seat. We instinctively have a sense of injustice about that. Aquinas believed natural law to be universal, unchangeable and eternal. Drawing from Aristotle's preferences for inward rational goodness over against legal justice, Aquinas asserted that the intellect of all individuals possesses naturally an inclination towards the good. It is up to each person to discover it. This is given by God: 'Hence in him [the moral agent] the eternal reason is participated in in such a way that he has a natural inclination to the fitting act and end.'[22] This emphasis on universal natural law and its divine point of origin is a concept that has stood the test of time and proved useful to the famous scholar of medieval and Renaissance literature, C. S. Lewis in his war talks, later assembled together as *Mere Christianity*.

Aquinas was a virtue ethicist. As bearers of God's image, we all possess, at least as a vestige, an instinctual feel for what is good and right. Aquinas borrowed from Aristotle an understanding of the four essential virtues as being wisdom, courage, temperance and justice. These virtues form themselves around good habits or dispositions and are good for society, while vices form around bad habits and are destructive of civil society. Aquinas was clear, however, that these virtues were not sufficient for salvation. For salvation, the higher virtues of faith, hope and love were needed, and these can only be given by divine revelation and are not available to human rationality alone.

Realism and nominalism

The supreme importance of this Aristotelian renaissance is the way its influence caused ontology and epistemology to change shape away from the abstract, metaphysical Plato into a more concrete, this-worldly direction and then finally move beyond even Aristotle to the beginnings of modernity. There are two key terms that unlock the thought of this period.

First, there is the word 'realism'. This is the belief that everything in the universe falls into a Form or category or 'universal' of which it is a particular instance, and, therefore, the way to truly understand a particular instance is to more truly understand the essence of it, the wider Form or category to which it belongs. And here is the crucial thing: that defining reality behind everything we see has a real existence, indeed must have in order to give real existence to everything that participates in it. This realism then refers to a mentally but not physically see-able truth or meaning behind the shadowy and transient world that we see and touch. As we encounter this idea in Plato, it greets us as a series of leading questions with no final or dogmatic answer. Plato's theory of Forms really amounts to the conviction that things are not what they appear, that reality is deeper than appearances. What today we would call critical thinking amounts to much the same mindset: the determination to find out the truth of what lies behind a phenomenon or a statement that somebody makes.[23]

By the early Middle Ages, Plato's writings had been mostly lost and his ideas transmitted only via the Neoplatonist influences on Augustine and Pseudo-Dionysius. As a result, the subtleties in Plato's concepts were also lost and much of his thinking had been synthesized with Aristotle thanks to the work of the Neoplatonic commentators of Late Antiquity. The concept of the Forms was understood to mean that even things like tables and chairs are an artisan's imperfect copy of the non-concrete ideal Form, which was actually located somewhere, in some kind of heaven of Forms. So these were actual things which existed in an actual place, a place increasingly seen as entirely separate from this earthly world. The concept of earthly things participating in transcendent realities had faded.

Arguably the most notorious outcome of this kind of realism was the way the doctrine transubstantiation was defended. The physical appearance of the elements of bread and wine were described as mere 'accidents', an Aristotelian term used by the realists to denote the tangible things in the world around us. These accidents were seen as something so distinct from real substances that it was claimed that the real substance of the bread and wine, their 'universal', their underlying reality, was transformed into the body and blood of Christ while the appearances of the bread and wine to our senses could remain unaltered. This version of realism was easily demolished by Peter Abelard as being entirely unnecessary and unhelpful to our understanding of the world around us, though no one yet questioned transubstantiation as such, and it was ratified at the fourth Lateran Council of 1215.

For Aquinas, nothing has a perfectly actualized existence apart from God: 'God's absolute perfection is to be identified with His complete actualization . . . He contains no unactualized potential'.[24] Aquinas's terms '*actus*' and '*potentia*' (which are dependent upon Aristotle's *energeia* and *dunamis*) form the very heart of his thought, just as much as teleology was so central to Aristotle. So, in Aquinas universals become goals, the ideal end point of the gradual and faltering process of 'becoming' that is our lot on earth. The goal of our lives is to become as actualized as possible as God's image bearers. Moral descent is a descent into something closer to non-being, a descent into incompleteness. But perfect completeness belongs to God alone. God is the supreme example of that full actualization, but more than that, as the only being that is simple, undivided, without particular instances – the Trinity involves relational distinctions but not divisions – he is on a higher plane than everything else, impossible for us even to define.

What happened next brings us to our other word: 'nominalism'. This was the belief of Oxford scholar William of Ockham. He took up the cudgel that Abelard had started to use against early medieval realism. He believed that classifications, of whatever kind, do not have any objective existence except as events in our thinking that are expressed in words. We note the things that something has in common with other things such as people, and we call them humans and humanity. Hence nominalism, from the Latin, *nomen*, is all about how we choose to put a name to things. It is a no-nonsense approach that places far greater value on our observations of things, so that we can indeed name what we observe accurately. Ockham contended that the idea of actual universals and actual particulars was a misunderstanding of the way we name things. Sometimes we might use 'terms that stand for terms'.[25] These are terms such as 'human'. They are our metalanguage. Then there are terms that stand for actual things, particular humans such as Bob. But these are only words, just two different types of words.

So the realist–nominalist debate resulted in a clear win for nominalism over realism, which, on the face of it, might seem perfectly fair. It resulted, however, in a view of the universe in which only the individual tangible things we encounter are really real. The realm in which God lives becomes progressively more removed from the world of actual things. The link is broken. Individual things are no longer enchanted by being seen as participating in a higher, God-given reality. And with the link between the earthly and the heavenly broken, the link between faith and reason was also broken, and the links between philosophy and theology, politics and the church, science and faith were now already severed conceptually. It would be only a matter of time before the familiar landscape of modernity would appear.

Discussion 1: Participation in Christ

Pauline scholars look at Paul's 'in Christ' terminology and call this the doctrine of our 'participation in Christ'. A classic passage is Romans 5.12–21. Have a read of this now. In order for our participation in Christ to work, Christ first had to participate in humanity according to Paul. Ockham insisted that there is effectively no such thing as humanity but only the word 'humanity'. What does nominalism do to Paul's participation in Christ teaching?

Discussion 2: The Nicene Creed

The Nicene Creed, written in AD 325, both appropriates and rejects elements of the popular Platonism of the time. Its boldest rejection of Platonism is in the strong insistence that the Son is of the *same* substance as the Father: 'God of God, Light of Light' and so on. It also affirms that Christ, 'for us humans and for our salvation came down from heaven, was incarnate, was made human' [τὸν δι' ἡμᾶς τοὺς ἀνθρώπους καὶ διὰ τὴν ἡμετέραν σωτηρίαν κατελθόντα καὶ σαρκωθέντα καὶ ἐνανθρωπήσαντα.]

Again, if humanity is not a thing, so to speak, what does the incarnation mean if viewed from a nominalist position?

Discussion 3: Justification in Christ

Going back to Paul again we have the doctrine of justification in Christ. The Reformers, who were all nominalists, were fond of saying that God pronounces us righteous even if we are not, that he, to quote Paul, justifies the ungodly. It is only sanctification that actually changes us. Justification is purely a 'declarative' act according to the Reformers. What happens to justification if we see it from a realist, and not a nominalist viewpoint?

Discussion 4: The Church

Again turning to the Nicene Creed, this time the longer version of AD 381, which is what we call the Niceno-Constantinopolitan Creed, we discover that it defines the church as 'one, holy, catholic and apostolic'. Many great writers on the subject of 'ecclesiology' – the theology of church, what the church is, what it does – have tried to define the *esse* or 'essence' of church. They believe it has a very being, an animating something or other. Other writers insist that there is no *je ne sais quoi*, no mysterious oneness or any other quality that defines all the people of God. There are, they say, only churches doing stuff. Churches are a functional thing not belonging to any wider 'church universal'. (See the *SCM Study Guide to Theology in the Contemporary World* (London: SCM, 2017), pp. 54–70 for a fuller discussion of this.)

Which side of this divide would we fall on if we were nominalists?

Notes

1 And probably only one-fifth of his total output has survived: Kenny, *History of Western Philosophy*, p. 75.

2 Jonathan Barnes, 2000, *Aristotle: A Very Short Introduction*, Oxford: Oxford University Press, p. 4.

3 Interest in Aristotle seems to be increasing. There are twice as many articles on EBSCO, a widely used journals database, about Aristotle as there are about Plato. Recent books include Christopher Shields, 2014, *Aristotle*, 2nd edition, London: Routledge; Gabriel Lear, 2004, *Happy Lives and the Highest Good: An Essay on Aristotle's Nicomachean Ethics*, Princeton, NJ: Princeton University Press; Lorraine Pangle, 2003, *Aristotle and the Philosophy of Friendship*, Cambridge: Cambridge University Press; David Bostock, *Aristotle's Ethics*, 2000, Oxford: Oxford University Press; Barnes, *Aristotle*. There is also a classic work by Sir David Ross, first published in 1923: *Aristotle*, 6th edition, London: Routledge, 1995.

4 Expounded to varying degrees of depth in *Categoriae* chapters 5–9.

5 Immanuel Kant, 1781, *Critique of Pure Reason*, tr. J. Meiklejohn, London: Dent, 1934, 'Transcendental Doctrine of the Elements', Part II.1, Book I.1.3,10.

6 This, and other options, are discussed in Paul Studtmann, 'Aristotle's Categories', available at https://plato.stanford.edu/entries/aristotle-categories/ in *Stanford Encyclopedia of Philosophy*. This is an excellent resource of scholarly, regularly updated articles introducing every topic in philosophy.

7 Aristotle, *Prior Analytics* II.16. A. J. Jenkinson translation, available at http://classics.mit.edu/Aristotle/prior.2.ii.html.

8 www.nizkor.org/features/fallacies/begging-the-question.html [accessed 15 July 2014].

9 Aristotle, *Prior Analytics* I.27b (lines 14–15). In Aristotle, *Categories. On Interpretation. Prior Analytics*, tr. H. P. Cooke and Hugh Tredennick, Loeb Classical Library 325, Cambridge, MA: Harvard University Press, 1938.

10 Aristotle, *Prior Analytics* I.27b (line 18).

11 See Roy van den Brink-Budgen, 2010, *Critical Thinking for Students*, Oxford: How To Books, pp. 57–62.

12 Aristotle, *On the Parts of Animals* I.5 (lines 645a2–4). From McKeon (ed.) *Basic Works*.

13 Aristotle, *On the Generation of Animals* 3.10 (lines 760b30-31). From Aristotle, *Generation of Animals*, tr. A. L. Peck, Loeb Classical Library 366, Cambridge, MA: Harvard University Press, 1942.

14 In *Physics* II.8 (lines 198b17–32), but he then rejects it in the paragraph following.

15 Andrea Falcon, 'Aristotle on Causality', http://plato.stanford.edu/entries/aristotle-causality/#FouCau. See also Aristotle's opening remarks in *On the Parts of Animals* where he distinguishes two causes: that 'for the sake of which' exists, e.g. webbed feet for the sake of the duck being able to swim, and that which is proper to the essence, that which is the ultimate good, e.g. the duck being able to swim is essential to it and an aspect of the good ends that the duck serves. Duck examples are from: Barnes, *Aristotle*, pp. 116–17.

16 Aristotle, *Eudemian Ethics* I.IV (lines 1215a32–1215b2). From Aristotle, *Athenian Constitution. Eudemian Ethics. Virtues and Vices*, tr. H. Rackham, Loeb Classical Library 285, Cambridge, MA: Harvard University Press, 1935.

17 Jonathan Jacobs, 2002, *Dimensions of Moral Theory: An Introduction to Metaethics and Moral Psychology*, Oxford: Blackwell, p. 92.

18 *Nicomachean Ethics* III.3, lines 1113b30–33. From Richard McKeon (ed.), *The Basic Works of Aristotle*, New York: Random House.

19 Jacobs, *Dimensions of Moral Theory*, pp. 94–5.

20 *Politics* III.8, 1279a4–10. From McKeon, *Basic Works*.

21 *Politics* III.8, 1281a14–19. From McKeon, *Basic Works*.

22 Thomas Aquinas, *Summa Theologica* vol. 1, part I–II, Question 91, Article 2. From Ralph McInerny (ed.) *Thomas Aquinas: Selected Writings*, New York: Penguin, 1998, p. 620.

23 Carré put it aptly: 'To attend to the common elements in abstraction from sensibly perceived objects is to think.' Meyrick Carré, 1946, *Realists and Nominalists*, Oxford: Oxford University Press, p. 33. The Platonist distinctive is that this process orientates us to realities, not just to thoughts or ideations.

24 John Shand, 2014, *Philosophy and Philosophers: An Introduction to Philosophy*, London: Routledge, p. 63.

25 Shand, *Philosophy and Philosophers*, p. 70.

3

Early Modern Philosophy and Science

Chapter Outline

1 The Starting Points of Early Modern Philosophy

Ancient philosophy had set the tone until now

From the patristic era onwards, Plato gave Christianity the main features of its theological vocabulary, with Neoplatonism defining its contemplative spiritual style. Aristotle, once rediscovered, gave medieval intellectuals new tools of logic and categorization by which to define the world and God.

William of Ockham broke with ancient philosophy

The Oxford scholar William of Ockham, whom we have already met in connection with nominalism, is associated with the phrase 'Ockham's Razor', which describes his style of logic, paring categories down to the bare minimum, thus filtering out a lot of Aristotelian scholasticism. Behind this, of course, lay his fundamental belief known as nominalism, the commonsense belief that categorizations of things are only linguistic and have no extra-mental or 'real' existence. Aristotle had already moved in this direction having asserted that these are merely 'categories' of things, not 'Forms' and that they never can be found anywhere other than in particular instances. There is a universal category called 'cat', but we know that only from the particular instances of furry clawed whiskered creatures that all have the same features. Ockham, however, went as far as to say that there are no actual universals, there are only names for universals, hence the term 'nominal', having to do with names. 'Man' is a name, and 'Fred' is a name: they are just two different kinds of name that serve two different purposes: 'Man' names the type of thing that 'Fred' belongs to, while 'Fred' has reference to something outside of language: an actual particular man called Fred. But both are only linguistic tools.

Even if you understand nothing else about Ockham then, it is him that ensures that modernity began in an atmosphere in which a fairly clean break with ancient philosophy was understood to be taking place. A new anti-Platonic and anti-Aristotelian mood took hold. As early as the mid 1500s, Luther himself had taken to deriding Aristotle as a 'mere sophist and quibbler', an 'inventor of fables', the 'stinking philosopher' or the 'blind pagan'.[1]

Nominalism seems to survive as a subliminal influence rather than a confessed standpoint. Were it not for nominalism's attentiveness to the meaning and function of words, for example, it is doubtful whether the linguistically focused methods of Russell, Moore and Wittgenstein would have come about. Having said that, realism of a slightly different sort has made a definite comeback in recent decades. The 'critical realism' of Roy Bhaskar, for example, insists that there are real 'causal structures' behind the phenomena that anthropologists and sociologists observe in human societies. These are more than mere sociolinguistic constructs. Critical realism has become a respectable option for those engaged in social science research today. We will see that there are also theologians and biblical scholars working with similar ontologies, which are also called 'critical realism'.

A new understanding of God and the universe was already taking shape

We now need to briefly introduce someone we have not introduced so far. His name is John Duns Scotus (c.1266–1308). Our word 'dunce' owes its origins to people who were followers of Thomas Aquinas (called Thomists) who didn't like the followers of John Duns Scotus (called Scotists) and used Scotus's middle name (which was simply the name of a town on the Scottish borders) as a term of derision. It eventually evolved into a not very nice term referring to anyone thought to lack intelligence. There are pictures of Scotus wearing what looks like the dunce's hat, so the hat probably owes its origins to him also.

Scotus, besides being a nominalist himself, threw some additional things into the late medieval philosophical soup that would also become familiar features of modernity. There is a tendency, by the way, among many philosophical theologians today, especially those sympathetic to Radical Orthodoxy, to read much greater significance into the thought of Ockham and Scotus than the received account of the origins of modernity normally does. This newer reading of late medieval thought seems to have its origin with Hans Urs von Balthasar[2] and has the effect of pushing back the date, philosophically, for the true beginnings of modernity to the early 1300s, rather than during the Enlightenment.[3] The effect of doing this is striking: suddenly the origins of the way the Western world thinks are explicitly theological, not scientific at all. What I mean by that are two things:

Univocity of being

This is the belief, propounded by Scotus, that God is not a higher order of being to other beings.[4] God is merely the being who possesses qualities that you and I share but to a qualitatively infinite degree. He possesses them most excellently, most supremely. This was a natural outcome of taking a nominalist stance and working from the bottom up from particular instances. The maximal version of these instances is God. 'Univocity', by the way, simply means 'with one voice'. Particular things that we can put a name to in the world around us have particular qualities. When we speak of God, in order for those descriptions to mean anything at all, we would need to know that we are referring to the same things, but just to a higher degree. We are speaking with 'one voice' about both. When we see somebody who loves someone it is that, and nothing more than that, which is what we mean when we say that God loves or that God is love. Fine, you might say, so far it just seems like a language-game. But there were some quite far-reaching outcomes to this, as follows.

Divine voluntarism and inscrutability

As a result of the univocity of being principle, it became necessary to distinguish God from us by saying that he is like us but much more powerful. He has absolute power. God's power to do whatever he wishes quite rapidly became God's defining attribute. In Plato, we met the Euthyphro Dilemma: the question of whether what we might call 'good' is to be considered good purely because God wills it or whether good has its own existence as though God himself were answerable to it. In late medieval philosophy, the former option, known as voluntarism, decisively prevailed. So, now we have an all-powerful, overwhelmingly wilful deity who is inscrutable, who moves in mysterious ways and is not answerable to our ideas of fair or unfair.

One of the most controversial results of this shift was the revival and eventual enlargement of the Augustinian doctrine of predestination and of the notorious 'double predestination'. Calvin and, even more so, Calvin*ism*, raised the inscrutable exercise of divine election of some to salvation and others to damnation to heights not seen before within Christian thought. This inscrutability, this all-powerful God moving in mysterious ways, had the net result of even further removing him from intimate involvement with his world, adding another secularizing factor to the sacred–secular divide already implicit within nominalism. The worlds of faith and reason were rapidly splitting asunder.

The quest for religious neutrality

Lastly, the early modern and Enlightenment philosophers were quite deliberately trying to do something theological or religious. All of them professed belief in God but tended to redefine the terms on which the idea of God could be allowed to continue. And generally, this involved placing God in the wings, putting him in the background somewhere. He was invoked only to explain the 'rational structure of the universe'.[5] Hence, the dominant religious outcome was deism, and the sacred–secular divide essentially begins here. God and religion, especially in Hobbes, are sealed off into the private realm and not allowed a voice in the public square. The reasons for this religious agenda mainly lay with the Wars of Religion and the religious factions that had torn Europe apart in the late Reformation. There was a new quest for tolerance, with Amsterdam leading the way as the greatest haven for freethinkers in the Western world.

We will tour the key ideas of the early modern philosophers, not by grouping them artlessly into rationalists and empiricists, but by using the chronological order of the game-changing published works that emanated from these thinkers. This will allow us to see arguments take shape as each thinker reacted to the thinking of their contemporaries or predecessors. For reference the key works we'll be dealing with are:

1637	Descartes, *Discourse on Method*
1641	Descartes, *Meditations*
1651	Hobbes, *Leviathan*
1677	Spinoza, *Ethics*
1689	Locke, *Essay Concerning Human Understanding*
1714	Leibniz, *Monadology*
1738	Hume, *Treatise of Human Nature*
1765	Leibniz, *New Essays on Human Understanding*

2 René Descartes (1596–1650) and His Legacy

It is almost impossible to exaggerate the significance of the Frenchman René Descartes (pronounced 'Day-cart') (1596–1650) to Western thought. Today, rather like Plato, he is more often despised than admired, yet, much as his ideas might be questioned, his importance is never queried.

He wrote at a time of great scepticism. Europe had just seen the Renaissance and then the Reformation and the religious wars that followed. The effect of the Reformation, in particular, was to create anxiety in people about what was true and real and how they may be sure that their particular beliefs were right. In Northern Europe, there was no longer a pope to tell people what to believe and the Protestant churches had themselves splintered into innumerable sects and confessional groups. Though Descartes himself remained a Catholic all his life, he felt this uncertainty keenly, especially in the freethinking city of Amsterdam where he did much of his writing.[6] It was a unique cultural moment for the West, and one that no other culture has gone through. It led, positively, to the birth of scientific method, which brought about the Enlightenment, the Industrial Revolutions and what is sometimes called the 'miracle of the West', its peerless technological advancement through one ground-breaking invention after another. Were it not for this positive effect of Cartesian (the verbal form of Descartes)[7] thought, it is likely that such things as the invention of antibiotics, anaesthetics, trains, planes, automobiles and computers would not have happened. Negatively, there are two things that may be said.

First, Descartes brought about a monolithic preoccupation with epistemology, the study of what can be known. This had the effect of further deepening an already entrenched intellectualism in European culture that dated back as far as the Greeks. Western intellectualism now threatened, despite Descartes' deep personal faith, to crowd out all non-rational avenues to knowing, including revelation, emotion and intuition. Second, Descartes confirmed the individualistic tendencies of the West. Individualism probably originates with Augustine's *Confessions*, which embodied what was at the time a uniquely introspective way of relating to God. Descartes' famous maxim, 'I think, therefore I am', is quite pointedly not 'We think'. Thinking and being are conceived of in unquestionably solitary terms.

Key text: Meditations on First Philosophy

Of the two most important philosophical works of Descartes – *Discourse on Method* of 1637, and *Meditations* of 1641 – it is the *Meditations* that reveal to us most clearly the anatomy of the new rationalism he was using.

We will now look at the key moments in his argument.

The dream argument

We come to the first stage in Descartes' use of 'methodological doubt' as his main means of arriving at something that cannot be doubted. He uses radical doubt against himself, as a way of unseating deeply held but unexamined assumptions. He uses doubt 'as an instrument which self-destructs, impelling him forwards on the journey towards certainty and truth'.[8] He explains: 'The eventual result of this doubt is to make it impossible for us to have any further doubts about what we subsequently discover to be true.'[9]

The dream argument is found in his First Meditation and is very straight-forward:

> How often does the nocturnal quietness convince me of familiar things, for example, that I am here, dressed in my gown, sitting by the fire, when I am really undressed and asleep in my bed? But at the moment I certainly see this sheet of paper with my eyes wide open, the head I shake is not asleep, I extend and feel this hand, carefully and knowingly; things which are as clear as this would not occur to someone who is asleep. As if I do not remember having been deluded by similar thoughts while asleep on other occasions! When I think about this carefully, I see so clearly that I can never distinguish, by reliable signs, being awake from being asleep.[10]

His conclusion from this is that only mathematical and geometrical facts can always be trusted: 'For whether I am awake or asleep, two and three added together make five and a quadrilateral figure has no more than four sides. It seems impossible that one could ever suspect that such clear truths are false.'[11] The merit of mathematical and geometric truths over against 'physics, astronomy, medicine, and other disciplines'[12] is that maths and geometry discuss 'only very simple and general things, and are not concerned with whether or not they exist in nature'.[13]

So, for as long as we base knowledge on the geometrically and mathematically measurable, all should be well.

The demon argument

But supposing the all-powerful God has so made me that even geometrical and mathematical judgements are a false suggestion to my mind. This, says Descartes, is unthinkable: God is to be trusted as the one who has so made me that I am not always mistaken in everything. A God who is truth would not make creatures that are always in error. But supposing, instead of a God of truth under-writing human rationality, there is instead an evil demon that has been deceiving me all along, and that none of the things I am sure of can be relied upon as real and true:

> I will suppose, therefore, that there is no God of goodness, the sovereign source of truth, but a malignant genius, as powerful as he is cunning and deceitful, who has used all his zeal to deceive me; and I will make myself think that the sky, the air, the earth, colours, shapes, and sound, indeed every external thing we perceive, are all no more real than the illusions of dreams, by means of which this Demon has laid traps for my credulity.[14]

So his thought experiment has now left him with nothing at all that can be relied upon as indubitable except one thing. He begins to notice that his mind, whether he is dreaming, doubting, being deceived or just thinking, is truly existing. He immediately equates all this mental activity with a locatable 'I', an individual personhood, which is also seen to be truly existing and generating the mental activity. He is a thinking thing: 'What am I? A thinking thing – a thing, that is to say, which doubts, understands, affirms, denies, wills, and does not will.'[15] In his *Discourse on Method*, where the argument appears without the demon argument preceding it, he puts it in a way that is now the most famous philosophical quote of all time:

> I realized that, in the very act of thinking everything false, I was aware of myself as something real; and observing that the truth: *I think, therefore I am*

[*je pense, donc je suis*. Latin: *cogito, ergo sum*], was so firm and so assured that the most extravagant arguments of the sceptics were incapable of shaking it, I concluded that I might have no scruple in taking it as that first principle of philosophy for which I was looking.[16]

He has now reached a point in his thought experiment where the whole universe has, for the moment, receded and he is, quite literally, left alone with his thoughts. The next task is to bring the world back again but on a more reliable basis free of the clutter of uncritically accepted ideas and habits of thought.

The wax argument

First, he proceeds in a way that relies on the thinking self rather than on the senses. It may seem that he has already done this in his dream argument with its rejection of the reliability of sense data, and to a certain extent he has. But to reinforce the non-reliability of observable phenomena, Descartes asks us to consider a solid lump of beeswax, fresh from the hive. It gives a solid sound when struck, it smells of flowers, tastes of honey, looks opaque and feels hard and cold. Bring the wax close to fire, however, and it changes in almost every respect: it becomes a liquid, starts to smell differently, would doubtless no longer taste of honey, it has become clear and hot to touch: 'all that was subject to taste, smell, sight, touch, or hearing has been transformed; and yet the wax remains'.[17] His confidence in his senses is diminished and must proceed with caution, relying always on a rational, not experiential, starting point: 'my conception of the wax can only be the conception of a human mind'.[18] He concludes:

> I now know that our perception of bodies is due neither to the senses nor to the imagination, but solely to the understanding, and that they are known to us not because we see them or touch them, but because we conceive them in thought; and so too I know clearly that there is nothing that can be known to me more clearly and evidently than my own mind.[19]

So, we may not proceed with the old assumptions about our perceptions of the material world but must start with what is clearly and distinctly perceived by the rational mind. It is the mind that knows the wax rather than the senses.

But there is one more thing, besides the thinking self, which Descartes' thought experiment allowed him to keep and take with him back out into the world: belief in God. Having served his purpose, the deceiving demon has presumably been exorcized. Errors may yet be possible, but God is not the cause of these since God cannot deceive us. Rather, we can safely assume that we are not customarily mistaken in our search for truth because God did not make us habitually erroneous. Here, Descartes does more than simply reaffirm what he wanted to affirm just before the demon argument got in the way. He now tries to prove, using rationality alone, that the God of truth really does exist, so there is now an argument for reassuring himself that he is not deceived by a demon. Following Anselm's ontological proof for the existence of God, Descartes also seeks to demonstrate the existence of God by the existence of the concept in our minds of a perfect being. Now, the cause of a thing cannot be a lesser thing that the thing itself, so if the concept is that of a perfect being then the cause of that concept must itself be at least that perfect. An attribute which God must possess at the very least, therefore, is existence, otherwise he would be lacking in the most fundamental perfection and could not be the unsurpassably great being that our minds take him to be.

What are we left with?

- *Mind.* Despite Descartes' belief in God, what we actually end up with is a mind–matter dualism since even God's existence is made to serve the purposes of the autonomous thinking self.
- *Matter as extension in motion.* For Descartes, the great criterion of an indubitable truth is that it is clearly and distinctly perceived with our minds. We make mistakes when our wills push ahead of our intellect and we make choices before we have developed a clear and distinct understanding of the facts. And our perceptions of material objects are so prone to being skewed by the physiology of our senses or by the perspectives we inherit that the only properties that we may clearly and distinctly perceive, as though from a vantage point outside the universe, are shape, size and movement. All of these are measurable using entirely indifferent mathematical and geometrical methods.

Some common objections

- Regarding the *cogito*, Descartes extrapolates from his doubt a full concept of an 'I'. Is he entitled to do this? On his own minimalistic terms, perhaps all he can really deduce is 'there are doubts'.[20]
- Isn't the *cogito* circular? Here is A. J. Ayer: 'If I start with the fact that I am doubting, I can validly draw the conclusion that I think and that I exist. That is to say, if there is such a person as myself, then there is such a person as myself, and if I think, I think.'[21] In other words, if objection 1 above is correct in that he infers too much, then all Descartes can really say is 'I am thinking, therefore I am thinking.'
- What about other people? Must we begin with a solitary doubter who has shut himself away in a stove before we can know anything clearly and distinctly?

Discussion

So Descartes may not have got everything right, but there is something admirable about subjecting himself to such a rigorous and potentially isolating thought experiment. What were the benefits? Were there some good points?

To what extent are we still under the spell of this individualistic notion of the autonomous thinking self? Collectivist cultures in Asia and Latin America are not at all like this. In what ways does Cartesian individualism impact the church in the West?

---

3 Other Early Modern Philosophers

Hobbes and materialism

Thomas Hobbes (1588–1679) was one of the foremost British intellectuals of the seventeenth century. Like Descartes, with whom he strongly disagreed, he was attempting to lay the foundations for science, except in his case he was facing more in the direction of empiricism, a word which is based on the Greek *empeiria*, meaning 'experience' while Descartes was helping to found rationalism.

The most striking thing about Hobbes is his view of the universe as 'body', and everything that goes on within it as 'motion'. Everything, even human emotion, is conceived in entirely mechanistic terms. The most important source to go to for his key ideas is his classic work of 1651, *Leviathan*.

All is body

Hobbes's materialism allows him to go in completely the opposite direction to Descartes. Instead of distrusting the senses, he claims that human memory and imagination itself, upon which all reasoning must base itself, consists of the fading memories of sensory experiences. The mind thinks in snapshots of past events that have been physically perceived in some way. Here again is that remarkable extract, so troubling to the Cambridge Platonists, but which has proved to be surprisingly prophetic of the modern secular outlook:

> Every part of the Universe, is Body, and that which is not Body, is not part of the Universe: and because the Universe is All, that which is no part of it, is *Nothing*; and consequently *no where*.[22]

Baruch Spinoza (1632–77)

Spinoza is illustrative of the way the thinkers that laid the foundations for the Enlightenment took the train from theism to atheism in stages, stopping at various stations along the way as each one preferred. Spinoza, a Jew by background who fled to Amsterdam with his family from the Inquisition in Portugal, chose to alight at pantheism. He threw out all of the things that an atheist might throw out – revelation, Scripture, sin and guilt, the afterlife and prayer – yet could still make this remarkable pronouncement: 'whatsoever is, is in God, and without God nothing can be, or be conceived'. Yet he could also affirm: 'By God, I mean a being absolutely infinite – that is, a substance consisting in infinite attributes, of which each expresses eternal and infinite essentiality.'[23] God is coterminous with nature and yet infinite. This apparent contradiction is partly resolved by the way he defines infinity as that which 'contains in its essence whatever expresses reality, and involves no negation'.[24] This may leave us puzzling, but the important thing for Spinoza was the ethical benefit of the pantheist option, and this is where his early liking for the Stoicism of Seneca comes in, with all its high regard for restraining emotion and ambition to achieve serenity. In a universe that is all already divinely infused and ordered, absolutely everything is already determined, and so the path to happiness is not prayer. Prayer is our way of constantly trying to get God to change the universe in some way that is more to our liking. Happiness comes not by praying but by accepting the things we cannot change. Relinquishing desires and choosing to acquiesce to the way things are is the way of the wise. In any case, God, in Spinoza's understanding, is not to be thought of as a personal being who personally has it in for us or particularly favours any of us. He neither loves nor hates, he simply is and cannot be swayed:

> I have explained the nature and properties of God. I have shown that he necessarily exists, that he is one: that he is and acts solely by the necessity of his own nature; that he is the free cause of all things and how he is so; that all things are in God and so depend on him, that without him they could neither exist nor be conceived; lastly, that all things are predetermined by God, not through his free will or absolute fiat, but from the very nature of God or infinite power.[25]

Some of his outcomes have been highly suggestive of the idealism which we will encounter later in this book. Spinoza was a favourite of the idealists.

> Hence it follows that the human mind is part of the infinite intellect of God, thus when we may say, that the human mind perceives this or that, we make the assertion that God has this or that idea.[26]

Discussion

So why do we pray? What are we implying about God's being when we claim that he answers prayer, that he, in some small way, changes the universe for us?

John Locke (1632–1704)

Locke's contribution lies in his rejection of the rationalists and their beliefs that human minds already have certain indubitable concepts printed on them from birth. For Locke, the mind was a blank sheet (*tabula rasa*, blank slate), utterly dependent upon sense data for everything. Like Hobbes, he argued that even when we recollect something, we reference what the senses have told us. When we imagine something we likewise remember something from the sensory world we have experienced:

> Let us then suppose the mind to be, as we say, white paper, void of all characters, without any ideas; how comes it to be furnished? Whence comes it by that vast store, which the busy and boundless fancy of man has painted on it, with an almost endless variety? Whence has it all the materials of reason and knowledge? To this I answer, in one word, from *experience*: in that all our knowledge is founded; and from that it ultimately derives itself. Our observation employed either about *external sensible objects, or about the internal operations of our minds, perceived and reflected on by ourselves, is that which supplies our understanding with the materials of thinking.*[27]

The mind does not innately have ideas, rather ideas come through the mind representing to itself what has been experienced. This is the representative theory of knowledge. It entails the fact that, because the mind has no way of bypassing the senses, it has no direct knowledge of the outside world but only of the representations it makes to itself on the basis of what the senses have experienced. Bishop George Berkeley would go even further with Locke's theory of knowledge and claim that not only is our only knowledge of things our perception of them but that the things themselves have no objective existence apart from our perception of them – an idea which is made slightly more sustainable by the fact that God is always perceiving everything so keeps everything in existence, but more on him later.

Like some other early Enlightenment philosophers, Locke was a person of devout faith who nonetheless cordoned off a God-zone in his thought, which those who followed his thought but lacked his devotion did away with altogether. For Locke, the resurrection of the dead was in the realm 'above reason'. Faith is derived from revelation, which is communication that has a special status because of the status of the communicator, i.e. God. The problem, as far as Locke is concerned, is with the claims we make on the basis of supposed revelation. Hence, he prefers to rely on natural religion, a commonsense, undogmatic reliance on what he hopes is plainly visible to all simply by looking at creation:

> Since then the precepts of natural religion are plain and very intelligible to all mankind and seldom come to be controverted, and other revealed truths, which are conveyed to us by books and languages, are liable to common and natural obscurities and difficulties incident to words, methinks it would become us to be more careful and diligent in observing the former, and less magisterial, positive and imperious in imposing our own sense and interpretations of the latter.[28]

It was largely down to the influence of Locke that deism and natural theology took such firm hold, first (with Lord Herbert of Cherbury) as a way of defending the faith, but latterly (with John Toland and Matthew Tindal) as a way of escaping any specifically Christian dogmas. However, John Wesley was also influenced positively by Locke in a very different direction: in the direction of affirming the value of religious experience to Christianity. It was this that prompted Wesley to include 'experience' alongside Scripture, reason and tradition to form his quadrilateral about how we gain certain epistemological access to the truths of the faith. Inspired by the writings of the Church Fathers, Wesley even seems to have developed his own distinct doctrine of the 'spiritual senses', unseen, internal but super-rational faculties by which we perceive God.[29]

Discussion

Where is the balance to be struck between affirming the revealed nature of the Christian faith while also not being 'magisterial, positive and imperious' about things we could be wrong about?

John Wesley interviewed over 600 participants in the Otley revival of the early 1760s and incorporated their testimonies into his doctrine of Christian Perfection as laid out in his book of 1765, *A Plain Account of Christian Perfection*. How much scope is there to incorporate people's spiritual experiences into the formation of theology?

Gottfried Leibniz (1646–1714)

Leibniz (pronounced 'Libe-nids') was a true polymath, belonging to the same class of genius as Aristotle. His two most enduring contributions were in mathematics and philosophy. In the area of mathematics, he co-invented calculus, pioneered the first calculator and laid the foundations for the binary mathematics that underlie computer science today. In philosophy, he pioneered the transposition of logic into mathematical notation that breaks down propositions into their smallest components. This was his most enduring contribution to philosophy, laying a foundation for the methods of the early analytic tradition which we will encounter much later on in this book.

Here, he is significant in that he takes on Locke, which means that we tend to lump him together with the rationalists. He ardently believes in the immateriality of the mind and that it is *not* a blank slate:

> Experience is necessary, I admit, if the soul is to be given such and such thoughts, and if it is to take heed of the ideas that are within us. But how could experience and the senses provide the ideas? Does the soul have windows? Is it similar to writing-tablets, or like wax? Clearly, those who take this view of the soul are treating it as fundamentally corporeal.[30]

Though he wrote these words while Locke was still alive, news of his death in 1704 meant that Leibniz lost the desire to publish. His *New Essays on Human Understanding* did not finally get into print until 1765.

Leibniz also provided a useful response to Descartes. Going to press not long after Leibniz's death in 1714, this was his most significant later work, and was called *Monadology*. In it he explains his philosophical monism, the belief that everything is ultimately one thing. This, it must be said, was after meeting Spinoza and some of the latter's pantheism may have rubbed off. Leibniz successfully identifies the main problem in Descartes, which philosophers have been moaning about ever since, and that is the dualism between mind and matter. The remedy is to conceive of the whole universe as made up of pre-programmed simple units which all play their part. These are not *necessarily* physical entities, which is where his concept most differs from the modern scientific concept of the 'atom'. Here is how he introduces us to the concept of the 'monad':

1   My topic here will be the monad, which is just a simple substance. By calling it 'simple' I mean that it has no parts, though it can be a part of something composite.

2   There must be simple substances, because there are composites. A composite thing is just a collection of simple ones that happen to have come together.

3   Something that has no parts can't be extended, can't have a shape and can't be split up. So monads are the true atoms of Nature—the elements out of which everything is made.[31]

Investigate

Leibniz is able to ascribe some sort of intelligence to even the simplest and tiniest of monads. The monad does what it is programmed to do so as to serve the purposes of the greater whole. He accounts for this by reference to God. Can you find out how modern scientists account for the programming that is found in cells and atoms? Articulate a response on behalf of faith.

David Hume (1711–76)

We have already detected the possibility of scepticism latent in some thinkers who were concerned that our knowledge of the world is all mediated via the senses so that we have no direct knowledge of it as such. Leader of the Scottish Enlightenment, David Hume, took this further:

> For my part, when I enter most intimately into what I call myself, I always stumble on some particular perception or other, of heat or cold, light or shade, love or hatred, pain or pleasure. I never can catch myself at any time without a perception, and never can observe anything but the perception.[32]

Hume possessed a more explicitly anti-religious and anti-dogmatic tendency in thought than the other Enlightenment thinkers and was concerned with the bigotry that accompanies the three monotheistic faiths. With regard to epistemology, his position was so sceptical that he seems to have even depressed himself with his thoughts until relieved by socializing:

> Most fortunately it happens, that since reason is incapable of dispelling these clouds, Nature herself suffices to that purpose, and cures me of this philosophical melancholy and delirium, either by relaxing this bent of mind or by some avocation. . . . I dine, I play a game of backgammon, I converse, and am merry with my friends; and when, after three or four hours' amusement, I would return to these speculations, they appear so cold, and strained, and ridiculous, that I cannot find my heart to enter into them any further.[33]

He went on to influence the great Scottish political thinker Adam Smith, who pioneered the idea of unregulated, free trade economies, a concept later to become important to the development of British economics. His influence was also crucial in the thinking of Immanuel Kant. Hume's scepticism famously woke Kant up from his 'dogmatic slumbers' in 1770, inaugurating Kant's critical period, which was when his most influential work was done, beginning with his famous *Critique of Pure Reason* of 1781.

4 Scientific Ethics

Utilitarianism, the main ethical product of early modern scientism, is the way of judging rightness or wrongness by whether or not it accomplishes the greatest possible happiness for the greatest possible number of people. This can involve a modern form of Epicureanism, the pursuit of pleasure and the avoidance of pain. Indeed, Epicurus (341–270 BC) is really the true originator of this style of ethical reasoning. However, properly speaking, we should say that Epicurus was an ethical egoist, not a utilitarian. And despite the associations of Epicureanism with unbridled hedonism, his is better termed 'austere hedonism'.[34] By using this term, we acknowledge that Epicurus himself made a clear distinction between the lower and short-lived pleasures of sensuality and the higher, more lasting pleasures of the intellect and relationships. Via Adam Smith, 'ethical egoism' has worked its way into modern life as the dominant moral climate of most capitalist societies. What we mean by that is that these societies tend to run, to a greater or lesser degree, along the lines of enlightened self-interest. Conservative politics is especially keen to harness this with a minimum of government interference and regulatory control. Hollinger points out in passing that even Christian conversion is necessarily based largely upon self-interest. People do not become Christians out of altruistic motives.[35]

Utilitarianism was deemed to be a scientific, even a mathematical approach to ethics. Jeremy Bentham even devised a mathematical model for making ethical decisions, known as his 'hedonistic calculus'. Pleasure and pain could be quantified using seven criteria: intensity; duration; certainty (the probability of a pleasurable or painful outcome); propinquity (how near in time the likely pleasure or pain is); fecundity (productiveness – it produces a lot of pleasure of the same kind); purity (how free of any pain alongside the pleasure, or additional pains on top of the initial pain); and extent (how many people will enjoy it or suffer from it).[36] 'Sum up all the values of the pleasures on one side', advised Bentham, 'and all the pains on the other. The balance, if it be on the side of pleasure, will give the good tendency of the act upon the whole, with respect to the interests of that individual person . . . Take account of the number of persons whose interests appear to be concerned; and repeat the above process.'[37] It was an honest attempt at addressing issues of the public good with complete impartiality. Utilitarianism is anti-heroic and resolutely pragmatic, radically questioning traditional moral norms in the light of whether those norms achieve the desired ends. This is a consequentialist ethic. If the results seem good, then the actions producing such happy results must be right. This has great appeal to the postmodern penchant for pragmatism and tends, unless checked, to become a default within medical ethics for the simple reason that medicine exists to reduce pain for as many people as possible. John Stuart Mill (1806–73) differed from Bentham in that he preferred to speak of the quality of human happiness or pleasure secured by our moral judgements about the public good rather than the quantity.[38]

Exercise

Try doing, with a group of peers, a hedonistic calculus on some contemporary morally charged issue, especially one that involves a dilemma, an either/or option. You will need to create a table with two columns:

one headed 'Pleasures' and the other headed 'Pains', and seven rows, one each for Intensity, Duration, Certainty, Proximity, Productivity, Purity and Extent. Try to get everyone to give a score of 1–10 for both pain and pleasure so that a figure appears in every box. Add up the columns and this will give you an answer that is likely to be weighted one way or the other. In my class, we did Brexit: 'Is Brexit good for Britain?' Despite the young average age of the class, the results were in favour of Brexit.

Probably a great many factors adversely affect the reliability of the results, but the exercise is fun and flexes our critical thinking.

A contemporary problem: Ethics and genetics

It is worth bringing ourselves up to date by dealing with one of the ethical problem areas that the scientific progress of the modern era has given us – the breakthroughs in genetics.

The key problem: A feared return to eugenics

Here is a statement many of us would find troubling today:

> What nature does blindly, slowly, and ruthlessly, man may do providently, quickly and kindly. As it lies within his power, so it becomes his duty to work in this direction. The improvement of our stock seems to me one of the highest objects that we can reasonably attempt.[39]

These are the words of Francis Galton (1822–1911), the famed founder of the Eugenics movement, which had its heyday in the first half of the twentieth century but which fell upon hard times in the wake of the disrepute brought upon it by Nazi aims at racial purity via enforced sterilization, euthanasia and artificial insemination. However, since the year 2003 when the Human Genome Project was completed, a whole new suite of possibilities, some of which are a dream come true and some of which are the stuff of science fiction and horror, have presented themselves to medical science. It has become the area more than any other where our moral reasoning has struggled to keep pace with technological progress. The only major reference point we have is the 1978 document called *The Belmont Report*, which offers three basic principles when making decisions about medical research carried out on living human subjects: respect for persons; beneficence; and justice.[40]

The main problem has been the vacuum created by the evacuation of old religious deontologies. These had been at the backbone of the medical profession's commitment to the healing imperative, which is enshrined in the Hippocratic oath. In the nineteenth century it became possible not only to heal but also to prevent disease through sanitation and vaccination. Only very recently has it become conceivable that medicine might also involve the taking of a human life. This signals a shift towards a hedonistic utilitarianism. It is a 'quality-of-life ethics as opposed to a sanctity-of-life ethics'.[41] There has also been a shift away from accepting the realities of chance, in favour of establishing more choice. This shift from chance to choice is encapsulated in the musings of John Harris:

> If it is not wrong to wish for a bonny, bouncing, brown-eyed, intelligent baby girl, with athletic potential and musical ability, in virtue of what might it be wrong to play fairy godmother to oneself and grant the wish that was parent to the child?[42]

Examples, in more or less descending order of controversy, of genetically orientated phenomena giving rise to ethical difficulties include the following:

- *Human admixed embryos.* These may be 'chimaeras', made by inserting animal cells into human embryos; 'cybrids' made by inserting a human nucleus into an animal cell; or 'true hybrids', which are made from combining both sperm and eggs of humans and animals respectively. This is the ultimate violation of a species boundary, and hence (it is argued) of a human right, but also of animal rights.
- *Cloning.* So far, aside from Dolly the sheep, cloning has proved very difficult and success rates are extremely low, but techniques are set to improve.
- *Embryonic stem cell research.* These cells are undifferentiated and totipotent. In other words, they have the potential, in the right environment, to become any type of cell – skin, heart, liver – hence their appeal as a potential treatment.

- *Germ-line gene therapy.* Germ-line genetic modifications (GGM) could help us to design our descendants, thus 'shaping the genetic future of our species'.[43]
- *Genetic enhancement.* Here, the difficulty lies in defining at what point therapy (as below) becomes enhancement. The new sporting crime of gene-doping is a clear case of the latter.
- *IVF embryo selection.* If there is a risk of passing on a genetic abnormality, pre-implantation genetic diagnosis takes place.
- *Saviour siblings.* IVF can be used to create a brother or sister to a sick child, from whom tissue is taken – usually umbilical cord blood – to help to treat the sick child. Later in life, the saviour sibling might be asked to donate bone marrow or organs.
- *Prenatal screening and diagnosis.* Some cite the 'subtle pressures'[44] that expectant mothers are put under to have certain prenatal tests. These have as their aim the potential termination of pregnancies that could lead to the birth of disabled children. Expectant parents can be made to feel that it is part of 'responsible parenthood'[45] to prevent the birth of disabled children.
- *Somatic gene therapy.* Pioneered in 1972, it involves injecting healthy genetic material into mutant cells in the hope of treating diseases such as Parkinson's disease. There has been some success in trials since 2006. Cells are taken from elsewhere on the patient's body, rather than from embryos.

Before we come to consider a couple of discussion questions, here are some examples of how various thoughtful people have tried to respond to the challenges of modern genetics.

The search for the right response: It's unethical not to

In this first group are those thinkers who would generally insist that whenever we are faced with a new opportunity of enhancing medical practice through genetics, it would be unethical *not* to take that opportunity.

Medicinal and procreative beneficence. On this view, 'We are to act in accordance with a vision for the future of what best enables human flourishing.'[46]

There are overwhelmingly powerful reasons to pursue therapeutic cloning, stem cell research and other research which therapeutic cloning will augment and probably make much more effective. The reasons for pursuing this research are so strong that it would be unethical not to pursue this research.[47]

Creativity is God-given. This is the line of Christian ethicist Ted Peters:

> We are condemned to be creative. We cannot avoid it. The human being is a tool maker and a tool user . . . We cannot be fully human without being technological. . . . despite its occasional deleterious consequences, we humans have no choice but to continue to express ourselves technologically and, hence, creatively.[48]

Who is to say what a 'person' is? On this view, researchers ought to be given the benefit of the doubt as to the moral status of an embryo: 'nature has not to date stood up and offered us a clear definition of a person, nor told us precisely when personhood begins'.[49] The criteria generally offered include consciousness, self-awareness, rationality, interests and moral agency. These mostly go back to John Locke,[50] and are patently inadequate since a good many adult human beings would be unable to fully satisfy all of these criteria, yet we would not for that reason judge them to be not persons or not human. It is claimed that, before the 14-day point, the human embryo is 'so profoundly unlike us that it cannot be one of us'.[51]

The search for the right response: It's unethical to

In this group are those who are more likely to argue that, whenever there is even the possibility that, in the pursuit of medical breakthroughs, we are taking a human life, it is unethical *to* pursue such research.

The beginnings of human life. UK legislation on embryo research stipulates that embryos cannot be used for research beyond the 14-day point. At that point the 'primitive streak' (the first sign of a spinal cord) has appeared and twinning is no longer possible. Before that point, it is considered to be only a blob and the very fact that it could even split into twins at that point seems to support the view that this is not yet a single 'person' using any of the conventional criteria for defining a person. Against this view, the Catholic Church, in particular, insists that from the moment of fertilization a new life has begun, which, though it is yet to develop nearly all the qualities of a human being, should not for that reason be discounted as non-human or a non-being:

> From the time the ovum is released, a new life is begun which is neither that of the father nor of the mother; it is rather the life of a new human being with its own growth . . . and each of its capacities requires time.[52]

Pope John Paul II has argued powerfully using a 'for all we know' argument. In other words, if there is even the slightest danger that by killing a human embryo we are taking the life of a fellow human being, we ought to refrain:

> what is at stake is so important that, from the standpoint of moral obligation, the mere probability that a human person is involved would suffice to justify an absolutely clear prohibition of any intervention aimed at killing a human embryo.[53]

An embryo may not have the qualities we would normally associate with personhood, but it has the qualities proper to its stage of development. The mere willingness to enter into the possibility of killing a person is a serious matter: 'to be willing to kill what for all one knows is a person is to be willing to kill a person'.[54]

Ethical contradictions. One of the chief objections to the selecting out and destruction of embryos deemed to be imperfect is the effect this potentially has on those already living with disabilities. It brings a contradiction: on the one hand, we are attempting to eliminate prejudice against those with disabilities and disfigurements; and on the other, we are eliminating the very possibility of such people even being born. The recourse to individual choice seems to make such contradictions inevitable.

Technological greed. Another tendency in bioethics has been the attempt to critique our 'insatiable desire for innovation'.[55] The desire itself seems to breed ever-increasing desires for control over nature and destiny. Again, this has brought a strange contradiction. Here in the West, our life and health expectancies are astonishingly good compared to the rest of the world, yet it is precisely here that the greatest health anxieties are to be found.

Strangely, at a time when life expectancies in the affluent West are at levels which would have astonished our grandparents, let alone our great grand-parents, we have become anxious consumers of stories which treat our health as a subject of intense interest and concern.[56]

Playing God. This is perhaps one of the more well-worn arguments and is one that holds less and less sway as society moves away from belief in God. In this type of ethical discourse, there is a distinction between acting in the *imago dei,* which emphatically includes creativity, innovation and discovery, and acting *sicut deus,*[57] 'like' God in a way that is a 'basic distortion in our relationship to God',[58] a distinction first highlighted by Bonhoeffer.[59] The basic idea is that of warning a choice-driven society, however unheeded that warning goes, that we are overstepping the mark, that we are guilty of hubris.

Attention to the greater good. It is often pointed out that Paul would not have chosen his 'thorn in the flesh' and begged God three times to remove it yet it is clear that, in his case, tolerating the thorn brought about the greater good of God's power in weakness (2 Cor. 12.7–10). This kind of reasoning has a long history going back at least as far as Irenaeus and is known as the 'Greater Good' argument. The Irenaean theodicy is a particular form of this that draws atten-tion to the way God uses suffering as a 'soul-making' tool. John Hick famously revived the Irenaean theodicy, going so far as to claim:

> A world without problems, difficulties, perils, and hardships would be moral-ly static. For moral and spiritual growth comes through responses to chal-lenges; and in a paradise there would be no challenges.[60]

Some good qualities in people depend logically upon the presence of certain evils. There could be no courage, compassion or forgiveness, for instance, with-out the existence of the evils that make those qualities necessary. And our lives would be much the poorer for want of these virtues. Disability is one of those evils that creates opportunities for us all to become more human, and its artifi-cial elimination would be to everyone's loss.

Discussion

1 How great is the danger that, like the Catholic Church excommunicating Galileo, we will find ourselves needlessly standing in the way of progress if we object to the endeavours of genetic science?

2 Would you be willing, if necessary, to defend a 'sanctity-of-life' ethic over a 'quality-of-life' ethic to a non-Christian scientist? Give an example of how you might do this with respect to a specific dilemma presented by modern genetics.

5 Theology and the Philosophy of Science

The epistemological revolution of the early modern era gave us two opposite poles: empiricism and rationalism. Immanuel Kant sought to find a synthesis, a middle position, which took the best insights of each. However, Kant is such a giant figure that we will deal with him in the next chapter. The point is, Kant's synthesis, for all its many merits, did not finally end the polarities of Western epistemology. In fact, by the mid twentieth century those polarities were more in evidence than ever, and still bore a remarkable resemblance to the empiricist–rationalist dichotomy of the seventeenth and eighteenth centuries. At the two extreme ends of the spectrum were the following:

Positivism

This is a type of realism which is these days often referred to as 'naive realism', though such a derogatory phrase does a disservice to the stature of the philosophers who contributed to the development of positivism's greatest glories in the mid twentieth century: Ludwig Wittgenstein, A. J. Ayer, Karl Popper and others. Positivism entails the belief that certain knowledge is limited to what is perceived via the senses, but this is then understood to be capable of interpreting in a way that exactly corresponds to the real world out there (hence 'realism'). It was asserted that, so long as the right words are used in making a claim and that all claims are verifiable and falsifiable using hard observable evidence, then the claim is valid: it has the potential to become justified true belief, it corresponds in an entirely objective and unproblematic way to the real world out there.

Phenomenalism

This opposing end of the spectrum in contemporary research methodologies really came into its own in the late twentieth century with the growing postmodern mood. Even in the face of hard empirical data, the phenomenalist will be reluctant to draw any generalizable conclusions. The phenomenalist sees only particulars and shrinks from creating any general theories based on the evidence. Why? Because there is no view from nowhere.[61] It is naive to presume that objectivity can ever be achieved. All we have are perspectives and social constructs and the arbitrary system of signs which we call language. All these things differ from culture to culture.

In natural science this position is not, in practice, embraced. In fact, McGrath reminisces on his own experience of working in a laboratory in Oxford. He claims that scientists mostly do not work with any *a priori* epistemological system. They poke and prod and repeat experiments until they are sure that something works. The exact opposite is true of social science, which goes out of its way to define the ontologies, epistemologies, data-collection methods, axiologies and rhetorical frameworks that it will use. Phenomenalists (or interpretivists) in social science are known generally as constructivists because they believe there is no such thing as the social order but only norms constructed by the behaviours and language-games of the agents (people) that make them up. If you go on to do postgraduate research in theology and want to do some empirical work using surveys or interviews, you will need to be aware that by doing so you will have strayed into the growing field of social science. You will be expected to speak the native language!

Roy Bhaskar

Reacting against the growing dominance of constructivism in social science, together with the knowing snobbery around ontology and metaphysics, Bhaskar developed a new mediating position.[62] It is, perhaps inevitably, not very different from Kant's mediating position between the empiricists and the rationalists. The main difference is that, where Kant (as we will see) uses the notion of structures that are inside us called categories which give us our only means of placing a meaning on sense data, Bhaskar locates these structures, not inside the mind of the knower, but within human societies. He calls them 'causal structures'. He insists there is no need to impose a positivist framework on culture and say it is this or that because the result will be biased. But neither is there a need to abandon overarching theories entirely in deference to local particulars and language-games. There are real factors 'out there' that cause cultures to take the forms they do at particular times and places.

Bhaskar has only lately begun to be noticed by theologians.[63] This is partly because theologians have their own very similar concept, which they also call 'critical realism'. To this we will shortly turn, but first, let's have some time-out.

Terminology time-out

The sheer fluidity of concepts and terms, many of which are, to all intents and purposes, talking about the same thing, is enough to make our heads explode. This is especially the case now that, with this chapter, we have made the transition into modern philosophy. The main problem is epistemology – the study of how we know stuff – which from here on becomes very nearly a total obsession within the Western tradition. What we will do here, then, is take terms that mean something ever so similar and group them all together (see Table 1).

It is interesting to note that at both extreme ends of the table you have extreme scepticism, extreme doubt. In those columns you have notions, in fact, that psychologists would associate with very poor mental health and even delusional states of mind. They entail a rejection of commonsense or of social reality. Yet the closer we get to the middle columns, the more we are in the realm of confidence: a confidence that is all too easily sniped at by those who would rather

Table 1.

A Priori Approaches[a]			A Posteriori Approaches[b]		
All I can be sure of is my own mind and its reasoning ability.	There are other minds besides my own. In fact, the whole cosmos is really a great big mind or spirit.	I am confident about how the universe really works because I can point to a transcendent realm above both mind and matter that gives existence to both.	There is a real world out there and I am confident that, if I get my language right, I can claim absolutely and objectively true theories about the world around me or the world behind a text.	There is a real world out there and I am cautiously optimistic about identifying how it works.	There might be a real world out there but all I can be sure of are my perceptions and arbitrary linguistic rules. I am sceptical about any theorizing about the phenomena of the world around me or of the referents in the text in front of me.
Rationalism Solipsism	Idealism	Platonism Medieval Realism	Positivism Medieval Nominalism Historical Criticism (literature) Foundationalism	Critical Realism Moderate Empiricism Kant	Phenomenalism Anti-realism Relativism Humean Empiricism Postmodernism Interpretivism (social science) Deconstructionism (literature) Constructivism (social science) Structuralism (literature) Post-Structuralism (literature) Antifoundationalism

a Thinking that, whether intentionally or otherwise, starts with concepts.
b Thinking that starts with experience and observation.

stay in the two sceptical extremes. And, admittedly, positivism, which ends up being right in the middle, is probably a case of far too much confidence!

Question

Is there a biblical position? Have a go at identifying which column or columns you think a particular biblical writer would fall into, for example, Paul.

Reflection

Let's think about that word 'confidence'. How important is what we know what we know? Or, put another way, would we ever feel confident about ourselves or about anything important to us if we never felt confident about what we know?

Critical realism and theological method[64]

There is a group of great thinkers in theology who have also had a background in science and who are, in various ways, advocates of 'critical realism', a term coined for scientific theology by Ian Barbour in 1966. The originators of the conversation are mainly Bernard Lonergan and Michael Polanyi, and then their thinking was taken up by the next generation, most notably T. F. Torrance (an avid admirer of Polanyi). Torrance, in turn, is the main inspiration for the work of Alister McGrath today.

The prime motivation behind the effort to place theology on the same epistemic footing as science is summed up by Arthur Peacocke:

> we still regard the natural sciences which feed technology as the paradigm of what constitutes reliable knowledge. The corollary of this is that other forms of enquiry are tacitly demoted relative to the sciences.[65]

Bernard Lonergan even hoped that, if only theologians could all unite behind an agreed method like scientists more or less have, then maybe theology might see the same kinds of success that science has. Michael Polanyi, in his *Personal Knowledge*, even classifies all disciplines besides science on a sliding scale of diminishing success relative to the natural sciences. These thinkers were and are united by the hope that natural science can do for theology today exactly what Plato did for patristic theology and what Aristotle did for medieval theology, namely be its 'handmaid'.[66]

Theological critical realists share the conviction that knowledge needs to rely first on *a posteriori* data that is allowed to stand free of any *a priori* judgements. Having said that, the arguably *a priori* assertion that God has already made himself known or knowable to us is the backbone of T. F. Torrance's work.[67] Indeed, all the scientific theologians would agree that there must be no bracketing out of ontology. Polanyi's whole project was founded on what he saw as a misunderstanding of what it means to be objective. He cites the examples within science of the discovery made by Copernicus that the earth revolves around the sun and not vice versa, and Einstein's theories of relativity. These were embraced for their rational beauty even while empirical evidence appeared unsupportive. Polanyi points out that, even in these most celebrated examples of scientific breakthrough, there are, at the heart of the scientific enterprise, strong rational constructs which are arrived at by *rejecting* rather than *relying* on sense data.[68] Sense data, for example, would absolutely lead us to conclude that the heavenly bodies revolve around the earth.

However, scientific theologians are agreed that models are imposed upon the data with the proviso that these are always contingent. With that contingency in view, theology, in seeking to explicate itself scientifically, should not be made to fit into any particular scientific theory or general worldview. Theories are created in the hope that an ontological reality will emerge. Models are always 'partial and inadequate',[69] yet, through an iterative process, working upwards, Lonergan would say, from experiencing to understanding to judging,[70] working hypotheses are refined:

> we discover knowledge not by imposing our own frames of meaning on objects of knowledge, but by progressively adapting our frames of meaning so that they increasingly conform to the ontological nature of such objects, thereby allowing them to reveal themselves to us. Theological science and natural science are thus both *a posteriori* activities.[71]

Critical reflections

1 Scientific theology is predicated on the inherent rationality of the universe. McGrath explicitly states that being able to appreciate such rationality entails a prior commitment to God's creation of the world *ex nihilo* (Alister McGrath, 2001, *Scientific Theology 1: Nature*, Oxford: Blackwell, p. 137). He even feels free to affirm, from the outset, that the same Logos that created the world was then incarnate in Jesus of Nazareth (McGrath, *Scientific Theology 2: Reality*, pp. 213, 309). How can he affirm these things from the outset while also claiming to be asking entirely open questions of the data before him, reaching only *a posteriori* conclusions?

2 'A theological method that does not differ in any fundamental way from the methods of other disciplines discloses a God who does not differ in any fundamental way from all other beings' (Edward Hogan, 'Divine Action and Divine Transcendence: John Polkinghorne and Bernard Lonergan on the Scientific Status of Theology' *Zygon* 44:3 (Sep 2009), 558–82 [at 578]). The writer here is criticizing scientific theology for the way it potentially makes God differ only in degree but not in kind from all other existing things. In other words, if anything about him can be known via scientific enquiry he is therefore reduced to *a being* rather than *being itself*, the definition and foundation of all being. Do you agree?

For Polanyi the quest for knowledge is driven by passion, and Lonergan's use of Archimedes running naked down the street following his 'Eureka' moment suggests similar deep-seated, all-consuming devotion to discovery. For Peacocke, it must also involve a community of learners. The fundamental point of all the scientific theologians is that these are the kinds of methods that both science and theology can and should share.

Critical realism and biblical studies

So, to recap, on the one hand there is uncritical realism, or positivism. This is the notion that it is possible, in an entirely unproblematic way, to explain in words the information our senses provide us with. The words we use should, in a simple and commonsense way, correspond to the real world out there. The other extreme is what we might call the phenomenological approach. We are drawn to this when, all of a sudden, our commonsense notions about the real world out there are not as unproblematic as we had thought. Other people of different worldviews, different sensitivities and different languages might describe the same real world in an entirely different way. Instead of accepting that there are variations born of varying perspectives yet still a real world out there, some have tended to become sceptical about the very notion of a sense-independent, extra-mental universe. We start thinking that perspectives are *all* we have. We have lots of different viewpoints but nothing out there that is being viewed.

When it comes to biblical studies, the first extreme has been the supposedly objective approaches of the historical-critical methods. Yet rather than providing us with a straightforward and ideologically neutral description of the way things are, these have proven themselves to be driven by agendas and worldviews that are far from objective, leading to the idea that biblical miracles must be explained away, for example. The other extreme in biblical studies has been the ever-increasing levels of interest in the dynamics of the text itself with no attempt to reconstruct a world behind the text, no interest in the historical context. A development of this has been a growing interest in what effect the text has upon the reader, even further subjectivizing the way we use the biblical text.

Tom Wright's critical realism

Tom Wright deplores both extremes:

> To the one side we can see the positivist or the naïve realist, who move[s] so smoothly along the line from reader to text to author to referent that they are unaware of the snakes in the grass at every step; to the other side we can see the reductionist who, stooping to look at the snakes, is swallowed up by them and proceeds no further.[72]

He recommends a version of critical realism as the fundamental angle of approach, though he nowhere makes clear to whom he is indebted for this, whether Lonergan, Polanyi, Bhaskar or someone else. In Wright's critical realism the overconfidence of historical approaches is shunned but without discarding those approaches altogether. And the excesses of the subjective phenomenalist approaches – from which he finds little that can be salvaged – is also rejected while also being aware of the need to be critically aware of what a reader brings to the text, hence 'critical' realism.

In the light of Wright, we would end up with all the main methods of New Testament interpretation arranged something like Table 2, and with this we finish this chapter:

Table 2.

Realist	Critical Realist	Perspectivist	Phenomenalist
Historical-Critical		Structural Criticism	Advocacy Readings
Source Criticism	*Biblical Theology*		Deconstruction / Poststructural Criticism
Form Criticism		Canonical Criticism	Reader-Response Criticism
Redaction Criticism		Narrative Criticism	
Rhetorical Criticism			
Social-Scientific Criticism			
	Theological interpretation of Scripture and similar approaches		

Notes

1 Brown, Colin, 1969, *Philosophy and the Christian Faith*. London: Tyndale, p. 43.

2 Hans Urs von Balthasar, 1991, *The Glory of the Lord: A Theological Aesthetics V: The Realm of Metaphysics in the Modern Age*, tr. O. Davies. Edinburgh: T & T Clark, B.1, 'The Parting of the Ways', pp. 9–48. See John Milbank, 2006, *Theology and Social Theory: Beyond Secular Reason*, 2nd edition, Oxford: Backwell, p. xxiv.

3 The acceptance or non-acceptance of this reading of late medieval thought is really only one of emphasis. It is a fact that these developments in thought occurred. The debate concerns how much significance we attribute to them and whether the received account of science and progress has deliberately suppressed these aspects of the story. Paul Tyson is convinced that the familiar 'Song of Modernity' has sidelined crucial developments in late medieval philosophy (see *Returning to Reality*, pp. 47–77).

4 This idea about God being of a higher and different order to anything else stems from Plato where the Form of the Good is 'not the same thing as being, but even beyond being, surpassing it in dignity and power'. *The Republic* Book VI, 509B. F. M. Cornford translation.

5 Brown, *Philosophy and the Christian Faith*, p. 49.

6 He lived and taught in various locations in Holland for 20 years.

7 You may have come across the term 'Cartesian' in mathematics. To Descartes we owe the existence of graphs, with their 'Cartesian axes'.

8 John Cottingham, 'General Introduction: The *Meditations* and Cartesian Philosophy', in John Cottingham (ed.), 1996, *Descartes Meditations on First Philosophy: With Selections from the Objections and Replies*, Cambridge: Cambridge University Press, p. xviii.

9 Cottingham, *Descartes*, p. xviii.

10 René Descartes, 2000, *Meditations and Other Metaphysical Writings*, tr. Desmond Clarke. London: Penguin p. 19.

11 Descartes, *Meditations*, p. 20.

12 Descartes, *Meditations*, p. 20.

13 Descartes, *Meditations*, p. 20.

14 Descartes, *Meditations* in Arthur Wollaston (tr. & ed.), 1960, *Descartes Discourse on Method and other Writings*, London: Penguin, p. 106.

15 Descartes, *Meditations*, Wollaston, p. 111.

16 Descartes, *Discourse on Method*, Wollaston, p. 61.

17 Descartes, *Meditations*, Wollaston, p. 108.

18 Descartes, *Meditations*, Wollaston, p. 115.

19 Descartes, *Meditations*, Wollaston, p. 116.

20 Brown, *Philosophy and the Christian Faith*, p. 51.

21 A. J. Ayer, 1956, *The Problem of Knowledge*, London: Pelican, p. 46.

22 Thomas Hobbes, 1651, *Leviathan*, 4:46, ed. C. B. MacPherson. London: Penguin, 1985, p. 698, discussed in McIntosh, 'Newman and Christian Platonism in Britain', p. 352.

23 Baruch Spinoza, 1677, *Ethics*, Part 1. Definition 2. Translated by R. H. M. Elwes. Available online at http://www.sacred-texts.com/phi/spinoza/ethics/eth01.htm [accessed 27 June 2018].

24 Spinoza, *Ethics*, Part 1. Definition 2.

25 Spinoza, *Ethics*, Part 1: Proposition 36.

26 Spinoza, *Ethics*, Part 2. Proposition 2.

27 John Locke, 1689, *An Essay Concerning Human Understanding* II.1.2, ed. Roger Woolhouse, London: Penguin, 1997.

28 Locke, *An Essay Concerning Human Understanding*, III.9.23.

29 Jacqui Hanover, 'The Role of the Spiritual Senses in Contemporary Mission with Particular Reference to John Wesley's Employment of the Spiritual Senses: A Revised Correlational Approach', Unpublished PhD Thesis, University of Manchester, 2017.

30 Gottfried Leibniz, *New Essays on Human Understanding*, 110. In Leibniz, *New Essays on Human Understanding, abridged edition*, tr. Peter Remnant and Jonathan Bennett, Cambridge: Cambridge University Press, 1982, p. 111.

31 Gottfried Leibniz, *Monadology* 1–3, tr. Jonathan Bennett, 2007. Available online at: http://web.archive.org/web/20060219031242/http://www.earlymoderntexts.com/pdf/leib mon.pdf, p. 1 [accessed 27 June 2018].

32 David Hume, *Treatise of Human Nature*, I, iv.6.

33 Hume, *Treatise*, I, iv.7.

34 Dennis Hollinger, 2002, *Choosing the Good: Christian Ethics in a Complex World*. Grand Rapids, MI: Baker, p. 29.

35 Hollinger, *Choosing the Good*, p. 31.

36 This series of succinct definitions is one of the better ones that can be found online: 'Intensity (I) – How intense is the pleasure or pain? Duration (D) – How long does the pleasure of pain last? Certainty (C) – What is the probability that the pleasure or pain will occur? Propinquity (nearness or remoteness) (N) – How far off in the future is the pleasure or pain? Fecundity (F) – What is the probability that the pleasure will lead to other pleasures? Purity (P) – What is the probability that the pain will lead to other pains? Extent (E) – How many persons are affected by the pleasure?' http://philosophy.lander.edu/ethics/calculus.html.

37 Jeremy Bentham, 1789, *The Principles of Morals and Legislation*, Darrien, CT: Hafner, 1949, I. Cited in Hollinger, *Choosing the Good*, 32.

38 John Stuart Mill, 1863, *Utilitarianism*, Indianapolis, IN: Hackett, 1979.

39 Francis Galton, 'Eugenics: Its Definition, Scope and Aims', *The American Journal of Sociology* 10:1 (1904), 1–25 [at 2]. Galton was a cousin of Charles Darwin and his theory of Eugenics was very much a response to Darwin's theory of evolution by natural selection.

40 National Commission for the Protection of Human Subjects of Biomedical and Behavioral Research, 1978, *The Belmont Report: Ethical Principles for the Protection of Human Subjects of Research*, Washington DC: US Printing Office, pp. 4–10. Available online at https://ia600404.us.archive.org/30/items/belmontreporteth00unit/belmontreporteth00unit.pdf [accessed 09 September 2014].

41 Agneta Sutton, 2008, *Christian Bioethics: A Guide for the Perplexed*, London: T & T Clark, p. 82.

42 John Harris, 'Liberation in Reproduction', in E. Lee (ed.), 2002, *Designer Babies: Where Should We Draw the Line?* London: Hodder & Stoughton, pp. 50–1.

43 Neil Messer, 'Introduction: Theological Anthropology and the Ethics of Human Germ Line Genetic Modification', *Christian Bioethics* 18:2 (2012), 115–25 [at 115].

44 Sutton, *Christian Bioethics*, p. 83.

45 Sutton, *Christian Bioethics*, p. 89.

46 Michael Peat, 2013, *Answering Mendel's Dwarf: Thinking Theologically About Human Genetic Selection*, Oxford: Whitley Publications, p. 16.

47 John Harris, 2004, *On Cloning*, London: Routledge, p. 143.

48 Ted Peters, 'Genes, Theology and Social Ethics: Are we Playing God?' in Ted Peters (ed.), 1994, *Genetics: Issues of Social Justice*, Cleveland, OH: Crossroad, p. 29.

49 Peters, 'Genes, Theology and Social Ethics', p. 191. I am indebted to Peat, *Mendel's Dwarf* for this citation.

50 Neil Messer, 2011, *Respecting Life: Theology and Bioethics*, London: SCM, p. 114.

51 Ronald Cole-Turner, 'Beyond the Impasse Over the Embryo', in Brent Waters and Ronald Cole-Turner (eds), 2003, *God and the Embryo: Religious Voices on Stem Cells and Cloning*, Washington, DC: Georgetown University Press, p. 91. See also, Michael Sandel, 2007, *The Case Against Perfection: Ethics in the Age of Genetic Engineering*, Cambridge, MA: Harvard University Press.

52 Sacred Congregation for the Doctrine of the Faith, 1974, *Declaration on Procured Abortion*.

53 John Paul II, *Evangelium Vitae* (25 March 1995), para. 60. Available online at https://w2.vatican.va/content/john-paul-ii/en/encyclicals/documents/hf_jp-ii_enc_25031995_evangelium-vitae.html.

54 Robert Song, 'To be Willing to Kill What for all One Knows is a Person is to be Willing to Kill a Person', in Brent Waters and Ronald Cole-Turner (eds), 2003, *God and the Embryo: Religious Voices on Stem Cells and Cloning*, Washington, DC: Georgetown University Press, p. 102.

55 Peat, *Mendel's Dwarf*, p. 4.

56 Michael Banner, 2009, *Christian Ethics: A Brief History*, Oxford: Wiley, p. 134.

57 An extract from the Latin of Genesis 3.5: 'Eritis *sicut deus* scientes bonum et malum'; 'You will be like God, knowing good and evil.'

58 Messer, *Respecting Life*, p. 103.

59 Dietrich Bonhoeffer, 1997, *Creation and Fall: A Theological Exposition of Genesis 1–3*, in *Works* Vol. 3, Minneapolis: Fortress, pp. 111–14.

60 John Hick, 1977, *Evil and the God of Love*, 2nd edition, London: Macmillan, p. 372.

61 A phrase first coined by the title of Thomas Nagel's 1986, *The View from Nowhere*, Oxford: Oxford University Press.

62 His writing is difficult to read, but the first chapter of his very last solo-authored work, the posthumously published, 2016, *Enlightened Common Sense: The Philosophy of Critical Realism*, London: Routledge, is not a bad place to start.

63 E.g. Alister McGrath, 2009, *A Fine-Tuned Universe: The Quest for God in Science and Theology*, Louisville, KY: Westminster John Knox. Bhaskar himself underwent a spiritual turn later in life, resulting in four books helpfully evaluated by Andrew Wright, 2013, *Christianity and Critical Realism: Ambiguity, Truth and Theological Literacy*, London: Routledge, pp. 21–38.

64 Probably a good starting point for this field would be J. B. Stump and Alan G. Padgett (eds), 2012, *The Blackwell Companion to Science and Christianity*, Oxford: Blackwell.

65 Arthur Peacocke, 1984, *Intimations of Reality: Critical Realism in Science and Religion*, Notre Dame, IN: University of Notre Dame Press, pp. 14–15.

66 Benjamin Myers's review article quoted in full in 'Alister McGrath's Scientific Theology', in Alister McGrath, 2006, *The Order of Things: Explorations in Scientific Theology*, Oxford: Blackwell, p. 4.

67 T. F. Torrance, 1969, *Theological Science*, Oxford: Oxford University Press. Barth's theology of revelation and hence the givenness of the object of theology's enquiry was absolutely formative of T. F. Torrance's scientific theology. See McGrath's work on Torrance, e.g. 'Profile: Thomas F. Torrance', *Epworth Review* 27:3 (July 2000), 11–15.

68 'We abandon the cruder anthropocentrism of our senses – but only in favour of a more ambitious anthropocentrism of our reason.' Michael Polanyi, 1958, *Personal Knowledge: Towards a Post-Critical Philosophy*, Chicago, IL: University of Chicago Press, pp. 4–5.

69 Arthur Peacocke, 1990, *Theology for a Scientific Age*, Oxford: Blackwell, p. 14.

70 Summarized neatly in Peter Beer, 2010, *An Introduction to Bernard Lonergan: Exploring Lonergan's Approach to the Great Philosophical Questions*, Glen Waverley, Australia: Sid Harta, p. 142 and elsewhere.

71 Wright, *Christianity and Critical Realism*, p. 50.

72 N. T. Wright, 1992, *The New Testament and the People of God*, London: SPCK, p. 61.

4

Kant and the Journey to Idealism

Chapter Outline

1 The Epistemology of Immanuel Kant

Following Immanuel Kant's *Critique of Pure Reason* (1781), the role of pure reason was undermined but, at the same time, so was pure sense experience. Kant claimed that human rationality is not equipped to understand anything that lies beyond time and space. His revolutionary move was to assert that 'objects conform to concepts and not concepts to objects'.[1] He divides our knowledge of the world into two types of knowledge:

- *A priori.* This is knowledge that we hold to be true at all times and under all circumstances. It is self-evidently true, like two and two adding up to four. It is the kind of knowledge that can be attained in a way that is absolutely independent of all experience. It is arrived at by 'pure intuition'.[2] An example of this kind of conception is a basic category such as space or time.

- *A posteriori.* By contrast, this is knowledge that is possible only through experience and tends to be of a more specific kind such as how much space is available for fitting a new dishwasher or how much time has elapsed reading Kant's *Critique* to raid it for nice quotes. It is knowledge I have to find out using my senses and cannot merely intuit it. However, were there no intuitive concept of time and space, I would have no way of making any sense of the numbers I see on my tape measure before acquiring a new dishwasher and no way of interpreting what my watch says: even if I knew how to tell the time, I wouldn't know what telling the time was for. Added to time and space are such things as quantity, quality and relation: not dissimilar to Aristotle's Categories.

One important thing that Kant did here was to limit the competence of human knowledge. Both the *a priori* and *a posteriori* kind of knowing were decidedly not knowledge of anything transcendent or of any grand metaphysics. This move effectively meant that knowledge of things beyond the realm of science was uncertain and therefore unimportant to us in our quest for certain knowledge. His system finally severed questions of God and theology from the world of scientifically acquired knowledge. And it is only in the realm of ethics that Kant has a filing cabinet for the idea of God, which he calls the *summum bonum*, the ultimate good, the perfect harmony of happiness and morality. Kant's thought flattened out the knowable world and partitioned religious knowledge into the realm of privately held convictions and moral acts. Thanks to Kant the vision of a world circumscribed by the disenchanted immanence of the scientific, political and social realms starts to look realizable.

A less intentional result of the mature Kant, however, was rather less stark. As we will shortly see, Kant's break with both rationalism and empiricism by highlighting the limits of both unintentionally paved the way for the Romantic Era, provoking an exploration of intuition and even emotion as alternative, possibly more profound, ways of knowing. Confirming this were the dehumanizing new developments of industrialization that arose from Enlightenment-inspired scientific breakthroughs. The Romantic turn, at its height in the first half of the nineteenth century, would leave us a rich literary legacy including Wordsworth, Goethe and Coleridge, Lord Tennyson, Byron and Keats – poets who also saw themselves as philosophers – who were on a journey to the hidden depths of the human soul.

2 Kantian Ethics

Kant divided his moral theory into the Categorical Imperative and the Hypothetical Imperative, later adding the Practical Imperative. The most important of these is his Categorical Imperative. It is an attempt to capture a moral inclination already latent in all people everywhere, independent of religious convictions or cultural influences, and chosen without any thought as to the benefits of so acting – the deed must be right in and of itself regardless of context or consequences; it must be pure duty and only duty.[3] In other words, he felt that he had discovered an absolutely universalizable moral principle or law by which we should all live.

This is how he defines the Categorical Imperative:

Act according to that maxim by which you can at the same time will that it should become a universal law.[4]

The Hypothetical Imperative is the 'practical necessity of a possible action as a means to achieving something else which one desires'.[5] Some contextual factor makes such acts necessary, whereas a Categorical Imperative is inherently necessary and obligatory. An example might be to act fairly in business. This is generally not an entirely pure decision but has partly selfish motives as well – namely, one wants to keep one's customers. This rendered it an inferior kind of morality for Kant, though clearly necessary for everyday life.[6]

Thankfully, he added the Practical Imperative, which is really a restatement in less abstract terms of the Categorical Imperative. It is as follows:

Act so that you treat humanity, whether in your own person or in that of another, always as an end and never as a means only.[7]

His emphasis was on the underlying will to do right rather than the ends in view, which could be construed as a kind of virtue approach, but this was not his intention. His intention was to establish ethics upon a firmly rational, self-evident basis. It is a deontological ethic, a principle ethic, because it makes us think of rights and duties external to us but to which we are obliged to respond.

> **Reflection**
>
> How useful is Kant's Practical Imperative as we seek to clarify what good conduct looks like whether in government, business, church or charity?

3 The Later Kant, Idealism and Georg W. F. Hegel (1770–1831)

Kant was the springboard for the ideas that would lead to the rise of idealism as the dominant nineteenth-century philosophy and thus contribute to romanticism as the dominant cultural mood. From here on, in the West philosophical movements will continue to walk side by side with cultural shifts, usually not each other's sole cause but each one feeding and encouraging the other, the most recent of which has been the postmodern shift. The first architects of idealism actually went to quite an obscure place in Kant to find the beginnings of their new philosophy: his *Dialectic of Teleological Judgment* no. 76–7. Here Kant concedes that the notion of a non-purposive, entirely mechanistic universe is not only undesirable but philosophically extremely strained. It seems far more natural to say that the universe consists of parts that exist for the sake of wholes, a universe that is 'intelligently designed'.[8] It was with great excitement that the young Schelling and Fichte thought they detected a change in Kant's later thought that had broken with Kant's earlier sharp distinctions between nature and spirit and now conceded an 'intuitive intellect' behind all of nature.

> it is at least possible to consider the material world as mere appearance, and to think something as [its] substrate, as thing in itself (which is not appearance), and so regard this thing in itself as based on a corresponding intellectual intuition (even though not ours). In that way there would be for nature, which includes us as well, a supersensible basis of its reality . . . Indeed, absolutely no human reason (nor any finite reason similar to ours in quality, no matter how much it may surpass ours in degree) can hope to understand, in terms of

nothing but mechanical causes, how so much as a blade of grass is produced. For it seems that judgement is quite unable to study, even if it restricts itself to experience as its guide, [how] such objects are possible, without [using] the teleological connection of causes and effects. [Yet] it also seems that for external objects as appearances we cannot possibly find an adequate basis that refers to purposes, but it seems instead that, even though this basis also lies in nature, we must still search for it only in nature's supersensible substrate . . . the character of human cognitive power forces us to seek the supreme basis for such combinations in an original understanding, as cause of the world.[9]

G. W. F. Hegel's first book, in 1801, was a comparison of the Kantian philosophers Fichte and Schelling. His most famous work was his *Phenomenology of Spirit* of 1806. In it he postulated a World Spirit, of which each particular human spirit was a manifestation:

Spirit is alone Reality. It is the inner being of the world, that which essentially is, and is *per se*.[10]

Not only the world as it now is but the development of human thought and all of history itself were the development or evolution of this World Spirit or Over-Soul. Shand comments: 'The world as determined by mental categories is one with the world itself. The world/concept dualism is collapsed.'[11] Matter is no longer unquestioningly seen as the most essential or basic feature of the universe. To the contrary, matter is queried and instead spirit or mind is affirmed as the fundamental substrate of reality, infusing all things with purpose and meaning.

Truth, for Hegel, was divine and dynamic. To demonstrate that truth had a life of its own, he invited us to imagine the most basic concept of all, the concept of being. This concept, because it has no content, inevitably slides into the concept of non-being. This is known as a dialectic, the idea of two opposite ideas that never reach equilibrium: a thesis and an antithesis. The only way to resolve the being and non-being is by way of the synthesis: Becoming. And this is the way truth manifests itself in all human history, since for Hegel everything is but a transitory expression of the Eternal Absolute. History itself is a process of thesis, antithesis and its resolving synthesis. A synthesis takes the best of both opposing elements to bring forth some new revelation of God, until the synthesis itself becomes a thesis and so on. This process is taking humanity nearer and nearer to the goal of perfect freedom. This was the part that the materialist Hegelians like Karl Marx were especially fond of, using it to devise some of the key aspects of the concept of the communist revolution.

Religion, defined by Hegel as God's self-consciousness,[12] does not struggle to find a place in Hegel's thought: at last, a philosophy to keep *everyone* happy perhaps. There was now not even any issue with the incarnation.[13] When, in 1859, Darwin's theory threatened to undermine the concept of a meaningful universe, Hegel's idealism promised to hold because it had all along posited that very thing: an ever-evolving world of nature, thought and human action. Indeed, it was not until 1865 that Hegel's ideas reached the British public. The idealism that had fed the Romantic movement had been that inspired by Fichte, Schelling and others who had already seen in Kant just enough idealism to build upon. Now, Hegelian idealism seemed to present 'a spiritual bulwark against the rising tides of materialism and secularism'.[14] Idealism was the dominant philosophical style in the British university departments until its eclipse in the early twentieth century by the rise of the analytic tradition with Bertrand Russell and Ludwig Wittgenstein, and then the extremes of logical positivism in the Vienna Circle of the mid twentieth century.

Reflection

Matter is a fiction. There is no material substance. No substratum. No extended unthinking substance. There are only minds and ideas. To think this way about the world, about persons, indeed about every created and uncreated thing, is to be an 'idealist'. Little else in philosophy provokes as many quizzical, brow-raising looks and sometimes outright ridicule, as one who claims to be an idealist. For contemporary philosophers of religion as well as theologians, idealism is peculiar to say the least. Yet idealism and its main thesis, that minds are most real and the physical world is mind-dependent, has proven to be extraordinarily resistant to refutation. (Joshua Farris and S. Mark Hamilton, 'Introduction: Idealism and Christian Theology', in Farris and Hamilton (eds), 2017, *Idealism and Christian Theology: Idealism and Christianity Volume 1*, London: Bloomsbury, pp. 1–7 [at 1])

Can you prove the existence of matter?

4 The Popular Influence of German Idealism

Nineteenth-century romanticism

Stimulated by the literary outputs of Schelling, Fichte and other Kantians, the nineteenth century was actually the time when the thought of the seventeenth-century philosopher Baruch Spinoza became popular. His pantheistic assertions were a source of inspiration. You may recall his assertion: 'Whatever is, is in God, and without God nothing can be, or be conceived.'[15] The idealists were now presenting one meaning-infused way that united God and humans. It was this immanence of God within the universe that was just the re-enchantment that a new post-Enlightenment generation was looking for after the cold logic of rationalism and empiricism. Romanticism was the new mood and would infuse the arts for most of the nineteenth century. In the case of music, the Romantic approach continued to thrive until Rachmaninov in the mid twentieth century. Philosophically, however, the idealism underlying romanticism did not survive the First World War. Darwinism, too – although Hegelian idealism initially seemed to answer it – made it harder and harder to sustain a belief in a purposeful universe. Philosophies that accommodated the blow to meaning held more promise: the initially abortive phase of pragmatism and the existentialism of Heidegger.

The metaphysical cults

Origins in Transcendentalism

Boasting Ralph Waldo Emerson as its most famous and eloquent exponent, Transcendentalism was 'the first intellectual movement in the history of the still-new nation'.[16] It was America's first home-grown philosophy and was profoundly and unashamedly influenced by Kant, Hegel and other German idealist philosophers filtered mostly through British writers in the Romantic tradition such as Samuel Coleridge and Thomas Carlyle. Added in were bits and pieces from Eastern religions. This produced the basic idea that humans are, at least potentially, divine. According to Emerson, Jesus himself paved the way for us to realize this divine potential:

> One man was true to what is in you and me. He saw that God incarnates himself in man, and evermore goes forth to take possession of his world. He said, in his jubilee of sublime emotion, 'I am divine. Through me, God acts; through me, speaks. Would you see God, see me.'[17]

Humans possess a higher faculty of reason, way beyond Lockean sense interpretation, that they called 'intuition' or even 'faith'. By this faculty, this faith, this 'spiritual intimation',[18] humans were capable of direct encounter with God. Many were from Christian backgrounds but had become Unitarians in their pursuit of 'nondogmatic experimentalism'.[19] The heart of the Transcendentalist idea, according to Buell, was 'the idea of a divinity latent within each person, whose ordinarily underactivated potential is not to be reasoned into being so much as ignited'.[20] They were reacting, as most Romantics were at the time, to the 'cool rationality of Enlightenment materialism and deism'.[21] One of the principal doctrines of the New England Transcendentalists was 'the supremacy of mind over matter'.[22] Transcendentalism helped fuel the optimistic 'can do' mentality of New England expansionism. It was a belief in the unlimited potential of the individual.

New Thought and Christian Science

The visionary self-actualizing outlook of the Transcendentalist movement, though it was confined to New England (especially Boston) and was at its height only from the mid 1830s to the mid 1840s, contributed significantly to the metaphysical cults such as New Thought and Christian Science. P. P. Quimby, the founder of New Thought, applied mind-over-matter idealism to the pursuit of happiness and wholeness:

> Now when people are educated to understand that *what they believe they will create*, they will cease believing what the medical men say, and try to account for their feelings in a more rational way.[23]

Quimby's main concern was with healing, yet it was clear that his beliefs about the powerful effects of thinking positively had much wider ramifications. Quimby had already described his beliefs as the 'Science of Life'[24] and the 'Science of Happiness'.[25] The implications of his message were soon noticed. Mary Baker Eddy, the founder of Christian Science, would be the best-known popularizer of Quimby's beliefs. A holistic philosophy of life emerged which perceived that the secret not only of bodily healing, but also of prosperity and well-being of every kind, was to exclude all negative thoughts and maintain a positive outlook on life.

New Thought advocates equated the positive with the divine: 'New Thought overcomes sickness by health, anger by love, evil by good, error by truth. The things of God are positive, any negation is lack of God.'[26] Becoming a positive person was a step towards the 'recognition, realization and manifestation of God in man'.[27] God was understood to be universal Mind; therefore, to get one's own mind into harmony with the positive divine Mind was to achieve union with the divine. Once this happened, you could create your life: 'the real cause of every event is an internal, non-material idea'.[28] And the key was 'faith'. For Ralph Waldo Trine, faith was 'the operation of the *thought forces* in the form of an earnest desire, coupled with the expectation as to its fulfilment'.[29] In Quimby, the very same idea is given the term 'Mind', to which he gives the meaning, 'matter held in solution'.[30] Mind can materialize its own reality. With Charles Fillmore, the founder of Unity, 'mind' and 'faith' are brought together: 'Faith is the perceiving power of the mind linked with a power to shape substance.'[31]

American metaphysics, then, was a constellation of idealist beliefs that found their genesis in an anglicized version of German idealism and shared a strong belief in the creative powers of the inner self. This creative force was able to bring to realization whatever positive state was mentally envisaged. I have covered this branch of popular idealism in some detail because of the strong similarities with much later 'name it and claim it' approaches to health and prosperity with which historical links have been demonstrated.[32] The nineteenth-century preacher E. W. Kenyon fell under the spell of New Thought and integrated it with his teaching. Kenneth Hagin then came across his work and appropriated it. He was then followed by Kenneth Copeland, Joyce Meyer and others.

Reflection

Can you think of instances that you have witnessed when a mind-over-matter, or a positive thinking and speaking approach was deployed in prayer or ministry to others? In what ways do these uses of faith correspond – or fail to correspond – to the New Testament concept of faith?

Discussion

Quantum physics has conclusively shown that the mind inherently has some tiny power, enough to cause light to act like a particle. The real question is how much more power the mind has naturally. (William DeArteaga, 1992, *Quenching the Spirit: Examining Centuries of Opposition to the Moving of the Holy Spirit*, Altamonte Springs: Creation House, pp. 161–2)

In the light of the findings of quantum physics, William DeArteaga argues that some form of 'Faith-Idealism' (DeArteaga, *Quenching the Spirit*, pp. 131–2, 212) is the only position a Christian should take. Discuss.

Marxism

The idealist view of the world not only gives us a way of re-enchanting it, but such a view also causes us to see the world as a malleable, plastic place, a place where things can change. Karl Marx took his inspiration for the communist revolution from Hegel, who believed that change can occur in society only through a process which, as we saw, is described as thesis, antithesis and synthesis. In Marxist political theory, revolution is seen as the populace freeing itself from the shackles of big business and religion. The 'bourgeoisie' were the thesis, the 'proletariat' were the antithesis and the communist revolution would be the synthesis. This would be the cure for human alienation. Alienation, according to Marx, comes about when workers no longer have any share in what they produce: it's all for someone else, a bourgeois businessman who has somehow acquired the right to buy what the workers produce and sell it at a profit which the workers themselves never see the benefit of. The proletariat then find that they need religion as an 'opiate' to dull the pain of their alienation and in some way compensate for what society is not giving them. Shared ownership of the means of production was the cure: 'From each according to his ability and to each according to his need.'

5 Christian Idealisms

George Berkeley (1685–1763)[33]

Berkeley can actually lay claim to being the very first modern idealist, predating Hegel by more than a century. His key maxim is fascinating to turn over in your mind:

> To be is to be perceived or to perceive.

Such an assertion is all the more intriguing given Berkeley's otherwise perfectly orthodox, creed-affirming Anglican faith. The springboard for his epistemic leap seems to be the thing that Locke admitted was the absolute frontier of his understanding. Locke, like Berkeley, affirmed that we can know nothing of the world around us but our perceptions. This being the case, for us to postulate some kind of real world out there requires us to place beneath these perceptions an underlying substrate of some kind, and it was this that Locke could only describe as an 'I know not what'. At this point, it is clear just how hard it is to prove to anyone the existence of matter. Supposing, Berkeley thought, there was no substrate called matter but a substrate that is simply another thinking and perceiving mind besides our own. This mind is continuously producing all the things that we, and all other perceivers, perceive. This mind, or spirit, is God. We need not posit the existence of matter in order for the world to make sense. In fact one difficulty, at least, is circumnavigated, namely the problem of how, as Christians, we are to understand divine, and hence non-material, interventions into a material world. Suddenly there are not two different kinds of stuff interacting but only one basic kind: spirit. A little like with Platonism, with which Berkeley became very enamoured later in life, Berkeley's idealism presents us with a re-enchanted universe, indwelt in the most intimate of terms with the being of God.

Having done away with Locke's 'I know not what' and put mind there instead, Berkeley then differentiates between ideas that are caused by the imagination of the perceiver and mental ideas that are not caused by ourselves but are perceptions of things over which we have no power and which other persons also perceive in the same way. These must be produced by some other mind, namely, the mind of God.[34] Further, it then becomes easy to explain God to the 'unthinking herd'[35] who insist that, because they cannot see God, they cannot believe in him. Berkeley brusquely insists that such people only need open their eyes. In just the same way that other human minds make their contents known to us through speaking – and this is the only evidence we have for the existence of other minds – so the great divine Mind makes himself known to us through his world. 'This Visual language', he asserts, 'proves, not a creator merely, but a provident Governor, actually and intimately present, and attentive to all our interests.'[36]

Jonathan Edwards (1703–58)

As a veteran of one of the greatest revivals of religion ever witnessed, the spectacular 'Great Awakening' which swept through several key towns in New England in the 1730s and 1740s, it is perhaps natural that Edwards would firmly believe that God is not distant but fills the world with his presence. He had witnessed especially remarkable phenomena in Northampton, Massachusetts in 1735–6 when he famously reported that 'the town seemed to be full of the presence of God'.[37]

Edwards did even more than Berkeley had done with the idea of God's mind speaking to us in nonverbal ways. Edwards was very fond of the idea of types and antitypes, greatly extending the concept. It is widely acknowledged by students of the Bible that certain aspects of Jesus and the gospel message are prefigured in the Old Testament. For example, the tabernacle is seen by the writer to the Hebrews as a type of Christ and the new covenant he inaugurated, but Edwards even thought that there are New Testament types that have their antitype in the present-day church, as well as types in the world of nature and human life that we may observe all around us now. Examples of this last kind include:[38]

- Meadows and gentle breezes = the sweet benevolence of Jesus Christ.
- Blue sky = the mildness and gentleness of Christ.
- Comets, thunders, rocks, mountains = God's awful majesty.
- Helpless new born babies = the nakedness and wretchedness of humans in their natural state.
- The unfailing rays of the sun = God's all-sufficient bounty and goodness.
- The pains of childbirth = the pains of the church in 'bringing forth Christ'.
- The waves and billows of the sea = the wrath of God.
- The rising of the sun = the resurrection of Christ bringing the world from darkness into light.

Edwards's doctrine of creation, perhaps inevitably, merges with his doctrine of providence: 'the universe is created out of nothing every moment'.[39] He seems to have in mind the teaching of the New Testament that Christ 'sustains all things by his powerful word' (Heb. 1.3), which in Edwards's version would have read 'upholds', implying perhaps a highly active, ongoingly creative act.

Reflection

Read Psalm 19.1–4; Colossians 1.17; Hebrews 1.3. To what extent is the biblical worldview an idealist one?

Does idealism, or some version of it, help us to be affirming of and to look for manifestations of the presence of God in our prayer life, church life or, as Edwards witnesses in 1735, in our local town centre?

Friedrich Schleiermacher (1768–1834)

At the very heart of the Romantic movement was Friedrich Schleiermacher. Schleiermacher attempted to show Enlightenment intellectuals that Christianity was reasonable, even indispensable. Raised as a Pietist, he greatly desired the kind of spiritual experiences he saw around him but never had them. However, his fellow Moravians were unable to answer his searching questions. As a result, he left and was virtually disowned by his father.

In 1799 he wrote *On Religion: Speeches to its Cultured Despisers*. In it, he argues that to be religious is part of what it means to be human, describing it as 'sense and taste for the infinite'. He sidestepped the rationalism of the period, threw himself into the Romantic movement then flourishing in Berlin and asserted the utter centrality of religion to human life. He agreed with Kant that we cannot know about God through the rational mind, or through experience but rejected his conclusion that religion should therefore be about ethical action instead of knowing. There was a third option. True religion was about 'feeling'. By this, he meant more than just emotion. He meant that the feeling of dependence on an infinitely greater being, the awareness of our own limitations, is the essence of religion. The Godness of God is revealed in the very humanness of humans and their helpless dependence on Him.

Schleiermacher was followed by Albrecht Ritschl (1822–89) and others at Tübingen to form the great nineteenth-century school of liberal theology.

John Foster (1941–2009)

Foster, an Anglican who converted to Roman Catholicism, was one of the few advocates for idealism in recent times.[40] His last work, *A World for Us* is dedicated, tellingly, to George Berkeley. Like Berkeley's idealism, Foster's vision is closely aligned to empiricism. It is a view of the world that is orchestrated by God to make empirical sense to us, so that it is a world 'for us'. He calls this 'phenomenalistic idealism'. He appears to see the alternative as a wholly unacceptable naive realism in which it is simply taken for granted that we have straightforward perceptual access to the world.[41] It is easy to become lost in his complex discussions of the nature of perception, but he occasionally condenses his argument: 'it is clear that it [phenomenalistic idealism] opposes these realist claims through and through. It takes all physical facts to be constitutively reducible to non-physical facts and all aspects of the character of the physical world to be logically dependent on facts about human mentality.'[42] His phenomenalistic idealism ensures, for him, 'the requisite empirical immanence of the world',[43] while citing God as the one who secures the necessary objectivity. In other words, the world out there is a real world but only in so far as it is the direct creation of a real God. And this real God has made our minds in such a way that we can rationally understand the world that he presents to our senses. God, he claims, makes this world into more than a 'virtual reality'[44] to us.

Discussion 1

> Mind as ultimate reality provides easy and natural explanations for the origin of the cosmos, cosmic and biological fine-tuning, the emergence of life, and the fact of consciousness, while naturalism struggles mightily to account for each of these things. (James Spiegel, 'Idealism and the Reasonableness of Theistic Belief', in Farris and Hamilton, *Idealism and Christian Theology Volume 2*, p. 18)

But what about Hiroshima, Nagasaki and the Holocaust? Does not idealism land us with some big questions to answer here? Everything is, literally, God's idea, right?

Discussion 2

Now read Ephesians 6.12. In line with this passage, an idealist would assert that there are other minds acting within the cosmos, including evil spirits. The Ephesians passage seems to ask us to open our eyes to this spiritual reality behind appearances. Does accommodating other wills, minds or spirits within the idealist universe help to answer the problem of evil?

6 Conclusion

Idealism provided a welcome reprieve to Christianity during the nineteenth century, delaying the full implementation of the findings of Kant, which was that human cognition simply is not competent to make any certain judgements about the realm of the sublime. Once idealism faded in the 1920s, the process could continue of bracketing out religion from public discourse and reserving it for the realm of private personal convictions. A new wave of positivism and empiricism swept the universities.

But there are problems with idealism. While it does seem to be the case that matter remains something that must be postulated and its existence cannot be conclusively proved, yet the consequences of *not* postulating it do seem to give us more problems than when we do postulate it. Idealism, without this matter-ist anchor point, becomes very slippery. It has a way of sliding into solipsism[45] in the high anthropology of the transcendentalists and metaphysical cults who saw themselves as divine and had an exaggerated view of what their own minds could achieve. But then idealism just as easily slides into pantheism in which everything is an emanation of God to the obliteration of all else. But then, supposing we steer clear of pantheism and allow for the existence of evil spirits? Go too far down that road and you end up with a terrifying dualism in which God and Satan are at war and, because there is no 'natural' realm absolutely everything that happens is deemed to be the direct product of divine or demonic activity (ever met anyone like that?). We could picture the situation using three circles. If any of the circles become too big we end up with a worldview that creates more problems than it solves (see Figure 1).

Figure 1.

Discussion

It seems clear that a theistic worldview would compel us to make the God circle bigger than the other circles but without swallowing them up. Have a go at drawing the circles for yourself, making each one the size you think it should be. Does this then give us something approximating a biblical worldview?

Notes

1 Cited in Simon Critchley and William Schroeder (eds), 1999, *A Companion to Continental Philosophy*, Oxford: Blackwell, p. 29.

2 Immanuel Kant, 1781, *Critique of Pure Reason*, tr. J. Meiklejohn, London: Dent, 1934, p. 42.

3 Immanuel Kant, 1785, *Foundations for the Metaphysics of Morals*, tr. Lewis Beck, Indianapolis, IN: Bobbs-Merrill, 1959, p. 16.

4 Kant, *Foundations for the Metaphysics of Morals*, p. 39.

5 Kant, *Foundations for the Metaphysics of Morals*, p. 31.

6 Hollinger, *Choosing the Good*, 39.

7 Kant, *Foundations for the Metaphysics of Morals*, p. 47.

8 Critchley and Schroeder, *Companion to Continental Philosophy*, pp. 37.

9 Immanuel Kant, 1790, *Critique of Judgment*, Part II, 'Critique of Teleological Judgment', §77, 409–10, tr. Werner S. Pluhar, Indianapolis, IN: Hackett, 1987, pp. 293–4.

10 G. W. F. Hegel, 1807, *The Phenomenology of Mind*, Preface para. 25, tr. J. B. Baillie, Digireads facsimile, 2009, p. 20

11 Shand, *Philosophy and Philosophers*, p. 165.

12 G. W. F. Hegel, 1832, *Lectures on the Philosophy of Religion*, tr. Peter C. Hodgson, Berkeley, CA: University of California Press, 1988, e.g. pp. 114–15.

13 Brown, *Philosophy and the Christian Faith*, p. 122.

14 Brown, *Philosophy and the Christian Faith*, p. 123.

15 Baruch Spinoza, *Ethics* Part I. 18.

16 Lawrence Buell (ed.), 2006, *The American Transcendentalists: Essential Writings*, New York: The Modern Library, p. xi.

17 Cited in Philip Gura, 2008, *American Transcendentalism: A History*, New York: Hill and Wang, p. 103.

18 Gura, *American Transcendentalism*, p. 54.

19 Buell, *The American Transcendentalists*, p. xviii.

20 Buell, *The American Transcendentalists*, p. xxiii.

21 Douglas Anderson, 'Idealism in American Thought', in Armen Marsobian and John Ryder (eds), 2004, *The Blackwell Guide to American Philosophy*, Oxford: Blackwell, p. 24.

22 C. S. Braden, 1963, *Spirits in Rebellion: The Rise and Development of New Thought*, Dallas, TX: Southern Methodist University Press, pp. 28–9.

23 H. W. Dresser (ed.), 1921, *The Quimby Manuscripts*, New York: Thomas Y. Crowell, p. 263 (italics original).

24 Dresser, *Quimby*, p. 241.

25 Dresser, *Quimby*, p. 253.

26 Robert Mitchell, 2011, *The Awakening Word*, Bloomington, IN; Author House, p. 176.

27 Mitchell, *The Awakening Word*, p. 176.

28 R. S. Ellwood, 1988, *Religious and Spiritual Groups in North America*, Englewood Cliffs, NJ: Prentice Hall, p. 64.

29 Ralph Waldo Trine, 1970, *In Tune with the Infinite*, New York: Bobbs-Merrill, p. 19 (italics his).

30 Dresser, *Quimby*, p. 234.

31 C. Fillmore, 1936, *Prosperity*, Kansas: Unity School of Christianity, p. 43.

32 See my, 2017, *Bold Faith: A Closer Look at the Five Key Ideas of Charismatic Christianity*, Eugene, OR: Wipf & Stock, pp. 67–87.

33 Excellent recent studies of the idealism of Berkeley and Edwards can be found in Joshua Farris and S. Mark Hamilton (eds), 2017, *Idealism and Christian Theology: Idealism and Christianity*, 2 vols, London: Bloomsbury.

34 George Berkeley, 1901, *The Works of George Berkeley* vol. 1, ed. A. C. Fraser. Oxford: Clarendon Press, pp. 29–30.

35 Berkeley, *Works*, 1, p. 148.

36 Berkeley, *Works*, 2: 4.14.

37 Jonathan Edwards, 'A Faithful Narrative of the Surprising Work of God', in Ola Winslow (ed.), 1966, *Jonathan Edwards: Basic Writings*, New York: New American Library, p. 101.

38 From William Wainwright, 'Berkeley, Edwards, Idealism, and the Knowledge of God', in Farris and Hamilton, *Idealism and Christian Theology*, Volume 1, p. 42.

39 Jonathan Edwards, *The Works of Jonathan Edwards* (New Haven, CT: Yale University Press, 1957–2008), vol. 6, p. 241.

40 John Foster, 1982, *The Case for Idealism*, London: Routledge & Kegan Paul; 2000, *The Nature of Perception*, Oxford: Oxford University Press; and, 2008, *A World for Us: The Case for Phenomenological Idealism*, Oxford: Oxford University Press.

41 Foster, *A World for Us*, p. 1.

42 Foster, *A World for Us*, p. 107.

43 Foster, *A World for Us*, p. 243.

44 Foster, *A World for Us*, p. vii.

45 The idea that, to all intents and purposes, only the self exists. The existence of other minds is doubted.

5

Philosophy in Revolt: Existentialism

Chapter Outline

1 Introduction

'Existential thinking' means thinking in a way which involves one's whole life. It means the attitude of one who is at every moment involved in the question at issue, that is, of one who is no spectator. 'Existentially' is the very opposite of all that is academic, abstract or theoretical. We think 'existentially' when we are conscious that for us matters of life and death are at stake.[1]

To a very large degree, existentialism may be defined as being, quite deliberately, the exact opposite of the philosophical system that had become orthodox across the universities of Europe right up until the outbreak of the First World War, namely, idealism. We can picture this as in Table 3.

Table 3.

Idealism	Existentialism
The universe is enchanted by spirit or mind.	The universe is an empty, random place into which I am born by chance.
Determinism dominates.	Free choice dominates.
Life is imbued with meaning and purpose.	Life is absurd and pointless.
Universal history is getting us somewhere good.	All that matters is my own history: Have I been living authentically or not?
Idealism essentializes human nature.	Existentialism emphasizes the estrangement of humans from their own essential nature.

It was not the only revolt against idealism that ended up dominating the middle decades of the twentieth century: this was only the Continental version of anti-idealism. The Anglophone version was the analytic tradition, which we will consider in the next chapter. Hence, the aftermath of the horrors of the First World War was the moment of a noticeable parting of the ways between the two traditions.

Existentialism was not only anti-idealist, however. There is more that existentialism was seeking to be the antidote to. It was seeking to be a philosophy of being, an ontology in the truest sense as opposed to a philosophy of science or a mere epistemology. In Heidegger, we encounter a frustration with attempts to describe all that there is to say about humans using scientific and epistemological categories. Scientific conceptions of humanity lower human beings to the level of *Vorhandenheit*, the being of things, substances, when really we should be looking at humans from the viewpoint of *Existenz*, the phenomenon of *human* being, of the understanding and consciousness of our existence that is given uniquely with *human* existence.

As we will see, Heidegger even developed his own set of existential categories to replace Kant's set of categories, which were designed for analysing the being of *things*. Heidegger would explain the failure of the human sciences to achieve success on anything like the scale of the natural sciences as being precisely due to this category mistake. We have been using the right lens for natural science: studying the being of *things* but then tried to use that same lens for the study of *human being*.

However, existentialism, as every introductory text book will say, is not a single philosophy united by a common doctrine. It is rather a mood or attitude towards the historic questions of philosophy characterized by a move away from the abstract and towards the immersive. It is a wallowing, if you like, in the terrifying matters of life and death as these actually confront us in real life. It is an attempt to get past the gridlock created by never-ending epistemological questions so as to arrive at a particularly raw and minimalistic kind of ontology. It is a study of pure being as self-consciously experienced by human beings, a study of *our* existence.

Existentialism proper does not really begin until Martin Heidegger but has some really important antecedents from the nineteenth century ranging from the Danish Christian thinker Søren Kierkegaard (pronounced 'kierk-a-gore') to the novelists Fyodor Dostoyevsky and Franz Kafka, both creators of bleak worlds inhabited by pathetic or sordid characters caught in hopeless situations. Friedrich Nietzsche's name also often appears in books about existentialism. Though none of these would have even been aware of the term 'existentialist', their influence upon the leading existentialist thinkers justifies including them in the general picture. This is especially so in the case of Kierkegaard, whom we will look at in a moment. Some existentialists were theists – Søren Kierkegaard (Lutheran), Nikolai Berdyaev (Orthodox), Gabriel Marcel (Roman Catholic), Martin Buber (Jewish) – and some were atheists – Martin Heidegger, Jean-Paul Sartre, Karl Jaspers.

Existentialism was popularized in the 1960s by Jean-Paul Sartre. His was a philosophy of self-actualization, an affirmation of being in the face of the absurdity that surrounds us. Inauthentic existence is life lived to please others or in a way that accepts limitations on one's freedom. Authentic existence results from a 'leap of faith'. Life as it presents itself to us is essentially without meaning, provoking Albert Camus to write that we should focus, above all else, on the question of why we should not all commit suicide.[2] Life is absurd, so there are no objective criteria for this leap in the dark, but we must make that leap if we are to live an authentic life. Until that happens, life will remain meaningless, for life, according to the existentialists, is what you make it. Meaning is what we give to life through the choices we make. And this need to make a choice means that

'The very thing that makes us unique among the vast array of things that exist in the world – *our freedom* – is also our biggest burden.'[3] We are condemned to be free.

In exploring the fundamental nature of human existence as it greets us every day, the existentialists shared a common quest to restore the task of philosophy to something more like what it looked like 2,500 years ago. The Greeks were interested in all of life, not simply the narrow and exclusive academic concerns of how we know things. And because of this conviction, many of the existentialists have written novels and plays that are not for other academics at all but for ordinary people, Sartre being a particular case in point.

Reflection

Thanks to Kierkegaard's faith and Heidegger's interest in the New Testament, it is almost inevitable that there are Christian resonances creeping in, despite the rather depressing starting points of existentialist writers. Did any doctrines of the Christian faith come to mind as you read this introduction?

---

2 Søren Kierkegaard (1813–55)

Kierkegaard, who spent all his life in Copenhagen, is an enigmatic writer whose works seem to resonate with people more than ever. In fact, he is quasi-postmodern in that he always resisted any claim to have authority over the meaning of his own writings, rejecting the idea that the author's intention, should be the final arbitrator of meaning. Meaning-making was something he did in conversation with the reader, as 'co-reader with his readers'.[4] Kierkegaard, being from a well-to-do family, did not need to work so was not part of an institution but was a prolific freelance writer.

Kierkegaard felt that his mission (not unlike Bonhoeffer in modern times) was to reintroduce true faith to a Christendom-dominated, culturally Christian society that did not live up to any Christian values. Coming from a strict Pietist background with a strict father, he was riddled with anxiety and melancholy, to such an extent that he broke off an engagement due to not wanting to subject his fiancée to his melancholy.

The notable thing about his work is the clean break with the rationalistic idealism of Hegel and a much more existence-orientated approach to doing philosophy.

Some key concepts of Kierkegaard include:

The aesthetic life

This was part of his critique of the superficial culture of his day. He observed that the lives of many of his contemporaries were an endless pursuit of spectacle, a leisure pursuit of the chattering classes that consume cultural products. The aesthetic life is life lived entirely for oneself. Aesthetic people are not interested in right or wrong but only in interesting or boring.

The ethical life

This is the life lived for others. Living this life involves one in a concern, not for the interesting or the boring but the right and the wrong. However, despair haunts this life of duty just as much as it haunts the imaginary worlds of wonder that the aesthetic life is always offering. While the aesthetic life might be too frivolous, the ethical life is too serious. This is described in his charmingly titled, *The Sickness Unto Death*.

The religious life

This is a life lived for God. Christianity is a communication of the possibilities of existence. It communicates a capability. It does not dictate belief but makes true belief possible. The life of faith is the ideal life described pseudonymously in *Fear and Trembling*. It is a life of simple devotion free from the allure of the aesthetic and from the expectations of others. In the life of faith, we die utterly to the world.

3 Martin Heidegger (1889–1976)

Heidegger began his philosophical journey as a follower of Edmund Husserl (1859–1938). Husserl was the inventor of 'phenomenology', which is the study of perception. Husserl saw himself as continuing the quest for certain knowledge that Descartes and Kant had been on. He saw himself as crowning their efforts with the assertion that it simply does not matter whether or not there is a real world out there. All that matters is that 'I take it to be' a real world full of real objects. What mattered was the 'intentional' content in the perception. He famously 'bracketed' off the question of real objectivity in order to examine what no previous philosopher of knowledge had done and focus on the 'aboutness' and 'directedness' of consciousness. It is impossible to think without thinking about something. Awareness is always awareness *of* something.

Heidegger was tired of the subject–object dualism that had been the leading preoccupation of Descartes, Hume and Kant, and now Husserl. Husserl was simply taking the old 'How do I make sense of myself as a subject in a world of objects?' question and trying to conclude it. He was still locked inside Descartes' world which consisted of two different kinds of being: mental and material. Husserl resolved this into a monism of consciousness but was still locked into that world where only those two things were ever an option for philosophy to consider. Heidegger pointed out that there is a whole aspect of existence which we are not even conscious of at all. In fact, most of the time we are not directing our consciousness out towards the world of objects at all. He uses the illustration of a carpenter using a hammer. The carpenter has got so used to using a hammer that he is not even conscious of what he is doing. Only if a problem arose – he picked up the wrong hammer, or the head came off – would he become conscious and his mind show the directedness and aboutness that Husserl seemed to think characterized all consciousness. Similarly with driving or with opening a door, these things fill our lives and yet we have no recollection of them most of the time. We are not conscious of any of the most routine aspects of our lives. The experienced carpenter can chat away to a fellow carpenter or think about his lunch and not need to concentrate on what he is doing. Heidegger describes this using such terms as 'transparent coping', 'primordial understanding' and 'ready-to-hand' entities where 'we just do not find conscious objects directed towards independent objects at all'.[5] Therefore, such epistemological preoccupations are not even addressing the most important questions of human existence. Humans are not spectators or passive observers of the world of knowable objects. Humans are always participants in the stuff of life. We are not knowing subjects but beings, and we care about what it means to be. 'Thinking is only one way of engaging with the world: acting upon it and reacting to it are at least as important elements.'[6]

Ontology, not epistemology is the primary concern then, hence Heidegger's best-known book: *Being and Time* of 1927. In taking up the question of ontology, Heidegger felt that he was taking up again the big questions of ancient philosophy and had spent a great deal of time in Aristotle just prior to writing *Being and Time*. Combined with this was an interest in Pauline temporality: how Paul's writings reveal the experience of a church living 'between the times'. Augustine, Luther and Kierkegaard also played a part in the formation of Heidegger's thought.

So, we are always already in the world, a state that Heidegger describes using, notably, a verb rather than a noun, the German verb *Dasein* (pronounced 'Darzine'), which can be translated as 'being-in', or 'being-in-the-world'.[7] Central to this whole concept is that of 'care'. The real stuff of being is to do with what we care about. For this reason, being is never static but is always pressing into new possibilities. In the second half of *Being and Time* he describes this active being-in-the-world in terms of a threefold structure:

- *Mood*. This aspect of *Dasein* is what causes things to matter, and to present themselves as threatening or attractive, difficult or useful. This attunement or mood describes the way our situation always already matters to us. Hence, we cannot start from a neutral mood-less standpoint, whether as individuals or as societies. Rather these are the givens of our situation, which require response.
- *Understanding*. By this he is referring to the fact that the world doesn't present itself dumb and awaiting our description. The world presents itself as already existing in a complex set of relations he calls the 'referential totality of significance'.[8] It is the 'articulation of the situation in which we currently find ourselves'.[9] 'Understanding' describes our present usage of things and present experience of the world, not as something passive but which rises up to meet us and compels our involvement. So, not only are we not neutral spectators, neither is the world a passive set of things.

- *Towards-which*. This is the future-orientated aspect of being that causes us to be always pressing in to new possibilities. We have plans and goals, whether these are big or small. Everything is done 'for-the-sake-of'[10] such goals.

So what?

The key outcomes of analysing our existence in these ways are:

For philosophy

This approach frees philosophy from the Enlightenment epistemological binaries and restores more of the holistic emphasis of ancient philosophy. It is not that Heidegger claims that the either thinking self or the real world do not exist. Rather, he is claiming that our very preoccupation with such things is a cul-de-sac that ultimately does not matter nearly as much as we seem to imagine. The old dualisms are replaced, supposedly, by a singular and holistic 'being-present-at-hand-together' of subject and object.[11]

For everyone

Heidegger's analysis of being leads him into some crucial explorations around the idea of authenticity. A new kind of binary emerges that we could describe as follows:

- *Anxiety.* Not being at home is the way he describes our slow realization of the groundlessness of the givens that we find ourselves always already in. We are plunged into a set of norms and practices that do not have to be that way. If we are to be intelligible to others then some level of conformity to this set of arbitrary norms is necessary, especially in light of the 'Understanding' aspect of *Dasein*. But too much conformity will lead to inauthenticity, a life that is merely the way it is because others expect it to look that way. Later in life, Heidegger would associate this anxiety specifically with the rootlessness of modern technological culture with its obsession with efficiency. He would go on to recommend doing enjoyable, non-efficient things that are not 'for-the-sake-of' anything.

- *Authenticity.* Because of the need to be intelligible, a radical break with the norms we find ourselves in is not advisable or sustainable but freedom from a zombie-like conformity is possible within the uniqueness of each situation as it arises. The authentic person has accepted the groundlessness, the arbitrariness and hence the freedom of their existence and, rather than looking for any ultimate meaning, has responded to their situation with a note of spontaneity. Here again, Heidegger was reacting against the dehumanizing results of modern, technological societies and the way these cultivate dull mass conformity. It was partly these sentiments that caused him, for a short time, to back what the National Socialists were promising.

Reflection

Despite the holistic aims of existentialist thinkers, Heidegger seems to make the human *will*, our capacity to *make a choice*, definitive of human being or at least definitive of authentic human being. But, is this not just as much of a distortion of human nature as the older ideas that made *rationality* the dominant aspect of being human?

---

4 Jean-Paul Sartre (1905–80)

The Frenchman Jean-Paul Sartre was greatly excited by aspects of Heidegger's *Being and Time* (which he read while a prisoner of war in Germany in 1940) and wrote his *Being and Nothingness* in 1943[12] in direct response to it, a publication that Heidegger himself read with dismay. What Sartre is accused of doing, being a Frenchman and more rooted in Descartes than the German Heidegger, is re-Cartesianizing Heidegger. Heidegger had got rid of the autonomous thinking self and the world out there as irrelevant to a discussion of what really matters about life. Sartre puts the autonomous thinking self back into the centre, making existentialism profoundly individualistic. For Sartre, 'Hell is other people.'[13] By that he meant that we can become imprisoned by what other people think of us, terrified by their gaze into our souls, not knowing what it is they see inside us but knowing that it can't be good. Like Part Two of Heidegger's *Being and Time*, he built a philosophy around death and the 'angst' or 'dread' that it brings. He understood the power of the fear of death and how this leads to a life that is not fully lived. It is a life controlled by fear.

The distinctive features of Sartre's thought are these:

- *Atheism.* Sartre's starting point is a phrase from Dostoevsky: 'If God did not exist, everything would be permitted.'[14] This is the basis for Sartre's belief that people must fend for themselves, must make up their own values.
- *Freedom.* Sartre believed we are 'condemned to be free'. Part of our 'nothing-ness' is this total freedom to choose combined with the absence of any criteria for making choices, yet there is a constant need to keep making choices any-way because life is always throwing them our way. This is what produces anxiety, which causes us to retreat into playing a role, acting a part, pursuing some destiny or identity which is really only diverting us from taking a long hard honest look at ourselves. This leads to 'failed dreams of completion'.

This concept of freedom is reinforced by Sartre's notion of three kinds of being:

- *Being-in-itself.* This is the kind of being that belongs to inanimate objects. It is characterized by the inability to make a choice. This kind of being is uncon-scious and not able to change its essential nature. When people live lives that are defined by their roles rather than by what they are (the example is given of a waiter who is far too attached to his role as a waiter) they are living in 'bad faith' because they need to realize that they should really be defined by the fact that they are a human being, not by the role they play in life.
- *Being-for-itself.* This kind of being is being that is always conscious and is true to itself. Good as this is, this state of being is characterized by the rather stark term: 'nothingness', or a blank canvas, because, unlike an inanimate being-in-itself, a human must actuate his or her being, must become what they choose to be based on the meaning that they give to their past and future.
- *Being-for-others.* This is a further consideration which is not given quite the same weight in Sartre as the previous two states of being but which is con-sidered as a factor that can lock us into a being-in-itself kind of existence. The look of others is often the look of people who see us as objects and think they can define us, or even shape us or imprison us by their judgements and norms:

Everything which may be said of me in my relations with the Other applies to him as well. While I attempt to free myself from the hold of the Other, the Other is trying to free himself from mine; while I seek to enslave the Other, the Other seeks to enslave me.[15]

5 The Reception of Existentialism

The English-speaking world has, perhaps predictably, been critical of this most Continental of philosophies. In predictable fashion, the analytical tradition (A. J. Ayer in particular) pulled to pieces what was felt to be a systemic misuse of the verb 'to be', though this in itself is to misunderstand the whole existentialist project. And, like Hegel, Heidegger is criticized for talking gobbledegook. Anglophone readers have suspected that the obscure language is a subterfuge for a lack of real content. This too is probably unfair. Heidegger is consistent and rigorous in his use of the terminology he invents, though, granted, he invents rather a lot of it.

Later, we will consider the theological adaptations of existentialism, but it is worth noting here that the existentialist approach to life seems to have trickled down into non-academic life in quite a pervasive way. This was partly thanks to Sartre's novels and plays but also due to the fact that the existentialist outlook entered currency at just the same time that Western culture was taking a rather nihilistic turn. In the early 1960s, the world lived with the danger of imminent death from an atomic bomb. The new cultural mood coincided with a new philosophical mood to the point where, to this day, existentialist assumptions remain embedded in popular thought, assumptions which all take their starting points from the imminence of death, the groundlessness of life's givens and the dizzying, anxiety-producing freedom that we are all thrown into. Take the idea, for instance, that 'life's what you make it', or the common big screen motif of the 'leap of faith'. And in popular Christian discourse, take the very close attention we pay to self-actualization, for example, John Ortberg's *The Life You've Always Wanted*, and his, *If You Want to Walk on Water You've Got to Step Out of the Boat*. The kind of existential concerns that are explored by Heidegger and Sartre are assumed by Ortberg, yet one wonders whether even the author himself is conscious of these influences or whether they have simply been absorbed by osmosis from the culture.

6 Existential Ethics

Joseph Fletcher (1905–91)

The ethical beliefs of Joseph Fletcher, an American thinker who travelled the path all the way from ordination as an Episcopalian priest to atheism, and who became an advocate of abortion, euthanasia, eugenics and cloning, were framed very much within the context of the growing popularity of existentialism in the 1960s. His name is associated with 'situation ethics', though he claims not to be the originator of the idea and cites many before him that have advocated a similar approach.[16] He is certainly the popularizer of the concept.

In situation ethics, love is the governing principle. There are no laws or rules to follow (whether this be the Catholic affinity for natural law, or the Protestant love of revealed or scriptural law[17]), but neither should there be a total absence of norms. Fletcher argued that neither legalism nor antinomianism works. He successfully demolished the closest thing within legalism to his own system, namely casuistry: the kind of case law that happens when there is doubt or perplexity when applying a given law. His own position is something more like 'neocasuistry'.[18] It is the kind of casuistry that approaches every situation fully prepared to alter the rules completely if that is the most loving thing to do. Fletcher's middle path was to put *people* first rather than *principles*. The end therefore justifies the means. A commandment may be broken for love's sake. This draws some inspiration from Augustine's maxim, 'Love, and do as you wish.'

Situation ethics was readily embraced during the permissiveness of the 1960s, though, in fairness to Fletcher, 1960s libertarian sexual ethics was a misunderstanding of true situation ethics. Fletcher made a clear distinction between philic, erotic and agapeic love, arguing only for a clear-headed agapeic love, which arrives at each situation in an open-minded way not forearmed with any preconceived ethical code. But this misapplication also brings us to the other pole from which Fletcher was keen to distance himself, since the sexual revolution was really only a form of antinomianism. The closest thing within antinomianism to Fletcher's system was the Moral Re-Armament movement, which arose out of the Oxford Group. Its claim to be able, through the Spirit and in any given situation, to live by standards of absolute purity, absolute truth, absolute unselfishness and absolute love is something he dismisses out of court and without proper argument.[19] Also, apart from asserting in the strongest of terms that love is not a virtue, he does not engage virtue ethics.[20] After all, to do so would somewhat spoil his nice neat system of the two poles of legalism and antinomianism with situationism as the middle way. Here he is in his own words, defining his middle position:

> The situationist enters into every decision-making situation fully armed with the ethical maxims of his community and its heritage, and he treats them with respect as illuminators of his problems. Just the same he is prepared in any situation to compromise them or set them aside *in the situation* if love seems better served by doing so . . . The situationist follows a moral law or violates it according to love's need . . . Our obligation is relative *to* the situation, but obligation *in* the situation is absolute . . . Situation ethics aims at contextual appropriateness – not the 'good' or the 'right' but the *fitting* . . . [I]n actual problems of conscience the situational variables are to be weighed as heavily as the normative or 'general' constants . . . There is only one thing that is always good and right, intrinsically good regardless of context, and that one thing is love. Augustine was right again, as situationists see it, to reduce the whole Christian ethic to the single maxim, *Dilige et quod vis, fac* (Love with care and *then* what you will, do). It was not, by the way, *Ama et fac quod vis* (Love with desire and do what you please)! It was not antinomianism.[21]

Situation ethics is a form of ethical consequentialism because the means, whatever they may be, are justified by the outcomes that are seen to be right for a particular situation. The key difference between him and Bentham and Mill would be that love rather than happiness is construed as the consequential criterion.
Problems with this system include the following:

- It lays great responsibility upon the ethical decision-maker. The expectation that such a decision-maker would be able to make the best and most loving choice without any firm hold upon anything prior is best answered by virtue ethics, which insists that the readiness required can only come as the result of long prior habituation.
- Despite the rhetoric in which situationism is so sharply distinguished from antinomianism, it seems really only to be a form of exactly that. The only difference is that a classic antinomian would make a point of not holding even

loosely to any ethical system, while in Fletcher's case there is the presence of an inherited morality, but it is discarded so readily as a situation demands that, it could be argued, one might as well not have bothered with it in the first place. There is a criterion – love – but other antinomian approaches would also claim not to be entirely criterionless: the criterion might be the leading of the Spirit, as in the Gnostics and Moral Re-Armament advocates he cites, or it might be the individualistic self-belief involved in the leap of faith required by the existentialists he cites.

Discussion

When you find yourself thrown into real-life situations, to what extent have you, at times, been a situationist and was that a bad thing?

Fletcher put people over principles and made love the criterion. What's wrong with that?

Free choice and the ethics of evangelism

While we are looking at a philosophical style that lays so much stress on free choice, it is worth looking at a subject that has come under fire largely because of the ethical position that advocating free choice brings about. In more general terms, there is also the clash of civilizations that has come with increased globalization. This has brought proselytizing and religious violence into centre stage, provoking strident denunciations of both. As different religions are brought into closer contact, the result seems to be insecurity in some adherents, resulting in the seeking of social confirmation of their insecure faith via the conversion of others to it.

The rights of the potential convert

In politics, rights campaigns seek the legislation of some way of being treated that is seen as universal and essential to the very nature of humanity. The idea of human rights originated with William of Ockham (1280–1349) and, during the urbanization, bureaucratization and democratization of society, was later embodied in the idea of the social contract. Rights were at the core of the French and American Revolutions. It is a dominant theme in today's politics. Autonomy and authority govern rights thinking, and consequently individual freedom and choice and the virtue of tolerance are paramount. There is also the issue of the painful and even deadly consequences for converts from Islam or Hinduism.

Perhaps a solution lies in making an explicit invitation to other religions to present their views to us, even to attempt conversion; otherwise, claims Greenway, we are guilty of the same intolerance that is often perceived in them.[22] A fundamental concept underlying our notions of what rights are is freedom. The fundamental freedom of a person to choose or not choose Christianity, without coercion, should, of course, be assumed to be inviolable.[23] Without this freedom, there can be no real responsibility on the part of the 'convert' to genuinely respond to God. The World Council of Churches has laid down guidelines against: 'Exploiting people's loneliness, illness, distress, or even disillusionment with their own church in order to "convert" them.'[24] However, 'the dignity and worth of persons', says Elmer Thiessen, needs to be balanced with 'their need for love and care'.[25]

The rights of the proselytizer

Thiessen also seeks to balance a person's autonomy – with all of its rights of self-determination – with 'our social nature and an inescapable degree of human interdependence'.[26] This means that there can be no blanket prohibition on persuasion, since, whether directly or subliminally, we all arrive at our beliefs by way of persuasion. The crucial thing is the method used to persuade. Despite the extensive criticisms levelled at Thiessen by Tillson,[27] this basic insight holds good. He defines both proselytizing and evangelism as the attempt to bring about 'a change of a person's belief, behaviour, identity and belonging',[28] an activity which, clearly, can include all manner of persuasive activity, religious and non-religious. And persuading others is a thing we are all doing all the time, in education and advertising, for instance. We are 'proselytizing animals'.[29] Where he seems to fall down is in defining exactly what ethical criteria need to be satisfied in the means we employ.[30] We are on broad philosophical ground, which goes back at least as far as John Stuart Mill, in affirming that the propagation of beliefs that are not in and of themselves deemed fundamentally harmful is permissible. The bigger questions arise from the means. Firmly in place from the start must be Kant's imperative that persons are ends in themselves and not means. The provision of companionship to the lonely, for instance, could be a form of inducement to convert.

The value of dialogue

Here, I take my inspiration from the greatest of the Apologists of the second century: Justin Martyr.[31] Justin used the Socratic technique of the dialogue with the aim of discovering the truth.[32] On this reckoning, a good evangelist will listen for the theology that is already going on in people's lives. In the wake of Vatican II, dialogue has become the primary approach to mission recommended by the Roman Catholic Church:

> Dialogue is thus the norm and necessary manner of every form of Christian mission, as well as every aspect of it, whether one speaks of simple presence and witness, service, or direct proclamation. Any sense of mission not permeated by such a dialogical spirit would go against the demands of true humanity and against the teachings of the gospel.[33]

Dialogue seems to be the only credible way of defending both the rights of the evangelized and the rights of the evangelist. Dialogue could also be an approach that the Spirit inspires in what is termed 'prophetic dialogue'.[34] Indeed, the widely acknowledged effectiveness of friendship evangelism is due in large measure to the very sure ethical footing it has that is altogether free from dehumanizing elements.

Reflection

In the context of evangelism, Paul was highly conscientious as can be seen from 2 Corinthians 4.2 and 1 Thessalonians 2.2–7. Take the time to reflect biblically on the ethics of evangelism. Are there biblical principles to reinforce what we have looked at here?

7 Christian Existentialisms

Neo-Orthodoxy

While Karl Barth certainly made it his aim to disentangle Christian theology from the fawning and anaemic version of it that had capitulated to the modernist temper, it is without doubt that his early work, in particular, has an existentialist colouring. His whole dialectical method – a method, that is to say, which finds the true message of Christianity between the 'No' of God pronounced on human effort and the 'Yes' of his redeeming love in Christ – owes much of its origins to his reading of Kierkegaard. This dialectical method was itself filled with existential concerns about the plight of humans before a God who is Totally Other and served as an antidote to the purely historical concerns of the liberalism of his training. This early Barth is seen very starkly in his *Commentary on Romans*, the first German edition of which came out in 1919. The later Barth – the Barth of the *Church Dogmatics* – tried to move away from ways of thinking which he regarded as too 'existentialist'. He softened somewhat the harshness of his earlier portrayals of the absolute lostness of man and the total inaccessibility of God, and he was critical of Bultmann's wholesale appropriation of Heidegger.[35]

Rudolf Bultmann (1886–1976)

A review of a fairly recent edited work on Bultmann expresses frustration that today, no less than when he was alive, there is a tendency to criticize Bultmann for his ideas about 'demythologizing' the New Testament to the point of allowing his demythologization project to overshadow his far more important contributions:[36] something that Heidegger, in a letter to Bultmann, once said that he hoped wouldn't happen. Partly related to this, there has been a tendency to not really try to understand Bultmann's engagement with Heideggerian existentialism. Demythologization alone, it seems, is enough to generate a lingering whiff of the age of nineteenth-century liberal scholarship – of the F. D. Strauss variety – and this is enough to put people off reading any further. The one interpreter of Bultmann that Bultmann himself seemed to have a high regard for was John Macquarrie. Bultmann praised him for being an example of someone whose criticisms are 'not dogmatically introduced from outside' but which are offered following an 'inner understanding of the existential interpretation, as the author takes part in it'.[37] We will, therefore, draw much from Macquarrie's appraisal of Bultmann.

What we have in Bultmann is a presupposition, which he openly deploys in his interpretation of the New Testament due to a firm conviction that this is a good kind of presupposition. This presupposition, according to Macquarrie, involves a 'pre-theological inquiry'[38] into the nature of existence which emerges, as Bultmann puts it, with the 'understanding of existence that is given with human existence'.[39] This posture means that we have a right way of putting the question.[40] Putting the question of human existence to the New Testament means that the answers we will get are 'significant for my existence'.[41] The *kerygma* or message of salvation presents us with 'an opportunity of understanding ourselves'.[42]

Everything in the New Testament starts to look decidedly anthropological rather than theological using this lens. This is, perhaps, what happens when you move from admitting that presuppositions *could* define the result to deciding that presuppositions *will* define the result because the presupposition is the right one to have. Bultmann would claim that this way of interpreting the message of the New Testament as being all about our own self-understanding need not limit our exegesis to what has been decided in advance. Because this is the right presupposition, it opens our eyes to the text.

Added to this general presupposition is a second strategy, which is to seek to understand the biblical worldview itself as categorically different from the modern Western scientific worldview. Such scientism uses categories drawn from the physical sciences to describe things, yet, as we saw in Heidegger, while these systems of thought have been the source of science's great successes, when applied to humanity they are a disaster. What the New Testament gives us is a way of looking at life which 'defies the kind of classification and generalisation which are appropriate only to the knowledge of the objects of nature'.[43] The modern scientifically orientated worldview thinks in the categories of 'substantiality' even when applying itself to theology, which results in abstract concepts of God as the Unmoved Mover, the First Cause or the Timeless Absolute. The biblical worldview understands human being in relation to God in the categories of 'existentiality',[44] not substantiality.

Specifically, Bultmann assumes this worldview to be a synthesis of Hellenistic Judaism and an early form of Gnosticism. So, the first move, the presupposition that the opening up of human self-understanding is the purpose of the New Testament *kerygma*, is then supported by the second move, which is the claim that the very world of the New Testament itself is a world whose chief concern is human existence. However, his assumptions about this alleged early form of Gnosticism – as far as we know, there was no such thing – cause Bultmann to assume that this New Testament view of life, though helpfully unscientific, is steeped in its opposite: mythology. This leads us to the most notorious aspect of Bultmann's thought: demythologizing.

So, what is demythologizing? The easiest way to grasp this is to start with the way Bultmann defines mythology:

> Mythology is the use of imagery to express the other-worldly in terms of this world and the divine in terms of human life, the other side in terms of this side.[45]

More recent theology, of the kind that engages with semiotics, would use the word 'metaphor' to describe the very same thing: it is the way in which language for the unfamiliar is developed which uses terms that are borrowed from the familiar. An example would be the New Testament metaphor of 'redemption', which pictures the achievements of the death of Christ in language borrowed from the then familiar first-century slave market. It seems that Bultmann needlessly problematized the New Testament's use of metaphorical or pictorial language and began to read into it a pervasively mythological (or pictorial, metaphorical) worldview. This worldview is quite unacceptable to modernity as it does not seem factual or scientific enough so, in the interests of making our message intelligible, it is necessary to isolate the core *kerygma*, or message, of Christianity – that is, the part of it that demands the response of faith – and leave the rest behind. However, because this *kerygma* must remain translatable into any given age or culture, not just the passing cultural moods of modernity, its content cannot be defined in any final way.

Ultimately, demythologizing is the negative or rearguard aspect of Bultmann's positive affirmation of the existential. It ultimately amounts to a severing of the core message of Christianity from history in an effort to make it ahistorical and transcultural. As one commentator aptly summarized, for Bultmann the only history that matters is 'significant-for-me' history,[46] history that is existentially significant for the present-day believer. Just as well, because he has closed the door to any other kind of history, especially the historical Jesus.[47]

We are left then not only with an ahistorical *kerygma* but a potentially contentless one that must be fit for travel and for rehoming in any culture. But this is where his Lutheran heritage comes into play. It turns out that the *kerygma* is not entirely devoid of fixed content. Standing firmly within the tradition of the Reformation, and a keen student of the apostle Paul, Bultmann was happy to emphasize the justification of the believer through faith alone. 'The kerygma', says Congdon, 'names the saving-event in which a person comes to participate in the new world of faith'.[48] This message, according to Bultmann, 'accosts each individual, throwing the person into question by rendering one's self-understanding problematic and demanding one's decision'.[49] In view of this kind of rhetoric, he has even been described as a 'liberal Billy Graham'.[50]

Reflection

Tent crusades and altar calls have been going out of fashion in Western evangelicalism for some time now, and there are many good reasons for this. Is it not the case, though, that Bultmann is onto something here? Is he not right to identify the preached message of the faith as entailing an urgent call to decision?

Paul Tillich (1886–1965)

Already a veteran of the trenches, Paul Tillich soon became a victim also of the repressions of Hitler and hence an émigré to the United States. His most important works were published at the height of the Cold War. It is not surprising, therefore, that Tillich joined the ranks of so many other mid twentieth-century thinkers who had also been somewhat traumatized by events and were trying to navigate a way through the angst of the times.

Two contrasting influences shaped the thought of Tillich: the idealism of Schelling and the horrors of the First World War, in which he served as a chaplain. These made him into a person who, in his own estimation, straddled a boundary between the increasingly strident questions of the secular rationality of his age and the fading world of his idyllic youth in rural Germany, imbued as it had been with a sense of connection to God, to the natural world and to the traditions of the Lutheran church of which his father was a minister.

For many today who have been influenced by the resurgent conservatism within theology and Christianity, Tillich's work seems to give far too much ground to secular culture and holds the historic Christian faith much too lightly. Indeed, to read his three-volume *Systematic Theology* for the first time can be a disconcerting experience since it is not really a systematic *theology* but a systematically arranged *philosophical theology*, which clings resolutely to the existential questions that Western culture is asking. Barely a Scripture is cited; hardly any theologians are engaged with in any depth: 'To pick up Tillich's *Systematic Theology* after studying traditional textbooks is like straying into a room full of Picassos. Everywhere the perspectives are strange.'[51]

Underlying his effort to straddle the boundary between religion and culture was his famous method of 'correlation', which first appeared in an essay for the *Journal of Religion* in 1947.[52] Correlation involves shaping the answers that Christian theology offers around the fundamental questions that the culture is asking: questions about our finite existence (to which the answer is God the eternal ground of all being), estrangement from our true selves (to which the answer is the new being in Christ) and the meaning of history (to which the answer is the concept of the steady realization of the kingdom of God). These are ultimate questions and, as such, are already essentially religious questions since religion is all about ultimate concerns:

> Theology has rediscovered its correlative and existential character. It has overcome a theology of objective statements and subjective emotions. It has become again a way of giving answers to the questions which are our ultimate concern.[53]

And this was what married his theological project so closely to existentialism. This philosophy, alone of all the philosophies, was religious despite the fact that, as he freely admits, existentialist philosophers were a mixture of theists and atheists. He chooses existentialism over Hegelian and empiricist alternatives, both of which create a 'methodological monism',[54] empiricism, in particular, inviting the absurd possibility of chemistry and theology being approached via a single methodological starting point. Existentialism, uniquely, is involved. It is immersed, like theology is supposed to be, and not theoretical or detached.

It is to the second volume of his three-volume *Systematic Theology*, published in 1957, that we must go to gain the best understanding of Tillich's engagement with existentialism.[55] Here we discover the influences of Heidegger (Tillich held a post at Marburg while Heidegger and Bultmann were there), Friedrich Nietzsche and Rudolf Otto, as well as the underlying influence of Schelling whom J. Heywood Thomas insists remained the chief influence on Tillich's thought.[56]

The way in which Volume 2 begins with an etymological definition of existence as involving a 'standing out' becomes definitive of the whole work: 'existence means standing out of non-being'.[57] This, he deduces, implies a split between 'potentiality and actuality'.[58] His preferred terminology for this is a split between the 'essential' (that is, to do with 'essences') and the existential, illustrating this from the idea of essential 'treehood' as distinct from an actual tree which participates in the treehood of all trees everywhere (evoking Plato).[59] Treehood does not 'exist' as such, but it does have 'being', whereas an actual tree *does* exist but derives its *essence*, its ideal essential nature, from treehood. In Platonic philosophy, existing things were a fallen and imperfect version of their essences, their ideal Forms. The Enlightenment reversed this order so that to 'stand out' from one's essence and to involve oneself in the material stuff of this-worldly existence was no longer a description of a fallen state but a goal. Then, according to Tillich, the pendulum swung completely the other way when Hegel created a system in which *all* was essence: everything was an emanation of a divine Mind but had no material existence. Real life existence was swallowed up by essence with the result that the difficulties and anxieties that come with human existence were glossed over by Hegel's naive optimism. With the existentialist revolt against Hegelian essentialism there came the fresh recognition, which Plato originally saw, namely that humans are in a state of estrangement from their essence, their ideal Form. Their existence is dislocated from their essence. They are caught between an 'is' and an 'is not', always trying to become something but always falling short. We are not truly ourselves, until that is, we are connected back to the ground of all essence and existence, the one who can comprehend in himself all potentiality and actuality: the being of God. Through the new way of being human that is found in Christ, we can stand out from non-being, from inauthentic existence and rediscover our essence; we can, to quote Ortberg, live the life we always wanted.

Discussion

As we now conclude this chapter, we return for a moment to John Macquarrie, the Anglophone world's keenest advocate of an existentialist vision of theology. He asks us to consider this:

> Confirmation of the affinity between the two [biblical understandings and existentialism] may be obtained from a consideration of some of the main themes in the biblical teaching about man. Among these may be mentioned: individual responsibility before God . . . man's fall from his true destiny into concern with the creature; his consciousness of guilt; the call for decision; the fleeting nature of man's temporal existence, and its termination by death. (Macquarrie, *Existentialist Theology*, pp. 19–20)

He refers us to these passages: Psalm 51.3; 103.15–16. There are doubtless many others that could be appealed to. Indeed, the whole book of Ecclesiastes is full of existential concerns. But how biblical is existentialism in your view? What, in biblical theology, does existentialism help us to see *more* clearly? What does it make us see *less* clearly?

Notes

1 Olive Wyon, 'Preface' to Emil Brunner, 1934, *The Mediator*, tr. Olive Wyon, London: Lutterworth, p. 11.

2 Albert Camus, 1942, *The Myth of Sisyphus*, tr. Justin O'Brien, London: Penguin, 1975.

3 Thomas Wartenberg, 2010, *Existentialism*, London: Oneworld, p. 2.

4 Critchley and Schroeder, *Companion to Continental Philosophy*, p. 129.

5 Bryan Magee, 1987, *The Great Philosophers*, London: BBC Books, p. 258, citing Hubert Dreyfus.

6 Kenny, *History of Western Philosophy*, p. 819.

7 Martin Heidegger, 1927, *Being and Time*, tr. John Macquarrie, New York: Harper & Row, 1962, p. 78. He seeks to elevate the idea of 'in' from being a merely spatial idea, like being physically or geographically located somewhere, into something more ontological, more like a total situation that I find myself involved in to which I cannot be indifferent.

8 Heidegger, *Being and Time*, p. 118.

9 Magee, *The Great Philosophers*, p. 264, citing Dreyfus.

10 Heidegger, *Being and Time*, p. 117.

11 Heidegger, *Being and Time*, p. 221.

12 Jean-Paul Sartre, 1943, *Being and Nothingness*, tr. Hazel Barnes. London: Methuen, 1957.

13 The climactic line of his play *No Exit*. *Jean-Paul Sartre, No Exit and Three Other Plays*, tr. Lionel Abel. New York: Vintage, 1989, p. 26. https://www.vanderbilt.edu/olli/class-materials/Jean-Paul_Sartre.pdf [accessed 27 June 2018].

14 Jean-Paul Sartre, 1946, *Existentialism and Humanism*, tr. Philip Mairet, London: Methuen, 1948, p. 33.

15 Sartre, *Being and Nothingness*, p. 364.

16 See especially John A. T. Robinson, 1964, *Christian Morals Today*, London: SCM.

17 Joseph Fletcher, 1966, *Situation Ethics: The New Morality*, London: SCM, p. 21.

18 Fletcher, *Situation Ethics*, p. 29.

19 Fletcher, *Situation Ethics*, p. 24.

20 Fletcher, *Situation Ethics*, pp. 77–8 is the closest. Here, his objection seems to be that virtues are just as prone to being unhelpfully universalized as rules are.

21 Fletcher, *Situation Ethics*, pp. 26–9, 60, 79.

22 Roger Greenway, 'Ethics of Evangelism', *Calvin Theological Journal* 28 (1993), 147–54 [at 152].

23 Greenway, 'Ethics of Evangelism', 153.

24 Central Committee of the WCC, 'Towards Common Witness', 1997. Available on-line at https://www.oikoumene.org/en/resources/documents/commissions/mission-and-evangelism/towards-common-witness.

25 Elmer Thiessen, 2011, *Ethics of Evangelism*, Downers Grove, IL: IVP Academic, p. 44.

26 Thiessen, *Ethics of Evangelism*, p. 57.

27 John Tillson, 'Elmer Thiessen and *The Ethics of Evangelism*', *Journal of Education and Christian Belief* 17:2 (2013), 243–58.

28 Thiessen, *Ethics of Evangelism*, p. 11.

29 Thiessen, *Ethics of Evangelism*, p. 143.

30 Tillson, 'Elmer Thiessen and *The Ethics of Evangelism*', 244.

31 A. Craig Troxel, '"All Things to All People": Justin Martyr's Apologetical Method', *Fides et Historia* 27:2 (1995), 23–43 [at 27]. All the Apologists were trying, not to Hellenize Christianity, but to 'formulate it in intellectual categories congenial to their age' (J. N. D. Kelly, 'Patristic Literature' under 'Christianity', 1989, in *Encyclopaedia Britannica*, Chicago: University of Chicago Press, 1989).

32 Sara Denning-Bolle, 'Christian Dialogue as Apologetic: The Case of Justin Martyr Seen in Historical Context', *Bulletin of the John Rylands Library* 69 (September 1987), 492–510 [at 503].

33 Secretariat for Non-Christians, 'The Attitude of the Church Toward the Followers of Other Religions: Reflections and Orientations on Dialogue and Mission', *Bulletin Secretariatus pro Non Christianis* 56:2 (1984), No. 29. Full text available online at www.shinmeizan.com/images/PDF/DialMiss.en.pdf [accessed 17 May 2018].

34 Roger Schroeder, 'Proclamation and Interreligious Dialogue as Prophetic Dialogue', *Missiology* 41:1 (January 2013), 50–61.

35 Karl Barth, 'Rudolf Bultmann: An Attempt to Understand Him', in Hans-Werner Bartsch (ed.), 1962, *Kerygma and Myth: A Theological Debate Vol. II*, tr. Reginald Fuller, London: SPCK, pp. 83–132.

36 David Congdon, 'Is There a Kerygma in this Text? A Review Article', *Journal of Theological Interpretation* 9:2 (2015), 299–311, reviewing Bruce Longenecker and Mikeal Parsons (eds), 2014, *Beyond Bultmann: Reckoning a New Testament Theology*, Waco, TX: Baylor University Press. See also David Congdon, 2015, *The Mission of Demythologizing: Rudolf Bultmann's Dialectical Theology*, Minneapolis: Fortress.

37 Rudolf Bultmann, 1955, 'Foreword', in John Macquarrie, *An Existentialist Theology*, London: SCM, pp. vii–viii.

38 Macquarrie, *Existentialist Theology*, p. 7.

39 Rudolf Bultmann, *Kerygma and Myth*, Vol. 2, p. 192.

40 Macquarrie, *Existentialist Theology*, p. 11.

41 Macquarrie, *Existentialist Theology*, p. 11.

42 Rudolf Bultmann, in Hans-Werner Bartsch (ed.), 1957, *Kerygma and Myth: A Theological Debate*, Vol. 1, tr. Reginald Fuller, London: SPCK, pp. 41–2.

43 Macquarrie, *Existentialist Theology*, p. 17.

44 Macquarrie, *Existentialist Theology*, pp. 20–1.

45 Rudolf Bultmann, *Kerygma and Myth*, Vol. 1, p. 10, n.2.

46 Claude Cox, 'R. Bultmann: Theology of the New Testament', *Restoration Quarterly* 17 (1974), 144–61 [at 151].

47 For a very brief introduction to Bultmann's views about the historical Jesus, see my 2017, *Theology in the Contemporary World*, London: SCM, 2017, pp. 10–11, plus passing references through that chapter.

48 Congdon, 'Is There a Kerygma in this Text?', 304.

49 Rudolf Bultmann, 2007, *Theology of the New Testament* vol. 1, tr. Kendrick Grobel, Waco, TX: Baylor University Press, p. 303.

50 Otto Heick, 'Rudolf Bultmann Revisited', *Concordia Theological Monthly*, 41:5 (May 1970), 259–78 [at 262].

51 Brown, *Philosophy and the Christian Faith*, p. 193.

52 Paul Tillich, 'The Problem of Theological Method', *Journal of Religion* 27:1 (January 1947), 16–26.

53 Tillich, 'The Problem of Theological Method', 26.

54 Tillich, 'The Problem of Theological Method', 16

55 A slightly old but particularly helpful introduction to Tillich's thought is Mark Kline Taylor, 1987, *Paul Tillich: Theologian of the Boundaries*, London: Collins.

56 J. Heywood Thomas, 2000, *Paul Tillich*, London: Continuum, 2000.

57 Paul Tillich, 1957, *Systematic Theology* Vol. 2, London: SCM, p. 21.

58 Tillich, *Systematic Theology* Vol. 2, p. 21.

59 Tillich, *Systematic Theology* Vol. 2, p. 21.

6

The Analytic Tradition

Chapter Outline

1 Introduction

Essence and existence, realism and nominalism, non-being and being, mind and matter, subject and object – philosophy has thrown up dozens of these dichotomies and then spent centuries agonizing over them. But are they not, in the final analysis, false dichotomies? Are these not more about the problems that philosophy has *created* than about the problems it has tried to *solve?* The way A. J. Ayer threw out existentialism at a stroke because it rested on a misuse of the term 'existence' is indicative of the whole project of analytic philosophy. Its advocates believed (and, to varying degrees, still believe) that if we would all try a little harder to frame the question rightly then we may find that it is either a non-question – that is, not a meaningful problem to be even worth bothering with – or that the question can be better answered if it is better analysed. Not surprisingly, this approach ended up being preoccupied with the use of language. It has, since then, moved in a more eclectic direction to embrace a range of interests from aesthetics to mathematics and has become more or less synonymous with English-speaking, predominantly Anglo-American philosophy. 'Analytic' has become the term used to contrast this tradition with the 'Continental' tradition, with the analytic tradition still more or less characterized by a liking for clarity and common sense. It looks upon the Continental tradition as needlessly complexifying issues and as encumbered by 'metaphysics' of the worst and most baffling kind. Continentals view themselves as deep and see the results of analytic philosophy as thin.

Recently, departments dominated by the analytic tradition have become relative havens for theism within some secular universities,[1] but this was not always the case. The early analytic tradition posed an immediate problem to Christian faith. It seemed quite willing to bracket the whole question of God and religion, placing it into the dustbin of questions that were not meaningful and therefore not answerable: 'Whereof one cannot speak, thereof one must be silent.'[2] The analytic tradition's firm weddedness, for a time, to a virulent form of empiricism did not help. However, as we will see, even the analytic tradition proved to be a useful, if unwilling, servant to theology. Its attentiveness to linguistics provided a new impetus to biblical studies as well as to the study of metaphor in religious language.

2 The Initiators: Moore, Russell and the Early Wittgenstein

From mathematics to logic

We now welcome a mathematician to this conversation between philosophy and Christian faith, though not by any means the first philosopher to have shown a keen interest in mathematics. He is Gottlob Frege (1848–1925, pronounced 'freega'). The actual form of Frege's 'propositional calculus' and his 'predicate calculus' is not useful to us here, but the significance of what he was doing helps set the scene for the approaches that Bertrand Russell and others would take under his influence. Frege wanted to reduce mathematics to logic and hence to provide a better way to understanding how logic works than Aristotle's syllogism.

He reduced all numbers to sets and then created logical statements made from those sets. This stimulated Russell to do something similar but in reverse: where Frege took mathematical formulae and made them into statements, Russell took statements and made them into mathematical formulae. Here is Russell himself describing the method:

> Modern analytical empiricism . . . differs from that of Locke, Berkeley, and Hume by its incorporation of mathematics and its development of a powerful logical technique. It is thus able, in regard to certain problems, to achieve definite answers, which have the quality of science rather than of philosophy. It has the advantage, in comparison with the philosophies of the system-builders, of being able to tackle its problems one at a time, instead of having to invent at one stroke a block theory of the whole universe. Its methods, in this respect, resemble those of science.[3]

From holism to atomism

G. E. Moore (1873–1958) and Bertrand Russell were Cambridge philosophers and originally Hegelian idealists influenced by the leading British idealist of the late nineteenth century, John McTaggart. Their interest in mathematics and the influence of Frege combined to move them away from the idealist notion that the way to understand reality was via holism. To the contrary, and in the manner of a mathematical equation which breaks everything down into the simplest possible sets, they came to believe that the way to a clearer grasp of the truth was via atomism. Atomism is the opposite of idealist essentialism. Here is the historian of philosophy W. T. Jones:

> The primary task of philosophy, they held, is the analysis of complex entities into the simple entities of which they are composed. Because the simple entities *are* simple, they are directly understandable whenever they are encountered. Accordingly, complex entities are completely explained as soon as their analysis into simples has been correctly carried out.[4]

Reflection

Biblical theology aims to start with individual texts throughout the canon, which are analysed one by one to build up a picture, for instance, of the biblical view of the poor. The big theological motifs emerge from small-scale analysis. It is bottom up.

Systematic theology, by contrast, already has a system: the doctrines of the Christian faith that have been thrashed out over the centuries. When systematic theology uses Scripture, it too will use the whole canon but will take it up into a theology already constructed for it, for example the doctrine of the Trinity. It is top down.

Is there a theological method that you think is better than the other?

Russell's student Ludwig Wittgenstein (1889–1951) developed atomism, this way of building complexity out of simples, into a method called 'logical atomism', which required the development of an ideal language, a special notation consisting of symbols, a language freed from all the ambiguities that keep cropping up in everyday language.[5] Like Frege and Russell, he enjoyed making mathematical-style formulae out of propositions. This is what he meant by ideal language analysis. In contrast to this, Moore (who, incidentally, gave to the analytic tradition the term 'analytic') preferred to accept ordinary language as the starting point for his analysis, an idea that would not surface again until the later Wittgenstein.

From idealism to realism

You may have picked up from that phrase 'directly understandable' in the extract above that Moore and Russell made the switch from idealism to realism. Once that transition was made, they never lost the commonsense conviction that there is a real world out there. Indeed, Russell describes the moment of this discovery vividly: 'It was with immense excitement, after having supposed the sensible world unreal, to be able to believe again that there really were such things as tables and chairs.'[6] He dates the change to the year 1898, when he and Moore both rebelled against all that they had been taught:

I felt it, in fact, as a great liberation, as if I had escaped from a hot house onto a windswept headland. In the first exuberance of liberation, I became a naïve realist and rejoiced in the thought that grass really was green.[7]

The significance of realism, especially for the early Wittgenstein who was a student of Russell's, was that it meant that language corresponded to reality. If, therefore, we could get the language of our propositions right, we could find that each element in the proposition corresponds exactly to elements out there in the world.

Moore famously refuted idealism, or at least its Berkeleian variety, by analysing Berkeley's aphorism: 'to be is to be perceived'. He focused on the word 'is' and pointed out how, in ordinary usage, we would usually use the word 'is' in a self-evident way to point out, for instance, that 'a bachelor *is* an unmarried man'. The 'is' brings together two units of language which have exactly the same meaning, so much so that we feel no need to even assert this. We do not normally feel the need to keep asserting that a bachelor is an unmarried man. Such is not the case with 'to be is to be perceived'. This phrase, likewise, would not even need asserting if it literally was the case that 'to exist' really is exactly the same thing as 'to be cognized'.[8] It would be obvious, yet clearly it is not.

3 Logical Positivism

Ernst Mach (1838–1916) provided the thinking that would eventually lead, in 1922, to the formation of the Vienna Circle. Mach wanted the philosophy of science to be so entirely free of metaphysics – that is, of the practice of theoretical system building – that it could focus entirely upon the data of sense experience, setting aside concepts like the laws of Newtonian physics that have no way of being verified by the senses. However, this radical empiricism did not function alone but in partnership with the same mathematical logic that had been pioneered by Frege, Russell and Wittgenstein's *Tractatus Logico-Philosophicus*.

Wittgenstein, whose *Tractatus* had been the set text for the Circle from the start, had already found common cause with natural science.[9] Now, two key concepts allowed the marriage between empiricism and logic to reach a new level. First, there was A. J. Ayer's 'verification principle'.[10] Using this principle, we might look at the statement: 'The trees outside are budding.' This is an acceptable statement because it is verifiable using sense data: I can go outside and have a look. However, the statement 'God created the trees outside' is not meaningful logically since there is no way I can empirically check this. It might be emotionally meaningful, but it is not worth any further examination. Hence it is not verifiable. Notice, however, that a factually significant statement need not have actually *been* verified – that comes later on as part of the scientific process – it is simply the assurance that, given the right conditions, it *can* be verified. Here is Ayer in his own words:

> We say that a sentence is factually significant to any given person, if, and only if, he knows how to verify the proposition which it purports to express – that is, if he knows what observations would lead him, under certain conditions, to accept the proposition as being true, or reject it as being false. If on the other hand, the putative proposition is of such a character that the assumption of its truth, or falsehood, is consistent with any assumption whatsoever concerning the nature of his future experience, then, as far as he is concerned, it is, if not a tautology, a mere pseudo-proposition. The sentence expressing it may be emotionally significant to him; but it is not literally significant.[11]

We need to pick up on this word 'tautology'. You might have heard this word used in a negative way as a kind of begging the question. You may recall how Descartes' *Cogito* was criticized – by A. J. Ayer himself – as a tautology: Descartes only appears to be deducing something when, if you look closely enough, he is merely restating something: 'I am thinking therefore I am thinking.' He has phrased his sentence (*Je pense donc je suis*) in such a way as to suggest that existence could be *proven* from thinking. According to Ayer, nothing verifiable can be deduced from thinking other than the observation that you are thinking. However, Ayer and the logical positivists mostly did not intend anything necessarily negative by the term 'tautology'. A tautology was simply any statement that was exempted from the verification principle. Such exemptions ranged from statements that about what was logically impossible such as stating that a ball cannot be a cube to stating that 2 + 2 = 4.

And all of this was not to test the truth of anything – this was no longer considered to be the job of philosophy – it was merely to decide whether something was even worthy of investigation in the first place, rather like a preliminary hearing before a court case.[12] However, a slight difficulty with the verification principle, as with so many other philosophical principles, is that it is self-refuting. The verification principle itself is not tautologous so would need verifying. There is, regrettably, no way to verify the verification principle!

To the verification principle was added Karl Popper's 'falsification principle', explained in his *The Logic of Scientific Discovery*.[13] This involved a recommended shift away from inductive methods in science. Inductive methods entail the steady accumulation of evidence that exemplifies a law. What can too easily happen is that we only collect evidence that supports a theory and tend to, perhaps unintentionally, ignore evidence that might falsify it. In this way, we can sometimes end up with great ideological constructs such as Marxism, Freudianism or Darwinism, all of which Popper described as examples of pseudoscience. They are pseudo-science because they have set themselves up in such a way as to be impossible to falsify. They become a picture of the world that, if adopted, we cannot get outside of. Class struggle, for example, is a lens through which all history is read by Marxists, yet no one is ever invited to test whether class struggle is entitled to be this all-defining lens in the first place.

Instead, Popper insisted that scientists should offer explanatory theories, which they then attempt to falsify. For that to happen, a statement of a problem must be in a form that suggests that, were certain evidence to present itself, it would be at least possible to falsify it. So this is just like the verification principle in this regard: propositions do not need to have already been verified or falsified in order to be worth the time of day; rather, they are not worth bothering with if it would never actually be possible to empirically test the claim and hence see it verified or falsified. And again, this principle does not apply to tautologous or 'analytic' sentences, such as that all balls are spherical or all triangles have three angles, which can stand by themselves without the need for anything outside of the words themselves to confirm or disconfirm their accuracy. So Freud's construct of the unconscious and subconscious mind is another example that could never be falsified. It is a system Freud built, which neatly accommodated what seemed to come out of people's mouths during hypnosis or emerge in people's dreams. Once constructed, the system is perpetually confirmed but cannot be dismantled empirically, only replaced by some other system.

Much of this seems fair enough, and we might quite admire the way Popper is willing to take on some of the great modernist monoliths that have proved so compelling to so many people. However, logical positivism was not at all kind to 'metaphysicians' – a category that included all religionists. The only significance that religious statements had, for them, was as expressions of attitude and feeling. They were value judgements akin to the vagaries of aesthetic statements about whether one likes a piece of art or admires a view. Rudolf Carnap, a prominent member of the Vienna Circle, made the link to aesthetics in a particularly un-flattering way, saying: 'metaphysicians are musicians without musical ability'.[14]

Reflection

If Carnap had directed that comment at you and your faith, claiming that you are only trying to express something you have feelings about but not even doing it very well, and that therefore all your claims about God are logically and scientifically meaningless, how might you respond? You know he is wrong, but why is he wrong?

If you feel stumped, then read to the end of this chapter and come back to this.

---

4 The Later Wittgenstein and the Philosophy of Everyday Language

So, to return to our story, Wittgenstein, having disabused philosophy of all its most cherished metaphysical projects and reduced it to a preliminary method for deciding what questions scientists should ask, left the profession in 1919. He gave away all his aristocratic wealth and trained to become a schoolteacher. After all, there was nothing more to be done in philosophy; it had now reached its *telos*. He had ushered in the new age and brought about the end of the world for traditional philosophy. Actually, this was not quite the reality. He appears to have thrown in the towel because of a series of psychological traumas arising from his involvement in the First World War and from the suicides of two of his brothers. There would later be the suicide of a third brother. His book *Tractatus Logico-Philosophicus* was also initially rejected for publication. However, there was no relief for Wittgenstein in elementary school teaching. He did not enjoy it. Things came to a head when Wittgenstein hit a child so hard that he was knocked unconscious, an event which was followed by an inconclusive police investigation.[15]

He eventually returned to philosophy at Cambridge in 1929 at the urging of former colleagues. By 1933, he was beginning a series of lectures that would eventually become the posthumously published *Philosophical Investigations* of 1953. His thinking following his return to professional philosophy is so markedly different from that of his earlier work that commentators have struggled to trace the lines of continuity.[16] This is why we always talk of the early Wittgenstein and the later Wittgenstein. In contrast to the early Wittgenstein, who devised logical notation in support of his ideal language analysis, the later Wittgenstein was more interested in using ordinary language as his starting point, just like Moore had been much earlier on.

There are two central motifs to the later Wittgenstein.

- Words mean what they mean when in use: 'The use of the word *in practice* is its meaning.'[17]
- Their use is context-dependent, varying according to the 'language-game' of a particular group. Sentences and propositions, then, are tools for social interface and cannot be interfered with or corrected by the philosopher, only described. The group itself provides the criteria for the correct use of its language. Here he is in his own words:

> The word 'language-game' is used here to emphasize the fact that the *speaking* of language is part of an activity, or of a form of life.[18]

In the 1940s to 1960s, Wittgenstein-inspired ordinary language analysis took hold in Oxford University, and the names of Gilbert Ryle, J. L. Austin, Peter Strawson and Paul Grice became part of what was called 'Oxford Philosophy'. Austin's student, John Searle, carried on this style of philosophy in America. 'Speech act' theory is the most famous outcome of this phase in analytic philosophy, and this has been flirted with here and there by New Testament scholars ever since.[19] Speech act theory is interested in the various social functions of language beyond merely denoting things. Words do things: we command, we pronounce, we confer and so on – phenomena that the biblical worlds are especially replete with. God, in particular, makes things happen creatively with only his words and can do things such as pronounce us righteous in Christ, and it is so.

The later Wittgenstein has been of interest not only to the Oxford Philosophers but also to theologians. From the late 1940s onwards, the logical and empirical strictures of the early analytic tradition eased. Logical positivism suffered a series of devastating refutations from W. V. O. Quine[20] and from Wittgenstein himself, not to mention the significant theological critiques that later flowed from Alvin Plantinga[21] and Richard Swinburne.[22] The later Wittgenstein, influenced as he was by Kierkegaard and often showing a decidedly mystical bent, proved something of an olive branch to Christian faith. This was in contrast to the hostility of Russell, whose views on religion had been collected together in his *Why I am Not a Christian* of 1927.[23]

5 God and God-Talk

There was a rash of publications during the 1950s to 1980s, almost all of which are now out of print, which sought to respond to the linguistic turn in philosophy by making a similar linguistic turn in theology and biblical studies. So, at about the same time that theologians and biblical scholars with a German accent were turning into existentialists and sounding like Heidegger, English-speaking scholars were busy trying on the garb of analytic philosophy to see if that would fit better.

Two things in Wittgenstein seem to have fired the imaginations of Anglophone theologians. The first was the language-games concept; the other was his words-as-pictures concept, which I have not introduced you to yet but will when we get there.

Language-games and Christian faith

Wittgenstein's views about the social function of words in language-games provided much food for thought. George Lindbeck, Hans Frei and Stanley Hauerwas would all be theologians directly influenced by Wittgenstein. They emphasize that, while language about God really is about God, it does not become intelligible except in the context of Christian practices where it is put to use in liturgy and so on. In the words of Lindbeck, doctrine is most usefully defined as 'communally authoritative rules of discourse, attitude and action'.[24] The relativistic outcomes of this, far from being a threat to theology, proved useful to Lindbeck when he was invited to participate in the Second Vatican Council deliberations. Ecumenically, treating doctrine as collections of differing language-games that meet the needs of different Christian communities is the starting point for doing a kind of theological therapy, disabusing us of the notion that our theological formulations really are expressive of the unchanging and unbending realities of orthodoxy. Experiences of what we take to be God vary from context to context, but the one constant is the grammar by which a community of faith articulates it and passes it on.

Lindbeck, Frei and Hauerwas belong to a movement which we call 'post-liberal' theology, also referred to as the 'Yale School' as all the most celebrated names were associated in one way or another with Yale Divinity School in New Haven, Connecticut. They were (and are) postliberal because, in agreement with Wittgenstein, they took issue with the subjective individualism assumed as foundational by the liberal tradition. In fact, because of Wittgenstein's disdain for systems-building – and doing so with the otherwise 'wonderful'[25] symbols of Christianity was something that disgusted Wittgenstein – the Yale School rejected all foundations. Hauerwas described vividly how he was cured by Wittgenstein of 'positions, ideas, and/or theories', preferring to return to the embodied, culturally and linguistically embedded 'rough ground'[26] of theology that is descriptive, not speculative, therapeutic, not theoretical. Theological truth is to be located in the public and embodied, not the private and subjective. It is to be found in the lives of Christians seeking to follow Christ in public.[27]

Reflection

Church and academy have been at a distance from one another ever since the Enlightenment. It seems the capitulations that liberal theology made to the modern outlook created something that has alienated a great many churchgoers. Might Wittgenstein, via the filter of Lindbeck and his friends, point the way back to theology that is at a more human level? Or are those of the postliberal outlook merely shaping Christian faith artlessly around yet another non-Christian philosophy?

Words and pictures

For Wittgenstein, religious beliefs, for example the Last Judgement, were really pictures that were designed to have a moral or practical force, inspiring us to live better lives. Religion consists in 'rules of life dressed up in pictures'.[28] However, this does not mean that, for Wittgenstein, pictures may be dispensed with. He admits that very often 'the whole *weight* may be in the picture'.[29] This kind of talk of pictures that carry the weight of meaning *as pictures*, without being converted into logical propositions forms the background music to a body of literature reflecting upon the nature and function of metaphor in religious language. Ian Ramsey,[30] John Macquarrie[31] and Janet Martin Soskice[32] would be among those who were particularly interested in the irreducibly metaphorical nature of religious discourse. They noticed, just as Aquinas had long ago, that religious language has a uniquely figurative or analogical quality. Even Jesus himself, after all, seems to have readily admitted that heavenly things cannot be described except in earthly ways (John 3.12). And it is this clarifying of what metaphors are and what they do which, by the time we get to Soskice's magisterial *Metaphor and Religious Language*, constitutes an impressively robust response on behalf of faith to the rigours of the early analytic tradition.

Our most ancient understandings of metaphor are Aristotelian. In his still widely cited *Poetics* in which he offers guidance to would-be playwrights and poets about how to use metaphor for maximum effect, Aristotle claimed that a metaphor (from the Greek *meta*: from, *pherō*: I carry, I bear. Hence: to carry over from, to transfer) is basically 'the application of an alien name by transference'.[33] Within the discipline of rhetoric, this gave rise to the 'substitution' theory of metaphor. However, Soskice, together with the linguistic philosopher Max Black, took serious issue with this, for the substitution theory implies that the substitution that has taken place in order to create the metaphor is artificial, not essential, decorative, not reality-depicting and reversible, not indispensable. The metaphor could be replaced with a straightforward and unambiguous way of putting it. Indeed, in higher education today, we instinctively correct students who want to use figures of speech because they lack precision. However, a good metaphor is one that, for both speaker and hearer, is readily comprehensible both as to the thing to which it refers (the 'tenor') and the thing that it is making use of as an aid to clarity ('vehicle'[34]). According to Ian Ramsey, it is all about 'a situation with which we are *all familiar*, and which can be used for reaching another situation with which we are not so familiar; one which, without the model, we should not recognize so easily'.[35] A bad metaphor is bad because it could so easily fail to make these familiar connections and so fails to be a cognitive aid. Good metaphors are absolutely ubiquitous to language and totally central to the way we learn about new and unfamiliar or abstract things. A good metaphor, far from being a frilly, aesthetic superfluity, is in fact the way we always grasp new truths, even scientific ones.

A metaphor, according to Paul Ricoeur, 'discloses a relationship of meaning hitherto unnoticed'.[36] Metaphors cannot be reverted back to the bare propositional entities that made them because *both* tenor and vehicle have been irreversibly altered in order to create the metaphor. Both have interacted in such a way as to create something new out of the features which the two things are now seen to share. Dissimilar features are left behind. There is hence an 'is' and an 'is not' tension about metaphors. Take the biblical metaphor that Christ is our ransom, for instance. An early misunderstanding of the metaphor assumed that the ransom must have been paid to someone. The prime suspect was the devil; and so it was that the 'ransom to Satan' theory dominated the first thousand years of the church's history. In fact, the metaphor leaves behind that part of ransom payments and focuses only on the concept of costly liberation. The metaphor by itself, as used in the New Testament, does not come complete with an instruction manual about the mechanics of the costly liberation. It does not delve into the common features of the manumission of slaves but is limited to awakening our gratitude over the cost of our freedom.

Soskice's definition is exhaustively argued for and seems difficult to surpass: '*Metaphor is that figure of speech whereby we speak about one thing in terms which are seen to be suggestive of another.*'[37] Soskice's definition may not have been bettered, but its scope has been much extended since her book. It has been noticed, especially now that we have transitioned (to some extent) into postmodernity with its preference for intuition, feelings and experiences over mere words, that metaphor speaks a language that conveys deep meanings and emotions not accessible through 'naked abstract formulations'.[38] Such would be dismissed by Soskice as a mere 'emotive' theory of metaphor because she fears that focusing on the emotive power of metaphors is a backdoor to the substitution theory whereby the frilly aesthetics that produce the emotions could too easily be understood as replaceable. To the contrary, theology of the arts writer David Brown claims that God is even able to *inhabit* well-chosen metaphors in just the same way that he is understood in some traditions to inhabit bread and wine. According to Brown, we see this sacramental dynamic in concentrated form in poetry (especially theistic poetry) where metaphors occupy a central place. Brown then applies the same appreciation for the metaphors found in the Bible. He uses John 1.1 as a case study, pointing out that efforts to paraphrase John's use of 'Word' to describe the incarnation, using terms such as 'expression' end up introducing a whole new set of associations not native to John's original 'Word' metaphor.[39] Brown thus adds a second layer of irreducibility to that established by Soskice: biblical metaphors are irreducible because God-inhabited. And this same logic can readily be applied to the purely visual arts. A painting works supremely because of its power as a metaphor, yet one that is precisely not a figure of speech at all but an actual figure, a visual form which speaks to our depths at a level that is pre-linguistic, a level that is too deep for words, rather like music. Yet we can still hold true to Soskice's urgency that what is said metaphorically 'can be expressed adequately in no other way'.[40] In fact, is this not the very reason for the existence of the arts? The arts express things in a way that can be expressed adequately in no other way.

Reflection

We have tried to facilitate a realism which is neither dogmatic nor presumptuous . . . Our concern is with conceptual possibility rather than proof, and with a demonstration that we may justly speak of God without claiming to define him, and to do so by means of metaphor. (Soskice, *Metaphor and Religious Language*, p. 148)

The study of metaphor by Soskice and others has been a thoughtful response to the analytic tradition's claims about logical propositions and their supposed correspondence to empirically verifiable and falsifiable facts. In response is the claim that figurative language, itself pervasive throughout the natural sciences, might also lay some claim to be reality-depicting. Others would go even further, giving metaphor a divinely owned cognitive and spiritual supremacy over sterile logic-chopping.

Go back to the challenge of Carnap in the Reflection on p. 134. How would you now like to answer Carnap?

Notes

1 See William Wood, 'On the New Analytic Theology, or: The Road Less Traveled', *Journal of the American Academy of Religion* 77:4 (December 2009), 941–60. See also the most important book Wood's article reviews: Oliver Crisp and Michael Rea (eds), 2009, *Analytic Theology: New Essays in the Philosophy of Theology*, Oxford: Oxford University Press.

2 Ludwig Wittgenstein, 1922, *Tractatus Logico-Philosophicus*, London: Kegan Paul, Tractatus 7.

3 Bertrand Russell, 1945, *A History of Western Philosophy*, London: Allen & Unwin, p. 834.

4 W. T. Jones, 1969, *A History of Western Philosophy: Kant to Wittgenstein and Sartre*, 2nd edition, New York: Harcourt, Brace & World, p. 332.

5 In his racy *Tractatus Logico-Philosophicus* of 1922.

6 Bertrand Russell, 1967, *The Autobiography of Bertrand Russell, 1872–1916*, London: Allen and Unwin, p. 135.

7 Bertrand Russell, 1959, *My Philosophical Development*, London: Unwin, 1959, pp. 61–2.

8 G. E. Moore, 'The Refutation of Idealism', *Mind* 12 (1903), 433–53.

9 'The correct method in philosophy would really be the following: to say nothing except what can be said, that is propositions of natural science . . .' Wittgenstein, *Tractatus*, 6.53.

10 First put forward in his highly influential *Language, Truth and Logic* of 1936. A second edition of 1946 sought to moderate some of its excesses.

11 A. J. Ayer, 1946, *Language, Truth and Logic*, 2nd edition, London: Penguin, p. 35.

12 Brown's analogy: *Philosophy and the Christian Faith*, p. 172.

13 New York: Basic Books, 1959.

14 Rudolf Carnap, 'The Elimination of Metaphysics through Logical Analysis of Language', in Sahotra Sarkar (ed.), 1996, *Science and Philosophy in the Twentieth Century* Vol. 2, tr. Arthur Pap, New York: Garland, p. 80.

15 This and previous incidents of hitting appeared to have plagued his conscience, and he returned in later years to attempt restitution with the families involved.

16 E.g. Anders Nygren, 1972, *Meaning and Method: Prolegomena to a Scientific Philosophy of Religion and a Scientific Theology*, tr. Philip Watson, Philadelphia, PA: Fortress, pp. 243–54. Wittgenstein's biography puts it down to the influence of Italian anthropologist Piero Sraffa: Ray Monk, 1990, *Ludwig Wittgenstein: The Duty of Genius*, New York: Penguin, p. 260, an influence that Wittgenstein acknowledges was significant in the preface to his *Philosophical Investigations*.

17 Ludwig Wittgenstein, 1960, *The Blue and Brown Books*, New York: Harper & Row, p. 69.

18 Ludwig Wittgenstein, *Philosophical Investigations*, 1953, tr. Elizabeth Anscombe. Oxford: Blackwell, p. 23.

19 Two relatively recent little studies using speech act theory are Eric Johnson, 'Rewording the Justification/Sanctification Relation with Some Help from Speech Act Theory', *Journal of the Evangelical Theological Society* 54:4 (December 2011), 767–85, and Lace Marie Williams-Tinajero, 2011, *The Reshaped Mind: Searle, the Biblical Writers, and Christ's Blood*, Leiden: Brill.

20 Especially his 'Two Dogmas of Empiricism' of 1951, in Quine, 1953, *From a Logical Point of View: Nine Logico-Philosophical Essays*, Cambridge, MA: Harvard University Press, pp. 20–46.

21 *God and Other Minds*, Ithaca, NY: Cornell University Press, 1967.

22 *The Coherence of Theism*, Oxford: Clarendon Press, 1977.

23 See also, prior to this, R. F. Alfred Hornle, 'The Religious Aspect of Bertrand Russell's Philosophy', *Harvard Theological Review* 9:2 (April 1916), 157–89, and much later, Arnold Weigel, 'A Critique of Bertrand Russell's Position', *Bulletin of the Evangelical Theological Society* 8:4 (January 1965), 139–58.

24 George Lindbeck, 1984, *The Nature of Doctrine: Religion and Theology in a Postliberal Age*, London: SPCK, p. 18.

25 Brian McGuinness (ed.), 1979, *Wittgenstein and the Vienna Circle: Conversations Recorded by Friedrich Waismann*, Oxford: Blackwell, p. 117.

26 Stanley Hauerwas, 1983, *The Peaceable Kingdom: A Primer in Christian Ethics*, Notre Dame, IN: University of Notre Dame Press, p. xxi. Also, Hauerwas, 1981, *Community of Character*, Notre Dame, IN: University of Notre Dame Press.

27 For an excellent survey of those theologians who have made notable responses – positive, negative and in-between – see Bruce Ashford, 'Wittgenstein's Theologians? A Survey of Ludwig Wittgenstein's Impact on Theology', *Journal of the Evangelical Theological Society* 50:2 (June 2007), 357–75.

28 Ludwig Wittgenstein's 1998, *Culture and Value*, revised edition, Oxford: Blackwell, p. 34. Here, he is specifically reflecting on Bunyan's allegory, *The Pilgrim's Progress*.

29 Ludwig Wittgenstein, 'Lecture on Religious Belief', in Cyril Barrett (ed.), 1966, *Wittgenstein: Lectures and Conversations on Aesthetics, Psychology and Religious Belief*, Berkeley, CA: University of California Press, pp. 53–72 [at p. 72].

30 *Religious Language*, London: SCM, 1957.

31 *God-Talk: An Examination of the Language and Logic of Theology*, London: SCM, 1967.

32 *Metaphor and Religious Language*, Oxford: Clarendon Press, 1985.

33 Aristotle, *Poetics* 1457b 7–8.

34 Tenor and vehicle are the terminology of I. A. Richards, 1936, *The Philosophy of Rhetoric*, Oxford: Oxford University Press.

35 Ian Ramsey, 1957, *Religious Language*, London: SCM, p. 61. Italics mine.

36 Paul Ricoeur, 'The Metaphorical Process', *Semeia* 4 (1975), 75–106 [at 78–9].

37 Soskice, *Metaphor and Religious Language*, p. 15.

38 Craig Ott, 'The Power of Biblical Metaphors for the Contextualized Communication of the Gospel', *Missiology* 42:4 (2014), 357–74 [at 362].

39 David Brown, 2008, *God and Mystery in Words: Experience through Metaphor and Drama*, Oxford: Oxford University Press, pp. 52–5.

40 Soskice, *Metaphor and Religious Language*, p. 31.

7

Postmodernism

Chapter Outline

1 Introduction

A first step in understanding postmodernism is to try to achieve some clarity about terminology. This is tricky because some of its keenest advocates resist classification and have never adopted the term for themselves. With the terms 'postmodernism' and 'postmodernity' and related term 'Deconstruction' bandied about so much, there is an urgent need for clarity; so urgent, I think, that it trumps the sensitivities of those who don't want their views essentialized. So here goes. It is necessary, for a start, to differentiate between postmodernity as an observable cultural phenomenon and postmodernism, the self-conscious movement within philosophy and the arts that is deliberately trying to encourage the onset of postmodernity by attacking all that is disliked about modernity. It is also worth noting that both postmodernism and postmodernity are on the wane. In other words, we are not transitioning into post-postmodernity, and neither is it especially helpful to try and tease out the elements in our culture that are still stuck in modernity and differentiate these from the postmodern bits. Christian writers have made quite an art of doing this over the past 20 years or so. Postmodernity and postmodernism should be considered to have mostly failed. Their central insights have simply been reintegrated into a thriving and virulent modernity.

Postmodernity: Origins

The postmodern condition emerged gradually after the Second World War. After the War, there was a pervasive weariness with dictators. The War had erupted as the result of a gigantic clash of modernist ideologies: capitalism, communism and fascism. By the time we get to the 1960s, there was the growing conviction, especially among the young, that perhaps no one was right in any absolute sense and that as soon as one man becomes convinced that he is, war breaks out. The revolt against modernity soon split into two streams: a moralistic stream, exemplified by the civil rights movement; and a nihilistic stream, which was the free love pop culture element. And we still see both these elements in our culture: the moralistic stream has transmuted into identity politics and equality legislation, while the nihilistic stream has become normalized into a pervasive consumerism. Meanwhile free love seems to be getting itself more and more of a bad press. But these two streams, I would argue, are no longer part of a wider revolt against modernity or the Enlightenment. Indeed, the last time this wider revolt was strongly visible was in the 1990s. During that decade, there was a clear postmodern cultural anomie, a dizzy and playful confusion about what was true and right. Now there is a monolithic certainty about the humanistic values that best hold our society together. Modernity is back.

It is worth briefly noting what Christian commentators were saying about postmodernity during the 1990s and early 2000s and seeing how this looks now. We will deal with the nihilistic features first as these are easier to understand as the direct product of the loss of confidence in the verities of modernity, then we will deal with the moralistic aspects. In the nihilistic category, we have Generation X, celebrity culture and consumerism. In the moralistic category, we have the spiritual quest, the quest for community and concern for the other.

Postmodernity: Nihilistic features

Postmodernity was an easygoing, and perhaps shallow cultural mood. TV shows and films were full of tongue-in-cheek humour. Nothing was serious because nothing meant anything anymore. There was a nostalgic look to previous decades, which was reflected in the way 1990s' Brit Pop sounded like music from the 1960s and the way fashion kept throwing backwards glances to the 1970s with its love of flares and platforms. This was symptomatic of a severe weakening of the optimism and faith in progress that had characterized modernity. In the year 2000, someone noted the contrast between the Eiffel Tower dominating the Parisian skyline in 1900 and the new London Eye dominating the London skyline. The one reached for the stars; the other went wearily round and round.

Postmodernity attacked that which was perceived to lie at the heart of modernity: the Enlightenment Project, with its quest for rational knowledge and scientific control. The basic idea behind postmodernity was that, as far as the kind of truths that really matter to us are concerned, there was no such thing as an absolute truth. There was no truth 'out there', it's all 'in here'. Truth is created. This was more than just relativism, the idea that by comparing like with like we will arrive at the truth. This was, more properly, extreme pluralism, the idea that everyone is right, and no one is wrong; there is no wrong answer. It entailed the rejection of authority at the profoundest level possible. Now, even the author of a book, or the painter of a picture, had no right to dictate to others how his or her work was to be correctly interpreted.

However, it is important to note that this position was not the rejection of all things that are truly the case. Two and two truly make four. It will not do to use the old trick of saying that the postmodern is self-defeating because it says there is no such thing as an absolute truth except the absolute truth that there is no such thing as an absolute truth! It is more correct to say that, for postmodernity, there was no position we could take up that was supremely privileged and neutral. The mistake lay in the next move that was made: therefore, we must abandon the very concept of a shared truth. Many Christians were ready to applaud the dismantling of the Enlightenment Project. We were ready to join in the mockery of the Enlightenment worldview, which entailed the

extravagant expectation that the arts and sciences would further not only the control of the forces of nature but also the understanding of self and the world, moral progress, justice in social institutions, and even human happiness.[1]

Some Christians looked forward to a post-secular age when we would no longer need to answer hard-headed rationalists who wanted a proof for everything. Full-blown atheism, we hoped, was now a thing of the past. We looked forward to being heard by people who are much more willing to recognize other ways of 'knowing': intuition, emotion – even revelation – as well as rational thought. The thing we needed to do, according to John Drane for instance, was to work at being *more* spiritual, and less rationalistic. Some were even recommending that we do away with the Sunday morning sermon as this was now too 'logocentric'.

Generation X

'Generation X' is the sociologists' term for the kind of postmodern people we have become. We are cynical about everything and everybody. We poke fun at and deflate anything which smacks of pomposity. We are pessimistic . . . we are deeply hesitant to commit ourselves to ideas or people.[2]

Gen Xers were contrasted with the previous generation, the Baby Boomers. The Boomers had vast opportunities and did extremely well for themselves. The Boomers wanted to keep their comfortable lifestyle so had few children. Those born during this time are the Baby Busters, the Gen Xers. They grew up in a society that was decaying and, initially, they did not do as well in life as their parents:

The term 'blank generation' embodies the popular media stereotype of Busters as bored, lethargic, and without the idealism which ought to characterize youth.[3]

This was a generation that had seen suicide rates among males aged 15–24 rise by 71 per cent. It was a generation that had lost its appetite for life. Starkey highlighted the impact of 'critical mass' on this generation:

For the first time, sufficiently large numbers of Generation Xers have experienced some sort of serious trauma at home and in society to have 'set off a chain reaction of pathology within the entire generation'.[4]

So many young people had now experienced broken homes as Boomer divorce rates soared, that even those that hadn't were put off marriage by the experience of their peers. Gen Xers typically married late in life, if at all, and then only after a prolonged period of cohabitation.

High levels of promiscuity were noted, as was the rising interest in substance and alcohol abuse. They were characterized as having 'McJobs' – 'low pay, low prestige, low benefits, low future',[5] for which they were often very over-qualified. They were over-educated and under-employed. They were portrayed as deeply resentful to their Boomer parents who had it so good yet had bequeathed to them a ravaged and totally unaffordable world:

> Sometimes I'd just like to mace them. I want to tell them that I envy their upbringings that were so clean, so free of futurelessness.[6]

Celebrity culture

To fill the Gen X void there developed an obsession with celebrity, especially with those who become celebrities because of *Big Brother* or *The X Factor*. Reality TV made stars out of nobodies virtually overnight: everything from celebrity vets to celebrity rat exterminators. TV camera lenses were happy to intrude into the private life or profession of just about anyone and make a TV series out of it. Consumers of celebrity lived the lives of the famous vicariously, finding fulfilment and value by proxy in another person's rise to fame.

The main driver was the loss of meaning, bringing in its wake a loss of identity and value. It had become hard to conceive of our lives as really mattering at all unless they could be made to matter to the masses.

Consumerism

Consumerism was the world's answer to the emptiness that Gen Xers experienced. Soon ranking as Britain's number one leisure activity, shopping had become a religion:

> A parallel with religion is not an accidental one. Consumerism is ubiquitous and ephemeral. It is arguably the religion of the late twentieth century.[7]

The English Church Census of 2005 revealed that more people could be found in Ikea on a Sunday morning than in church.

Consumerism is capitalism creating its own market. It is the result of over-production and over-efficiency. It has to work by generating false needs. Advertising convinces us that the goods we own are obsolete or inadequate, and so we buy new products that seldom address any real need. Only a fraction of many people's incomes goes on bare necessities such as food and bills. Most goes on luxury goods and services. Mass consumption of luxury goods and services is a phenomenon that began in America during its post-war economic boom:

> After the Second World War, rising standards of living, full employment, technological advance, and innovative marketing spearheaded the American revolution that has led to its [consumerism's] cultural dominance and imitation ever since.[8]

Consumerism is a way of dealing with overproduction in a way that ensures the economy keeps growing.

Advertising has the effect of raising the stakes on products. People no longer purchase a car, they purchase an *identity*, and this is the crucial thing to grasp about how consumerism works. The real need it is seeking to meet is that of a lost identity. The Jaguar S-Type, which came out in 1998, was a deliberate attempt at targeting young men. Traditionally, Jaguars had been bought by older business-men. Now, the advertising was geared up to fast-living, womanizing Gen Xers – the few that were making that kind of money. Music sales also are highly identity-loaded. The 1990s were the last great decade of the pop music megastars such as Oasis and the Spice Girls, both helping a lost and blank generation by modelling a brash over-confident manner.

Reflection

Listless young people lacking the naive optimism that ought to char-acterize youth and either turning to sex and drugs or losing them-selves in the lives of the famous; rampant retail therapy in which shoppers spend money they haven't really got on things they think will give them an identity. To what extent are these features still with us? Have we recovered in some ways from these things, or got worse?

Postmodernity: Moralistic features

The spiritual quest

One of the convenient names for a disparate collection of spiritualities that had emerged since the 1960s was the New Age Movement. It had no headquarters, no creed and no leadership but was increasingly well established with its own shops and conventions. The New Age was a melting pot of Eastern and occultic beliefs, first-nation beliefs such as those borrowed from Native American Indians or the Druids, and a deep ecological concern for the environment. The shop window of the movement was the various alternative therapies on offer. People often become involved via a yoga class, or by receiving acupuncture, aromatherapy or crystal therapy.

John Stott summed up New Age in the aphorism: All is God, All is one, All is well.[9] Adherents believed that the dawning of the Age of Aquarius was upon us, which spelled the end of the Age of Pisces – the Christian fish. The Age of Pisces was very masculine and aggressive; the Age of Aquarius, the mermaid, would be more feminine and understanding.

John Drane was an outspoken advocate for New Agers, searching as they were for something that the Church ought to be giving them:

> It is ironic, to say the least, that the church is in serious decline at exactly the time as our whole culture is experiencing a rising tide of spiritual concern – and that many of today's spiritual searchers dismiss the church, not because it is irrelevant or old-fashioned, but because in their opinion it is unspiritual.[10]

The quest for community

With the loss of consensus, and the break-up of families, we had formed, it was said, our own quasi-families: small groups who all share our own particular interest. Commentators called this 'tribalism'. Society was no longer a unity but a composite of many discreet societies each having their own subculture rarely penetrated by anyone from another social grouping. Similarly, and more dangerously, religious groups were carrying on their existence, almost unnoticed and certainly unheard, from the margins. This was where radicalization was already occurring, which was soon to erupt in acts of terror.

Literature advocating postmodernity often came back to community as definitive of what postmodern society ought to look like even if it had not yet taken that form. Millennials, the generation following the Xers, may be characterized as those that have intensified the quest for community, making full use of social media in pursuit of that. Though they probably attain their ideal only rarely, their commitment to it marks them out as those that especially value relationships.

Concern for the other

The postmodern age opened the door to all those who were marginalized by modernity. There was a wholesale effort, stridently demanded by lobby groups and enacted time and again in legislation, to bring those on the margins into the centre. There was a recognition that the totalizing narratives of modernity's quest for science and progress always had its shadow side. Success benefitted a few but created many silent victims. There was something about modern ideologies, therefore, that was inherently violent and oppressive.

Reflection

The search for spiritual fulfilment and for real community that beats our alienation and isolation, the desire to reach out to the Other, the marginal, the downtrodden. In what ways do you think these features have developed since the 1990s?

Postmodernism as a philosophy

In many ways, postmodern philosophy is most at home when talking about language, which makes it like and yet very unlike analytic philosophy. The fundamental difference would be the realist epistemological framework undergirding the analytic tradition in contrast to the radically anti-realist epistemology of postmodern philosophy. It was Nietzsche who first introduced questions of language and interpretation that became very difficult for modernists to answer. This questioning of, first, whether language as a whole has any 'real' or 'objective' meaning beyond the meaning that we give to it, and second, whether individual words have any real meaning when divorced from their context led Nietzsche to a loss of confidence in the whole idea of truth:

> What, then, is truth? A mobile army of metaphors, metonyms, and anthropo-morphisms – in short a sum of human relations . . . coins which have lost their picture and now matter only as metal, no longer as coins.[11]

To Nietzsche, the harbinger of postmodernism we now turn.

2 The Prophet: Friedrich Nietzsche (1844–1900)

The son of a German Lutheran pastor, Nietzsche (pronounced 'Neetsha') be-came an atheist in his youth. He has become important in recent philosophy as the first philosopher to begin the process of dismantling modernism. All the assumptions of the various modern worldviews, such as belief in human pro-gress, were all based on supposedly incontrovertible truths, Christianity being one of them. Nietzsche questioned whether anyone could really be so sure of the things we once assumed. Indeed, with the 'death of God' as he put it, that is, the demise of religion in the West, can we even be sure anymore of what is right from what is wrong?

> God is dead. God remains dead. And we have killed him. How shall we, the murderers of all murderers, comfort ourselves?[12]

He foresaw that the rejection of moral norms could and would lead to the collapse of Western civilization into a state of barbarism in which everyone tries to over-power everyone else. 'Might', in a world without God, is the only 'right'. This, he termed the 'will to power', the ability to turn what one wills into the power to bring it into being. The only way of avoiding anarchy and chaos descending on the West was for each individual to become a 'superhuman'. Each individual must realize their own potential by making choices based on their own personal philosophy of life. This would enable them to 'transcend' themselves, thus, in some sense, mastering or harnessing their will to power so that it is no longer so destructive of others. He thus invented a new kind of ethic: an ethic no longer of good versus evil but of noble versus base, of self-affirmation versus resentment of others. He was opposed to the Christian morality of meekness and humility. This he termed a 'slave-morality', which, in the end, only encourages resentment towards the strong on the part of the weak masses. He looked forward to the emergence of a superhuman race with as much fervour as Marx looked forward to a communist revolution. The first superhuman person would be a highly intelligent, fit and cultured individual with a strong, unshakeable will. His fictional *Thus Spoke Zarathustra*, which was put to music so famously by Nietzsche's friend Richard Strauss, was his fanciful exploration of the superman idea.

Nietzsche's staunch individualism anticipated the dominant role that existentialism would play decades after his death. His rejection of absolute truth-claims and moral norms anticipated by over a century the onset of postmodernism: 'There are many kinds of eyes . . . and consequently there are many kinds of "truths", and consequently there is no truth.'[13] Yet the enigmatic quality of his writings has permitted many and varied interpretations. He has been hailed not only by postmodernists, but also by Nazis and psychoanalysts. Unfortunately, insanity brought an end to his writing career in 1889. He died in 1900.

3 The Definer: Jean-François Lyotard (1924–98)

Here is Lyotard's famed definition of the postmodern:

> I define the postmodern as incredulity toward metanarratives.[14]

To help us understand what a metanarrative is, Lyotard very kindly defines what he means by 'modern': 'I will use the term *modern* to designate any science that legitimates itself with reference to a metadiscourse . . . making an explicit appeal to some grand narrative.'[15] Although we end up with another 'meta' mouthful, we start to get his point a little. Lyotard takes issue with a feature of modernity that, sadly, is still with us and seems to be on the rise. Modernity keeps producing monolithic and monochrome definitions of reality, always hankering after 'the realization of the fantasy to seize reality'.[16]

The most important thing, then, is to get a feel for what Lyotard's 'meta-narratives' *do*. One of the chief tools by which defenders of a particular meta-narrative silence the Other is language, language that is given one fixed meaning. Such metanarratives, according to Lyotard, need pluralism as their antidote and safeguard. One of the most noticeable developments since Lyotard's day, however, has been the way a now resurgent modernity has itself taken up diversity, equality and tolerance as its own cause. It is as though the leaven of anti-modern feeling with its 'war on totality' and its celebration of differences has merely been folded back into the dough of modern secular rationality and bureaucratized as legislation. The postmodern has been folded back into the modern.

So what exactly *is* a metanarrative. Many Christian authors claim that Lyotard never thought of a metanarrative as being just any big story, but only those big stories that aggressively assert a privileged status as arbitrator of all other truths. Christianity is not Lyotard's target, they say, but the total political explanations that have resulted in fascism and Marxism. But in fact, Thacker[17] has pointed out that Lyotard emphatically *did* think that Christianity is a metanarrative displaying all the same qualities that make any other metanarrative 'a terror'[18] to millions of people. However, it is also true to say that Lyotard's main target, and the thing he was asked by the University of Quebec to write his report on, was the special status we give to scientific knowledge. The key is in the word 'legitimation' that Lyotard uses in his definition of the modern, and the way he links this to science. According to Lyotard, science alone purports to be able to point to a legitimization of itself that stands outside of all human stories, all narratives, reducing all else to just that, nothing but myths, stories we tell. Lyotard points out that science is not honest enough with itself to admit that it too is a narrative, a myth built up over time and the accumulation of certain commitments and beliefs. It cannot articulate why it alone has a source of legitimation outside of itself. For all those of Lyotard's generation (and nationality) who lived through the horrors of what modern science could do during the war years, and what it threatened in the Cold War years, science's way of placing its legitimation beyond scrutiny was very troubling.

This is not to say that science is the only modern metanarrative, though it may well be the worst of them. The advent of the metanarrative is simply a result of the transition from pre-modern cultures where small communities told small stories about their own culture. To invoke Wittgenstein, they each had their own language-game. With the transition to modernity, these small communities broke up and we became a mass culture needing massive totalizing explanations of the way things are, explanations claiming to be self-evident and universal, not particular, or biased, or contingent. Postmodernity has become, quite rightly, incredulous of these. As we groan beneath a totalizing secularity, we see that this postmodern turn was potentially good news for faith but hopes of postmodernity 'providing new spaces for religious discourse'[19] have not materialized.

Lyotard does more than merely diagnose the postmodern condition. He inevitably ends up needing to offer some alternative to the metanarrative, which almost inevitably ends up being a micronarrative. Narratives imposed from on high are replaced by local convention. Whatever one particular people consider to be right and just is what must be accepted. However, Lyotard points out that even Nazism could command 'near unanimity' for one particular population. 'From where,' he asks, 'could one judge that it was not just?' He admits: 'This is obviously very troublesome.'[20]

4 The Pioneers: Foucault (1926–84) and Derrida (1930–2004)

Reflection

Thinking back to the view that Christianity is a metanarrative: at its best, the very genius of Christian faith is its ability to contextualize itself in very particular contexts and not be a one size that fits all, not an enforcer, not a terrifying grand narrative. At its worst, it uses divine and eschatological backing to terrify people. To what extent is Western Europe still smarting from the effects of very bad Christianity? What can we do about this?

Foucault the historian

Foucault drew massive inspiration from Nietzsche's concept of the will to power. This is the kind of power, you may recall, which kicks in once all other constraints are gone and 'God' is long dead. For Foucault, power is knowledge. He explains: 'power and knowledge directly imply one another . . . there is no power relation without the correlative constitution of a field of knowledge, nor any knowledge that does not presuppose and constitute at the same time power relations'.[21] That power is knowledge is exemplified by what we take to be progress in knowledge as we narrate to ourselves the all-too-familiar story of the West's unstoppable rise to super-sophistication and super-power. Foucault disabuses us of this hubris through a series of historical treatises often in areas he could hardly have been an expert in. He is widely criticized for the inaccuracies and distortions that are introduced into his historical accounts as he tries to make the history say what he wants it to say. His subjects included the history of mental illness and its treatment, a history of clinical practice, a history of the human sciences, a history of the criminal justice system and a three-volume history of sexuality. Part of his approach was to radically dispense with the whole way of doing history as a supposedly neutral observer. Rather, his historical method is genealogical. He wants to do archaeology on the origin and progress of key ideas and trace an unbroken chain of influence, leading up to the present day. In this way, he shows us that the very ideas we take for granted (and do history with for that matter) did not come from heaven but may be seen as contingent, particular and tainted by hubristic motives.

Possibly his most convincing and potentially far-reaching example is his history of prisons, *Discipline and Punish*. He points out how we assume the criminal justice system today to be far more humane than in, say, the medieval period when people were hung or mutilated for quite minor offences. However, that older way of doing things was a very public affair. People could, and often did, start rioting if they felt that someone had been wrongly executed. Now, all is behind closed doors. The state can exercise its power in an unaccountable way. So really, the invention of prisons was not a move towards being more humane, and it patently is not to do with the moral reform of the prisoner's character. Rather, it is simply a way of avoiding a riot while still exercising enormous disciplinary power over a population. Brutality decreased, while levels of intrusion and intervention steadily increased.[22] And the prison, according to Foucault, is an especially pristine example of what a modern social system is trying to do to us all of the time. As levels of control increase, power 'produces reality';[23] it normalizes and forms us into the kind of citizens it wants us to be. Power does not merely supress or censor like other postmodern philosophers note. It disciples us, it creates us.

He gives us an Orwellian picture of panoptic surveillance administered by a Kafkaesque bureaucracy:

> it [penal reform] was an effort to adjust mechanisms of power that frame the everyday lives of individuals; an adaptation and a refinement of the machinery that assumes responsibility for and places under surveillance their everyday behaviour, their identity, their activity, their apparently unimportant gestures.[24]

Reflection

According to Foucault, the use of power by the modern state means that we are always seen without seeing (Foucault, *Discipline and Punish*, p. 200). The seer remains inscrutable. These days perhaps it is not so much the state apparatus that does this to us but the data-harvesting social media giants. What, in your view, is a Christian response to this level of intrusion?

Derrida the deconstructionist

At the forefront of the beginning of postmodernism was a movement in literary criticism that developed in the 1970s called deconstruction. The chief architect of deconstruction was Jacques Derrida, an author of some 40 books on a vast array of topics. All of Derrida's writings have a certain 'iconoclastic' quality.[25] At the heart of his work is the querying of privilege for one thing over another. He queries why we tend to privilege words over pictures, or rationality over feeling, yet his concerns for otherness are readily applied to more general queries about why we privilege certain kinds of people over others. Indeed, this concern may be at the root of Derrida's entire project: as an Algerian Jew he himself knew what it felt like to be always on the margins, always second class to some other race or religion.

Deconstruction itself involves a search for hidden meanings within a text, based on the idea that, even if you refer to the supposed intentions of the author, or try instead to point to the things in the world that the text refers to, the meanings in the text are in the eye of the beholder. Our perspectives as readers make impossible any indubitable, universally agreed meaning. Meaning is made by each interpreter. He is famous for saying, 'There is nothing outside the text',[26] or, a more literal translation is 'There is no outside-text' (*Il n'y a rien en dehors du texte*), which Smith accurately interprets as saying, not that there is literally nothing real beyond texts, but that, 'there is no reality that is not always already interpreted through the mediating lens of language'.[27] Derrida was often misunderstood as making out that there was 'nothing beyond language', or that we are 'imprisoned in language', or 'submerged in words'. He corrected his critics by saying:

> The critique of logocentrism is above all else the search for the 'other' and the 'other of language' . . . to distance oneself from the habitual structure of reference, to challenge or complicate our common assumption about it, does not amount to saying that there is *nothing* beyond language.[28]

He rejects the notion that language could ever be a straightforward expression of truth; to make it central to the quest for knowledge is to be guilty of logocentrism (a word that you might have heard some Christian thinkers use as they critique the wordiness of a typical church service, which is perhaps not quite what Derrida had in mind in his coining of the term). He means that all we have to work with are interpretations, so we had better be a lot less sure of our supposedly rational discourse than we were and become more attuned to otherness in the process.

So what use is reading? It involves, after all, making use of a limited perspective further limited by a fixed form of words. Well, instead of a search for some kind of meaning which the words are somehow assumed to be in possession of, there is the possibility of a 'hermeneutic of suspicion'. In deconstruction, every text is scrutinized for 'power' language: power that keeps certain people and views central and keeps relegating others to the periphery. Texts keep some people on top and others below. Hermeneutics that is attentive to this is a useful or 'edifying' moral result of the act of reading. We read attentive to the marginalized, those who are on the underbelly of modernity, with a view to social and political activism that can bring those on the margins into the centre. Smith again: 'deconstruction is interested in interpretations that have been marginalized and sidelined, activating voices that have been silenced. This is the constructive, yea prophetic, aspect of Derrida's deconstruction.'[29]

And so we see here again the oft-overlooked moral urgency of some postmodernism. It may, quite understandably, be viewed, as Noam Chomsky does, as completely amoral,[30] but remember that one of the chief concerns of Lyotard, Foucault and Derrida is with what we call 'alterity'. This is a little like the word 'altruism' but without going quite that far! These guys are far from altruistic – they loved being celebrity philosophers appearing on the front cover of *Le Monde* and dazzling people with their shocking ideas. But to varying degrees, they show a real concern for the Other, a concern for 'those people excluded by the culture of Coke and Cleverness' as one Christian interpreter puts it.[31]

It is also worth cautioning, however, that the later Derrida would seem to belong to the nihilistic stream in postmodernism, not the moralistic stream. After having so strenuously insisted that he is not claiming that a text can mean simply anything, he then goes on to exegete Revelation 22.17 ('the Spirit and the Bride say "come"') as though it were about how the word 'come' is used in sexual slang. Anthony Kenny concludes, in no uncertain terms, that the later Derrida is not even worthy of any scholarly attention at all.[32] Some would place Foucault in the same camp, though reception of him has been inevitably coloured by his nihilistic lifestyle.

5 Richard Rorty (1931–2007) and Neopragmatism

All postmodern philosophers have worked hard to discredit the correspondence theory of truth, the idea that there is an objective truth 'out there', which language in some way corresponds to. That there are as many different perspectives on things as there are people is something Christians can accept. The existence of four Gospels in some way supports that. Philosophers like Rorty, however, will say that all is a matter of perspective, all is contingent, all is particular. No general, timeless principles or universals can be discovered that will not be discredited by the next generation or by some other community in a different context. Here is Rorty's most quoted aphorism:

> There is no difference that makes a difference between saying that something is true because it works or that something works because it is true.

Reflection

In 1 Corinthians 1, Paul does not argue with sophist ideas by proving that the gospel is true. His only concern was to point out that it worked, that the message of the cross is, to 'us who are being saved', the 'power of God' (1 Cor. 1.18). But compare Os Guinness: 'The Christian faith is not true because it works; it works because it is true . . . It is not simply "true for us"; it is true for any who seek in order to find, because truth is true even if nobody believes it and falsehood is false even if everybody believes it.' (Os Guinness, 2000, *Time for Truth*, Grand Rapids, MI: Baker, pp. 79–80.) To what extent can we say that Paul, or any other biblical author, was a pragmatist?

So, back to Rorty's aphorism, one might think that there is not a lot more to say once you have so set aside the whole business of epistemology as to reduce everything to its 'cash value' as it were. In order to see his distinct contribution, it is helpful to briefly look at the tradition he is invoking here. At some point in the late 1960s, Rorty became disillusioned enough with the analytic tradition to begin looking at the often-overlooked American philosophers who were active just before the analytic tradition eclipsed them. These we term the classical pragmatists. Those inspired by Rorty are neopragmatists. Here are some key points that can be gleaned from the classical pragmatism, which proved such an inspiration to Rorty as he altered his philosophical convictions:

- Any given theory is an *instrument for adaptation*. It is a way of coping. The very reason for a theory's existence is that it facilitates adaptation to changing conditions. Theories can quickly be left behind by changes in culture. When this happens, the pragmatist 'turns away from abstraction and insufficiency, from verbal solutions, from bad *a priori* reasons, from fixed principles, closed systems, and pretended absolutes and origins. He turns towards concreteness and adequacy.'[33]

- Classical pragmatism moves beyond both coherentism (assessing an idea by the strength of its internal logic and consistency with itself) and foundationalism (using some external principle to legitimate a claim) to affirm that truth is discovered in *a process of verification* in which something is tried out and works. And even this is contingent.
- Theories are judged by the *consequences of accepting them*. A utilitarian ethic is assumed, but there is a utilitarian approach to everything else as well.
- Ideas are *plans of action*.[34] We evaluate a theory by its fitness for purpose. Does it get us to where we need to go?[35]

Interestingly, Rorty is one of two postmodern philosophers (the other one being Lyotard) whom Thacker singles out as particular examples of the moralistic type that are primarily motivated by a concern for the other, as opposed to those whose incredulity leads them to more nihilistic outcomes.[36] And it is this moral quest that seems to have driven Rorty away from realism towards pragmatism:

> Pragmatists think that the question to ask about our beliefs is not whether they are about reality or merely about appearance, but whether they are the best habits of action for gratifying our desires. On this view, to say that a belief is, as far as we know, true, is to say that no alternative belief is, as far as we know, a better habit of acting. . . . We cannot regard truth as a goal of inquiry. The purpose of inquiry is to achieve agreement among human beings about what to do.[37]

This is where he parts company with classical pragmatism. Peirce, for instance, insisted that, while perspectives inevitably differ, truth is so 'whether you, or I, or anybody thinks it is so or not'.[38] The realism Rorty rejects, however, is not a realism that says 'there is a world out there'; he clearly accepts that there is, but the realism that says 'the truth is out there', since, like Derrida, he does not believe anyone can take up a position outside of words and texts. In the place of delusions of objectivity, Rorty recommends solidarity, by which he means that we enlarge our 'we' to include ever-widening circles of we-ness that include those we had previously referred to as a 'them':

Solidarity is not discovered by reflection but created. It is created by increasing our sensitivity to the particular details of the pain and humiliation of other, unfamiliar sorts of people. Such increased sensitivity makes it more difficult to marginalize people different from ourselves by thinking, 'They do not feel as *we* would,' or 'There must always be suffering, so why not let *them* suffer?'[39]

The new collectivity thus created becomes the locus for working out what's best. Neopragmatist Cornel West puts it this way:

> the validation of knowledge claims rests on practical judgments constituted by, and constructed in, dynamic social practices. For neopragmatists, we mortal creatures achieve and acquire knowledge by means of self-critical and self-correcting social procedures rooted in a variety of human processes.[40]

However, because of his insistence that a given construal should only be accepted on pragmatic grounds and not imposed upon anyone, Rorty leaves himself open to the charge that even his pragmatic option need not be accepted by anyone if, in their view, it does not work. In other words, he traps himself into having to hold his pragmatism pragmatically, rather than dogmatically. Thacker believes that, so concerned is Rorty to forward his liberal utopia of social justice, that he sees this contradiction as the necessary price to pay.[41]

Terminology time-out

- *Alterity.* Concern for the Other and for otherness.
- *Deconstruction.* Everything comes to us interpreted and requiring hermeneutics. Interpretations do things like keep certain people on top and others below so the right hermeneutic is a hermeneutic of suspicion. Thus deconstruction is concerned about the underside of dominant interpretations. It is unconcerned about trying to find original or real meanings to which an interpretation refers.
- *Logocentrism.* Because the powerful have so much to gain from their interpretation of the way things are, their version has dominated the texts which appear in print. A way out of this is to be less ruled by the printed page and more ruled by other modes of expression such as image.

- *Metanarrative.* A narrative that is claiming to not be merely a narrative but to have some unique purchase upon reality itself. It is legitimized by some neutral external reality that allows it to repress and silence other voices.
- *Nihilism.* Literally, nothingness. It is the result of abandoning the quest for ultimate meaning and consequently living life, like the existentialists and Nietzsche recommended, on the basis that one is therefore thrown back onto one's own resources to make something out of your life without any guiding principles.
- *Pluralism.* The belief that all beliefs are to be given equal value and none are to be excluded as untrue or wrong.
- *Relativism.* The belief that every belief has a partial grasp of the way things are and that beliefs that claim otherwise are to be critiqued by being set alongside a contradictory alternative. It is a way of problematizing big truth-claims and avoiding epistemic closure.

Reflection

Can you think of a movie or a novel that messes with your head, that unsettles you by playing around with what you take to be true and real? Or have you seen a film or read a book that moralistically opens your eyes to the Other, making you enter the world of a person who society looks upon as strange or different? Write down how these help to illuminate the postmodern condition. (Incidentally, if you are stuck here, in *Who's Afraid of Postmodernism?*, James K. A. Smith begins each chapter with a film that (unwittingly) helps to illustrate the thinking of the postmodern philosopher he is about to introduce.)

---

6 Postmodernism and Ethics

Alasdair MacIntyre (1929–)

MacIntyre is a celebrated name in ethical reflection today. He is the modern rehabilitator of the original Aristotelian virtue theory. MacIntyre advocates a return to Aristotle's emphasis on the virtues of an individual's character as the primary source and motive for acting for the good of others. His landmark work, *After Virtue*,[42] first came out in 1981, yet his critique of the sorry state of moral philosophy in the late twentieth century still feels remarkably current in many ways. He describes accurately the way moral debates had become unresolvable:

> Every one of the arguments is logically valid . . . the conclusions do indeed follow from the premises. But the rival premises are such that we possess no rational way of weighing the claims of one as against another . . . From our rival conclusions we can argue back to our rival premises, but when we do arrive at our premises argument ceases and the invocation of one premise against another becomes a matter of pure assertion and counter assertion. Hence perhaps the slightly shrill tone of so much moral debate . . . Corresponding to the interminability of public argument there is at least the appearance of a disquieting private arbitrariness. It is small wonder if we become defensive and therefore shrill.[43]

We have arrived, says MacIntyre, at a situation in which 'All moral judgments are *nothing but* expressions of preference, expressions of attitude or feeling'.[44] He blames this lack of any agreed premises or warrants on modernity rather than, as more recent writers would, on postmodernity. It is the very value-free neutrality of modern rationality that renders value judgements – ethics in other words – impossible. Not only that, but the very view-from-nowhere neutrality of modern academia makes academic historians unable to see that there has been a wholesale tearing up of the entire morality rule-book. They cannot see that all we are left with are incoherent fragments of more ancient assertions about the good and the true. These we now reassemble eclectically and according to whim. The modern attachment to the autonomous thinking self has contributed to the moral confusion. It meant that moral questions were solved in an abstract way, detached from community, as in Kant. This, for MacIntyre, was the beginning of the end. Now, that same autonomy is not even rational anymore and has led to the spread of ethical emotivism and the total collapse of moral consensus.

His proposal is that we get back our sense of *telos*, the goal that Aristotle used to speak of as essential to moral progress, which is human happiness. We need to ask ourselves again: What sort of people do we want to become? What sort of people are our current moral choices making us into? And we need to ask these kinds of questions in a grounded, embedded (not abstract) way within communities that tell stories. It is these stories, MacIntyre believes, that have the power to form virtuous inclinations in us. This emphasis on communal story-telling has made MacIntyre sound very postmodern and given him continued currency. He is someone who might help us to navigate our way along the cliff edge of nihilism to a safer place.

Stanley Hauerwas

Hauerwas picks up where MacIntyre leaves off, making up the shortcoming in MacIntyre, which is that he is not very specific about what goodness, character and virtue actually are. Where MacIntyre speaks of the importance of story gen-erally to the nurture of the virtues of a community, Hauerwas speaks specifically of the story of Jesus and the ethic of the kingdom of God:

> To be like Jesus is to join him in the journey through which we are trained to be a people capable of claiming citizenship in God's kingdom of nonviolent love.[45]

And the community context that MacIntyre felt was so crucial becomes the church. Beyond this outworking of the character of Christ in the church, Hauerwas is not interested in establishing the rational foundations for morals like Kant did. Like MacIntyre, he considers all such Enlightenment thinking, which disembodies morals from real life, to be where it all began to go wrong: 'our convictions embody our morality; our beliefs are our actions'.[46] Even in the case of hard decisions, Hauerwas is convinced that the decision 'makes itself' if we know who we are and what we need to become.[47]

Merold Westphal on Derrida

Moving further away from MacIntyre, we have Westphal's sympathetic treat-ment of postmodern philosopher Jacques Derrida. Westphal acts as a kind of 'yes, but' to MacIntyre's devastating critique of the current state of moral reason-ing. In many ways, the situation could be seen as having got even more dire than in MacIntyre's day because of the full onset of postmodernism, the philosophy with deconstruction at its heart. Deconstruction, of the kind championed by

Derrida, could be seen as rendering impossible any objective judgements about anything at all. Entire legal systems can be deconstructed, stripped of their supposed neutrality, critiqued for what they unjustly exclude and shown to be by no means synonymous with justice as such. This potentially leaves 'ethics to be a matter of personal preference and ethical language to be the expression or evocation of emotion',[48] which is exactly what MacIntyre feared. Derrida, however, insisted 'a deconstructivist approach . . . does not necessarily lead to injustice, nor to the effacement of an opposition between just and unjust'.[49] To the contrary, 'Deconstruction is justice'.[50] This is precisely because it interrogates 'the origin, grounds and limits of our conceptual, theoretical or normative apparatus'.[51] Because of this querying function, Derrida does not wish to define positively what this justice is that deconstructs what we take to be just. If he did that, he would be creating something just as problematic as the construct being deconstructed. Westphal helps us out. He defines justice in Derrida using a phrase of Kierkegaard: 'thoughts which wound from behind'.[52] He continues:

> Though we cannot get them in front of us where they are fully present to us and we can master them, they nevertheless insinuate themselves into our thinking, disturbing its complacency in ways we can neither predict nor control. They ambush our absolutes. On Derrida's view it is precisely as deconstruction that the idea of justice in itself wounds our legal systems, both as theory and as practice, from behind.[53]

This certainly provides the basis for self-critical moral deliberations but, in the end, it is in such a negative register that it cannot progress the discussion to any very assured positions.

Reflection

Paul often reinforces his pneumatological virtue ethics – that is his insistence that walking in the Spirit will be enough to ensure that we bear the fruit of the Spirit – with very specific moral guidance. Paul makes full use of the law of Moses – telling the story, if you like – as he tries to disciple former pagans in the way of Christ (see his imperative sections, e.g. Rom. 12.9–21; Eph. 5.1—6:9). With which of the above three ethicists – MacIntyre, Hauerwas or Westphal – does Paul's teaching seem to sit with the most comfortably?

7 Postmodern Church

The emerging church

The emerging church movement had its first tentative beginnings in the UK, with the now discredited Nine O'Clock Service being a forerunner of it. It began as a number of people with historic links to the house church movement began to describe themselves, in the words of Dave Tomlinson, as 'Post-Evangelical'.[54] Anglican Graham Cray also emerged during this early phase of the movement and John Drane, of the Church of Scotland, became significant. Under the auspices of Doug Pagitt, a number of conferences were held in America in the 1990s that spawned several churches that were decidedly of an 'emerging' flavour, that is, they actively engaged with postmodernity: Solomon's Porch (Doug Pagitt), Mars Hill (Mark Driscoll), Vintage Faith (Dan Kimbal) and Emergent Village (associated with Brian McLaren). A key turning point was Mark Driscoll's 1997 paper at a Leadership Network Conference: 'Generation X: Three Myths and Realities', which argued for the need to move beyond discussions about Gen X to discussions about the much bigger shift that was behind Gen X – postmodernity – a point that Brain McLaren was also keen to make. Placing only a generational interpretation on the changes that were becoming noticeable as Gen X began to dominate culture in the 1990s was seen as too short-sighted, not taking into account the cataclysmic epistemological shift that underlay it. However, the emerging church was, arguably, also being too short-sighted by assuming the transition to postmodernity was ushering us into a new setting that would not itself be succeeded by anything else.

The emerging church was an overt postmodernizing of the faith:

> The church is a modern institution in a postmodern world, a fact that is often widely overlooked. The church must embody the gospel within the culture of postmodernity for the Western church to survive the twenty-first century.[55]

And further:

> The majority of current church practices are cultural accommodations to a society that no longer exists.[56]

These churches showed a desire to live out an authentic Christian life that improved people's lives in the here and now: 'It's not about the church meeting your needs', said McLaren, 'it's about joining the mission of God's people to meet the world's needs.'[57]

There were many critics, especially of McLaren. One review of McLaren's *A New Kind of Christian* feared that: 'If the views promoted in the book are adopted, the church will be amalgamated within its culture and quickly lose its scriptural foundation and authority.'[58] McLaren would respond by saying that it is simply a matter of time before churches start to catch up with the reality that Scripture cannot be appealed to in any way that anyone other than the people of God would recognize as authoritative. And even for the people of God, who is to say that an infallible Bible (fallibly interpreted) has any more claim on Christians than an infallible pope and Christian tradition?

Throughout the fictional dialogue that makes up *a New Kind of Christian*, McLaren tries to wake the reader up to the new philosophical paradigm that had been unfolding throughout the 1990s and which could no longer be ignored: 'I'm supposed to be preaching the truth, but I'm not even sure what the truth is anymore,'[59] says Dan the disillusioned pastor. McLaren was convinced that we are living through a 'deep rift', a moment in which 'a new kind of Christianity' needed to be born.[60]

Reflection

Take a look at the website for either Solomon's Porch, Mars Hill, Vintage Faith or Emergent Village. What kinds of things are these churches offering that you would perhaps not expect to find in a regular church?

Radical Orthodoxy

The postmodern is the site of the post-secular; it's an opportunity for people to develop critiques of modernity and its brash rejection of the divine.[61]

John Milbank, together with Catherine Pickstock and Graham Ward, who all originally were based at Cambridge, initiated a new movement in theology called Radical Orthodoxy (RO). It is described as a 'new theological mood',[62] It is almost completely encapsulated in the opening line of the first chapter of the founding document of the movement, John Milbank's *Theology and Social Theory*:

Once, there was no 'secular.'[63]

Even this tiny statement gives us quite a commanding view of what RO is up to. We have here a genealogical or archaeological approach, which, in the manner of Foucault, seeks to uncover the historically dubious origins of ideas our society takes for granted. It undermines the taken-for-granted assumptions about a fundamental division between religion and secularity, together with the assumption that secularity is not itself a religious commitment.[64] And here RO sounds a similar note to Lyotard. Secular reason is not honest with itself. Its protagonists in social science seem to believe that only a secular vision of society, cleansed of all contentious religious bias and delusion, has any incorrigible legitimacy. Secularity, in other words, is not a mere narrative among other narratives but has scientific and objective legitimacy. RO sounds a resounding 'no' to this idea. The secular narrative certainly has no more claim upon us than the Christian one.

Further, RO sympathizers would claim that, whenever Christianity tries to do 'correlation', that is, whenever it tries to go to something external to itself within the world of modern philosophy to find legitimation, it goes astray. It pays for such unholy alliances with a loss to its core structure, a liquidated religion.[65] RO, instead seeks to do theology from the resources of revelation alone. This does not mean that they, like Tertullian, would refuse all liaison with the philosophies of this world. This would be inconsistent since they love Aquinas and Augustine,[66] both of whom dialogued closely with non-Christian philosophies. Rather they reject the fawning idea that Christianity must survive in a hostile world by shaping itself around something foreign to it. Both Aquinas and Augustine were very selective in their use of Aristotle and Plotinus respectively. Only by decoupling from correlative relationships will Christianity stand on its own two feet as a narrative that can have something to say to every other narrative. It could even have something to say about the metanarrative of science. One RO theologian has done exactly that and written a theology book about the scientific idea of motion.[67]

> ### Reflection
>
> The news of modernity's death has been greatly exaggerated. The Enlightenment project is alive and well, dominating Europe and increasingly North America, particularly in the political drive to carve out 'the secular' – a zone decontaminated of the prejudices of determinate religious influence. (Smith, *Introducing Radical Orthodoxy*, p. 31)
>
> What are we up against? From whence comes the resolute indifference to faith with which we are so familiar? Is it postmodernity, or is it secularity?

What is secularity?

The secular, according to the account of Catherine Pickstock in particular, is a worldview invented in the late Reformation at the end of the Wars of Religion, which advances non-religious and non-theistic attitudes and lifestyles and which invented a term for the worldview that it opposes: the term 'religious'. Once, there was no secular and there was consequently no 'religious'. In science, education and the media, God is kept out of view by dint of sheer silence on all matters of religion and theology except when contemplating religious violence and in-fighting. The events of 9/11 and the jihadism that has followed go some way, perhaps, to explaining why, instead of a more religiously and spiritually open mood that the 1990s promised, there has, instead, been a renewed vigour to the secular agenda. But is this the whole picture?

Canadian philosopher and Templeton Prize winner Charles Taylor asks the question: 'why was it virtually impossible not to believe in God, in say, 1500 in our Western society, while in 2000 many of us find this [that is, non-belief] not only easy, but even inescapable?'[68] He sees secularity as not only entailing a separating out of realms: religious and secular, with all the power vested in the secular realm. He believes a more fundamental shift has happened in the 500 years between 1500 and 2000, which has changed the conditions, changed the atmosphere (my term), in which faith is likely to flourish. He explores the fact that we no longer believe in an enchanted universe in which God must be called upon as the dominant spirit to overcome evil spirits. Another part of the changed atmosphere is the way society is now structured: more around the individual than around the givens of a society centred around church. And he looks at how our lives were once dominated by the liturgical year with its ordinary time and high days. In modernity, our sense of time is not organized around key religious moments in the year. All this was gradually swept away, says Taylor, not so much by something external to religion but by a secularity that was actually born within religion itself. The Reformation and the advent of deism were prior to the Enlightenment and unwittingly began the process of 'excarnation', the evacuation of religious interests from the realm of fleshly, embodied, this-worldly reality, opening the way for that realm's colonization by belief systems which made no reference to anything transcendent.

These ideas gradually transformed an enchanted cosmos into an impersonal and mechanistic universe. As a result of this, we began to see ourselves as living within a purely 'immanent frame' with no access to the transcendent, though we may continue to seek and enjoy experiences very much like transcendence without shedding the immanent frame. The way we extoll the emotional highs around falling in love as though this were some quasi-religious encounter is a case in point. People have not stopped longing for transcendence. But, within this immanent frame, our view of ourselves as 'buffered' and no longer 'porous' selves also developed. We are no longer porous or vulnerable to a world of spirits and God. Our sense of connection to community and nature is much diminished as a result. Consequently, we have a stronger sense of our own agency, which is not a bad thing in itself; yet here again, the gravitation to experiences of abandonment mostly using chemical highs of one sort or another, is evidence that the Buffered Self survives with a sense that something is missing.

Secularity, therefore, is more than merely the absence of something: the absence of religion from public life, or the absence of people from church. Thanks to Taylor, it takes on certain names such as the Immanent Frame and the Buffered Self, which more positively define what it is we are dealing with when we try to encourage people to believe in God in the midst of these taken-for-granted features of modern life.

Discussion

In what ways does Taylor's terminology around the Immanent Frame and the Buffered Self potentially change the way you would do ministry and mission within the secular West?

8 Summary

One of the most notable features of postmodernism is that it is centred around incredulity. Because of its incredulity it specializes in critique. It is very good at showing up the hidden agendas within modernity for what they are. It is almost like a conspiracy theory. It likes to uncover the dark forces of power and control that have made the West what it is. The relentless critique means that many of the leading postmodern philosophers have felt the pressure to do more than deconstruct what they don't like about modernity. They have tried to offer something in its place. In every case, they end up with a potentially show-stopping self-refutation but carry on with the show anyway. Lyotard seems to get trapped in needing to offer some kind of mini-narrative as an antidote to the metanarrative but soon realizes that localized conventionalism can be no better than the totalizing normalizations that have silenced the Other on a bigger scale. Foucault shows us how sinister power structures based on knowledge can be and helps us to recover our own sense of free personal agency, creating space for the transgressive and for the Other. But what do we do with a world filled with transgression, with the anti-structural? He himself became disillusioned with revolutionary ideals after Paris 1968. Derrida complicates notions of language giving us unproblematic access to truth. All we have are interpretations. So, presumably, everything he says is also only an interpretation with no privileged access to truth. Rorty corners himself into a place where no one needs to accept his pragmatic principle except on a pragmatic basis. He does not claim special epistemic access to truth, so someone could simply decide that his pragmatism does not work. Undaunted, he continues to champion the values of solidarity and liberal politics, values that could just as easily be championed on some other philosophical basis.

As Christians, however, the postmodernists have handed us two helpful points. First, they have shown us how to do worldview critique. We can use the techniques of genealogy and archaeology that Foucault showed us to do our own interested history of the ideas that we want to critique. This is exactly what RO have done. They have found common cause with postmodernism's incredulity and articulated their own incredulity towards the metanarrative of the secular. Second, we can engage with the moralistic strand within postmodernism, but, unlike the postmodern philosophers, we would not end up at a self-refuting cul-de-sac. As Christians we believe in a transcendent reality that provides the starting point for ethical judgements. These starting points allow us to do more than merely critique the West for its marginalization of the Other. We can offer positive reasons why others matter so much.

Notes

1 Jürgen Habermas, 'Modernity: An Unfinished Project', in C. Jencks (ed.), 1992, *The Post-Modern Reader*, New York: St Martin's Press, pp. 162–3.

2 David Cook, 1996, *Blind Alley Beliefs*, Leicester: IVP, pp. 12–13.

3 Mike Starkey, 1997, *God, Sex and Generation X*, London: Triangle SPCK, p. 28.

4 Starkey, *God, Sex and Generation X*, p. 33.

5 Douglas Coupland, 1991, *Generation X: Tales for an Accelerated Culture*, London: Abacus, p. 5.

6 Coupland, *Generation X*, p. 98.

7 Craig Bartholomew, 'Christ and Consumerism: An Introduction', in Craig Bartholomew and Thorsten Moritz (eds), 2000, *Christ and Consumerism*, Carlisle: Paternoster, 2000, p. 2, quoting Steven Miles, 1998, *Consumerism as a Way of Life*, London: Sage, p. 1.

8 Andrew Walker, 1996, *Telling the Story: Gospel, Mission and Culture*, London: SPCK, p. 143.

9 John Stott, 'Conflicting Gospels', *Church of England Newspaper* (8 December 1989), 6.

10 John Drane, 2000, *Cultural Change and Biblical Faith: The Future of the Church – Biblical and Missiological Essays for the New Century*, Milton Keynes: Authentic, p. 179.

11 Friedrich Nietzsche, 'On Truth and Lie in an Extra-Moral Sense', in Walter Kaufman, (ed. & tr.), 1976, *The Portable Nietzsche*, New York: Penguin, pp. 46–7.

12 Friedrich Nietzsche, 1882, *The Gay Science*, tr. Walter Kaufman, New York: Random House, 1974, Section 125 'The Madman'.

13 Friedrich Nietzsche, 1901, *The Will to Power*, tr. Walter Kaufmann, New York: Random House, 1968, p. 291.

14 Jean-François Lyotard, 1979, *The Postmodern Condition: A Report on Knowledge*, tr. Geoffrey Bennington and Brian Massumi, Manchester: Manchester University Press, 1984, p. xxiv.

15 Lyotard, *The Postmodern Condition*, p. xxiii.

16 Lyotard, *The Postmodern Condition*, p. 82.

17 Justin Thacker, 2007, *Postmodernism and the Ethics of Knowledge*, Aldershot: Ashgate, pp. 8, 23, referring to his earlier, 'Lyotard and the Christian Metanarrative', *Faith and Philosophy* 22:3 (July 2005), 301–15.

18 Jean-François Lyotard, 1985, *Just Gaming*, Manchester: Manchester University Press, p. 99, and elsewhere.

19 James K. A. Smith, 2006, *Who's Afraid of Postmodernism?* Grand Rapids, MI: Baker, p. 72.

20 Lyotard, *Just Gaming*, p. 74.

21 Michel Foucault, 1975, *Discipline and Punish: The Birth of the Prison*, tr. Alan Sheridan, New York: Vintage, 1977, p. 28.

22 Foucault, *Discipline and Punish*, p. 75.

23 Foucault, *Discipline and Punish*, p. 194.

24 Foucault, *Discipline and Punish*, p. 77.

25 Stanley Grenz, 1996, *A Primer on Postmodernism*, Grand Rapids, MI: Eerdmans, p. 139.

26 Jacques Derrida, 1967, *Of Grammatology*, tr. Gayatri Spivak, Baltimore, MD: Johns Hopkins Press, 1976, p. 158.

27 Smith, *Who's Afraid of Postmodernism?* p. 39.

28 Jacques Derrida, 'Deconstruction and the Other', in Richard Kearney (ed.), 1984, *Dialogues with Contemporary Thinkers*, Manchester: Manchester University Press, pp. 105–26 [at 123].

29 Smith, *Who's Afraid of Postmodernism?* p. 51. He even likens this to the Old Testament concern for widows, orphans and strangers.

30 Chomsky seems mainly to take issue with the French-ness of the main postmodern philosophers. See a number of talks and recorded seminars on YouTube.

31 Kevin Hart, 2004, *Postmodernism*, London: One World, p. 13.

32 Kenny, *The History of Western Philosophy*, pp. 824–8.

33 William James, 1907, *Pragmatism*, London: Longmans, Green & Co., p. 51.

34 James, *Pragmatism*, p. 46, citing Pierce.

35 An excellent six-part summary of pragmatism's tenets can be found in the *Encyclopaedia Britannica*: www.britannica.com/topic/pragmatism-philosophy of which my four points are an adaptation.

36 Thacker, *Postmodernism and the Ethics of Theological Knowledge*, pp. 7–9.

37 Richard Rorty, 1999, *Philosophy and Social Hope*, London: Penguin, p. xxiv–xxv.

38 C. S. Peirce, 'Why Study Logic?' in *The Collected Papers of Charles Sanders Peirce* (8 vols), vol. 2, para. 135. Discussed in Paul Murray, 2004, *Reason, Truth and Theology in Pragmatist Perspective*, Leuven: Peeters, p. 6.

39 Richard Rorty, 1989, *Contingency, Irony, and Solidarity*, Cambridge: Cambridge University Press, p. xvi.

40 Cornel West, 2000, *The Cornel West Reader*, New York: Basic Civitas, p. 183.

41 Thacker, *Postmodernism and the Ethics of Theological Knowledge*, p. 9.

42 Alasdair MacIntyre, 2007, *After Virtue: A Study in Moral Theory*, 3rd edition, Notre Dame, IN: University of Notre Dame Press.

43 MacIntyre, *After Virtue*, p. 8.

44 MacIntyre, *After Virtue*, p. 11.

45 Hauerwas, *The Peaceable Kingdom*, p. 76.

46 Hauerwas, *The Peaceable Kingdom*, p. 16.

47 Hollinger, *Choosing the Good*, p. 53, citing Hauerwas, *The Peaceable Kingdom*, p. 126.

48 Merold Westphal, 2001, *Overcoming Onto-Theology: Toward a Postmodern Christian Faith*, New York: Fordham University Press, p. 219.

49 Jacques Derrida, 'Force of Law: The Mystical Foundation of Authority', in Drucilla Cornell, Michel Rosenfeld and David Gray Carlson (eds), 1992, *Deconstruction and the Possibility of Justice*, New York: Routledge, p. 19. Cited in Westphal, *Overcoming Onto-Theology*, p. 219.

50 Derrida, 'Force of Law', p. 15.

51 Derrida, 'Force of Law', p. 20.

52 Westphal, *Overcoming Onto-Theology*, p. 228.

53 Westphal, *Overcoming Onto-Theology*, p. 228.

54 Dave Tomlinson, 1995, *The Post-Evangelical*, London: Triangle.

55 Eddie Gibbs and Ryan Bolger, 2006, *Emerging Churches: Creating Christian Community in Postmodern Cultures*, Grand Rapids, MI: Baker, p. 17.

56 Gibbs and Bolger, *Emerging Churches*, p. 19.

57 Brian McLaren, 'The Emergent Mystique', *Christianity Today* (November 2004), p. 39. Brian McLaren's first book was his famous, 2001, *A New Kind of Christian: A Tale of Two Friends on a Journey*, San Francisco, CA: Jossey-Bass.

58 David Mappes, 'A New Kind of Christian: A Review', *Bibliotheca Sacra* 161 (July–September 2004), 291.

59 McLaren, *A New Kind of Christian*, p. 18.

60 Brian McLaren, 2011, *A New Kind of Christianity: Ten questions that are Transforming the Faith*, London: Hodder & Stoughton, p. 14.

61 Hart, *Postmodernism*, p. 14.

62 John Milbank, Foreword to James K. A. Smith, 2004, *Introducing Radical Orthodoxy: Mapping a Post-Secular Theology*, Grand Rapids, MI: Baker, p. 12.

63 John Milbank, 1990, *Theology and Social Theory: Beyond Secular Reason*, Oxford: Blackwell, p. 9.

64 Smith, *Introducing Radical Orthodoxy*, p. 57.

65 Graham Ward, 2003, *True Religion*, Oxford: Blackwell, p. 115.

66 Smith describes Milbank's *Theology and Social Theory* as a kind of 'postmodern translation of Augustine's *City of God*', citing especially *Theology and Social Theory*, pp. 380ff.

67 Simon Oliver, 2013, *Philosophy, God and Motion*, London: Routledge.

68 Charles Taylor, 2007, *A Secular Age*, Cambridge, MA: Harvard University Press, p. 25.

Postscript

Before I conclude, it seems that a postscript is in order. I have brought this on myself by insinuating that both the analytic tradition and postmodernism are on the wane. I would first qualify that by pointing out that the influence of both philosophical movements is still very much with us. Wittgenstein and Foucault are both still being thickly referenced in all manner of academic discourse. But I have set myself up to need to say something about what is going on in philosophy now. What is the latest thing? As Christians, we want to know. Is something brewing within philosophy departments now that is about to spew its contents into the world of popular culture? Can we ready ourselves in some way?

Though it is probably only beginning to be felt within the discipline, the impact of globalization on philosophy looks set to increase significantly. Increasing numbers of non-Western philosophers are now appearing in various 'Top Ten' lists of rising stars in philosophy today.[1] There is an already dated Handbook to introduce readers to this new phenomenon.[2] This dimension adds to the already pronounced advocacy emphasis to so much recent philosophy, with non-Western philosophers bringing a postcolonial perspective. Ghanaian-born Kwame Appiah is probably the most famous non-Western philosopher today and speaks to issues not only of colonialism but of identity, sexuality and gender. And among Western philosophers too there is a growing tendency to speak directly and in an involved way about gender, otherness and politics. For the first time, a number of women philosophers such as Martha Nussbaum, Gayatri Spivak and Judith Butler have become prominent. The general trend is away from armchair philosophy towards a more involved and interested approach to thought. Philosophers who speak out on real social justice issues tend to be the ones who enjoy celebrity status today.

So, it is very much the moralistic stream that, having begun as a trickle within an otherwise somewhat amoral postmodernism, has now flooded its banks and is the resounding note common to most philosophical pronouncements uttered from platforms today.

Reflection

The shrill tones of confused assertion and counter assertion that Alasdair MacIntyre said had begun to characterize moral debates look set to be replaced by strident moral certainty of a generally liberal hue and shared by a large consensus of people, countered only by bigoted corners of right-wing populism. We are likely to see these values all but dominate public discourse, especially on social media. What might a Christian response to moral certainty look like?

Notes

1 E.g. *The Culture Trip*: https://theculturetrip.com/europe/united-kingdom/articles/top-10-living-philosophers/ [accessed 15 May 2018].
2 William Edelglass and Jay Garfield (eds), 2011, *The Oxford Handbook of World Philosophy*, Oxford: Oxford University Press.

Conclusion

I promised that learning philosophy would be a lens, a language and a skill. In order to see what lenses, languages and skills we have acquired, it will be good to go over the highlights. My selection of these highlights is subjective, and you may well have found other concepts and thinkers more useful, but here goes.

We were first ushered into the once-familiar world of Plato. Our ancestors found him a much more accessible critical friend than we do, and our faces frown when we encounter his theory of Forms. However, some Christian Platonists have helped us to see the significance of Plato. Uniquely of all the philosophers, he saw the world as consisting not only of mind and matter but also a transcendent realm. In fact, he concluded that, given the fact that everything we see in this life is not fully what it ought to be, it is to this transcendent realm that we should be looking for an understanding of the fully real, the definitively real. He believed this realm could be accessed through Socratic dialogue in which presuppositions are pressed more and more, and through the act of contemplation in which the mind reattunes itself to the realm where it truly belongs. For Plato, our heads are in heaven, and belong there, while our bodies are tied to earth. Aside from the silly dualisms between the spiritual and the bodily that all too easily result, Plato seems to give to Christianity for the first millennium or so of its existence a helpful way of making itself intelligible to the world and to itself.

Understanding Plato, then, gives us at least two things. It gives us a lens and skill with which to grapple with the aspect of theology that students typically find the hardest or remotest: patristic theology, the theology of the church fathers, all of whom were steeped in various kinds of Platonism and were trying to see Christian faith in the light of it but also in contrast to it. Second, Christian Platonism gives us a potential answer to Taylor's immanent frame of secular culture. It gives us language to speak of a transcendent realm.

Aristotle gives us an ancient basis for asserting the ethical system that has the most claim to being truly Christian: the virtue ethic, the inward ethic of the Sermon on the Mount and the Spirit-led lifestyle of Paul's letters. He is also the one who started the conversation about logic, beginning to lay the kinds of ground rules that we find laid out in any number of study skills guides or guides to critical thinking that abound today. He also starts many other conversations not covered in this book such as the importance of friendship and what happiness is. He is the go-to person whenever we want to begin to talk intelligently about the things that matter to people. He gives us a shared language about such things, language emanating from an ancient philosopher whose name is still respected by believers and unbelievers alike. Using that shared language, we can start to introduce the Christian perspective on such important matters.

Alister McGrath would be the most prominent today of a number of theologians that have discovered that the philosophy of science – which, in Chapter 3, we explored via the thinking of the early modern philosophers – can impart a skill, a methodology for thinking about God. Science remains the most illustrious of academic pursuits, earning continued reverence and awe from the general public as they welcome ever more advanced technological devices into their homes and pockets and hear with delight about the latest medical breakthrough. The thinking behind it might lift the practice of theological thinking to new heights, taking the guesswork out of theology and making it efficacious. And knowing the language of the philosophy of science seems to be a prerequisite to being able to engage in the ethical ramifications of scientific research.

When we came to idealism, we were back in the world of the strange. Like Platonism, idealism has not been a widely held position for a long time, and there is some difficulty in trying to imagine how anyone ever could have not believed in matter and preferred to see everything as a universal Mind or Spirit. But we got ourselves into the shoes of those who sincerely believed this and discovered that some devout Christians held to an idealist worldview. For Jonathan Edwards, the revival veteran, an intimately present and involved God was the only God that he could worship. We pondered whether idealism in fact opens our eyes to an aspect of the biblical worldview not otherwise visible. Its writers assumed that God was actively involved in all he had made. Perhaps some kind of moderate idealism helps to reinstate the doctrine of the providence of God and re-enchants our world with the expectation of his presence.

Existentialism threw out all of that idealism but gave us a few useful things in its place. Many theologians have found immense resources within existentialism. It appeals to us because of its way of always coming back to the issues of life and death, freedom and choice. These are the very things that preachers have always built their sermons around and pressed their listeners for a verdict on. Bultmann builds his theology around this very thing, making Christianity all about that call to authentic existence. However, as a language that resonates with those outside the church, the language of existentialism has somewhat lost its urgency. People are more comfortable now than they were in Sartre's day. People who have not lived through the Cuban Missile Crisis do not feel the threat of sudden death quite so keenly as that generation did.

Almost the opposite style of philosophy to existentialism was analytic philosophy, the practice of logic-chopping and atomizing, of responding to every question with the retort 'It depends what you mean', of reducing logical propositions to mathematical equations and claiming that this made them clearer!

Initially, the flourishing of analytic philosophy was only bad news for faith, and Bertrand Russell was extremely dismissive of religion. Then came the later Wittgenstein with his talk of pictorial language that could sometimes carry the whole weight of meaning without needing to be put another way and of language-games in which it is only the community that must use a given discourse that is entitled to judge the correct or incorrect use of their terms. These opened up a chink of light to theology and led to a brief linguistic turn but perhaps most importantly to the advent of postliberal theology, theology that was recovering its nerve. Using language well is a skill that this tradition within philosophy can help to impart to us, a skill that is perhaps most important when dealing with biblical texts, filled as they are with pictorial language. And understanding language-games allows us to engage with real respect in ecumenical work.

Lastly, even postmodernism can teach us much. Its nihilistic outcomes give us the chance to be better than merely faithful consumers and obedient hedonists. We can show a higher principle by living in a way that is not like that. However, postmodernism's moralistic outcomes are a lot more challenging. We are ahead of the game with nihilism but always behind the curve with alterity. It is difficult to outdo the world's preoccupation with otherness at the moment, and, for the moment at least, alterity is the moral benchmark by which the world judges the church. Mostly, it finds the church wanting. Tomorrow the benchmark might be something else, so wisdom is needed. But thanks to studying philosophy, at least we can speak the language and understand the lens through which we are being judged.

I encourage you to continue the dialogue with philosophy and keep looking through its lenses, using its language and applying its skills.

Select Bibliography

Plato

Augustine of Hippo, *Confessions*, tr. P. S. Pine-Coffin, London: Penguin, 1961.

Carey, Philip, 'The Mythic Reality of the Autonomous Individual', *Zygon* 46:1 (March 2011), 121–34.

Cooper, John (ed.), 1997, *Plato: Complete Works*, Indianapolis, IN: Hackett.

Corrigan, Kevin, 'Mysticism in Plotinus, Proclus, Gregory of Nyssa, and Pseudo-Dionysius', *The Journal of Religion* 76:1 (1996), 28–42.

Doering, E. Jane and Eric Springsted (eds), 2004, *The Christian Platonism of Simone Weil*, Notre Dame, IN: University of Notre Dame Press.

Fiebleman, James, 1959, *Religious Platonism*, Westport, CT: Greenwood Press.

Gaskin, J. C. A. (ed.), 1996, *Thomas Hobbes, Leviathan*, Oxford: Oxford University Press.

Gerson, L. P., 1990, *God and Greek Philosophy: Studies in the Early History of Natural Theology*, London: Routledge.

Hare, R. M., 1982, *Plato*, Oxford: Oxford University Press.

Hill, Jonathan, 2003, *The History of Christian Thought*, Oxford: Lion.

Inge, W. R., 1926, *The Platonic Tradition in English Religious Thought*, London: Longmans.

Kenny, Anthony, 2010, *A New History of Western Philosophy*, Oxford: Oxford University Press.

Luibheid, Colm (ed. & tr.), 1987, *Pseudo-Dionysius: The Complete Works*, New York: Paulist Press.

Mays, Wolfe, 1977, *Whitehead's Philosophy of Science and Metaphysics: An Introduction to His Thought*, The Hague: Martinus Nijhoff.

McIntosh, Mark Allen, 'Newman and Christian Platonism in Britain', *The Journal of Religion* 91:3 (2011), 344–64.

Mesle, C. Robert, 2009, *Process-Relational Philosophy: An Introduction to Alfred North Whitehead*, West Conshohocken, PA: Templeton Foundation Press.

Plotinus, *The Enneads*, ed. John Dillon, tr. Stephen McKenna, London: Penguin, 1991.

Sadler, Ted, 'Apophaticism and Early Christian Theology', *Phronema* 7 (1992), 13–22.

Turner, John, 'The Gnostic Sethians and Middle Platonism: Interpretations of the *Timaeus* and *Parmenides*', *Vigiliae Christianae* 60 (2006), 9–64.

Tyson, Paul, 2014, *Return to Reality: Christian Platonism for our Times*, Eugene, OR: Cascade.

Wassermann, Emma, 'The Death of the Soul in Romans 7: Revisiting Paul's Anthropology in Light of Hellenistic Moral Psychology', *Journal of Biblical Literature* 126:4 (2007), 793–816.

Wassermann, Emma, 'Paul Among the Philosophers: The Case of Sin in Romans 6–8', *Journal for the Study of the New Testament* 30:4 (2008), 387–415.

Wassmer, Thomas, 'The Trinitarian Theology of Augustine and his Debt to Plotinus', *Harvard Theological Review* 53:4 (1937), 261–8.

Weil, Simone, 1957, *Intimations of Christianity Among the Ancient Greeks*, tr. E. C. Geissbuhler, London: Routledge & Kegan Paul.

Whitehead, Alfred North, 1929, *Process and Reality: An Essay in Cosmology*, corrected edition, ed. David Ray Griffin and Donald W. Sherburne, New York: Free Press, 1979.

Aristotle

Aristotle, *Eudemian Ethics*, in *Athenian Constitution. Eudemian Ethics. Virtues and Vices*, tr. H. Rackham, Loeb Classical Library 285, Cambridge, MA: Harvard University Press, 1935.

Aristotle, *Generation of Animals*, tr. A. L. Peck, Loeb Classical Library 366, Cambridge, MA: Harvard University Press, 1942.

Barnes, Jonathan, 2000, *Aristotle: A Very Short Introduction*, Oxford: Oxford University Press.

Bostock, David, 2000, *Aristotle's Ethics*, Oxford: Oxford University Press.

Brink-Budgen, Roy van den, 2010, *Critical Thinking for Students*, Oxford: How To Books.

Brown, Colin, 1990, *Christianity and Western Thought*, Vol. 1. Downers Grove, IL: IVP.

Carré, Meyrick, 1946, *Realists and Nominalists*, Oxford: Oxford University Press.

Dyke, Christina van, 'An Aristotelian Theory of Divine Illumination: Robert Grosseteste's *Commentary on the Posterior Analytics*', *British Journal for the History of Philosophy* 17:4 (2009), 685–704.

Falcon, Andrea, 'Aristotle on Causality', http://plato.stanford.edu/entries/aristotle-causality/#FouCau

Haas, Frans, 'Did Plotinus and Porphyry Disagree on Aristotle's Categories?' *Phronesis* 46:4 (2001), 492–526.

Harrington, Daniel and James Keenan, 2010, *Paul and Virtue Ethics: Building Bridges Between New Testament Studies and Moral Theology*, Lanham, MD: Sheed & Ward.

Jacobs, Jonathan, 2002, *Dimensions of Moral Theory: An Introduction to Metaethics and Moral Psychology*, Oxford: Blackwell.

Lear, Gabriel, 2004, *Happy Lives and the Highest Good: An Essay on Aristotle's Nicomachean Ethics*, Princeton, NJ: Princeton University Press.

Lennox, James, 'Aristotle's Biology', http://plato.stanford.edu/entries/aristotle-biology/

Pangle, Lorraine, 2003, *Aristotle and the Philosophy of Friendship*, Cambridge: Cambridge University Press.

Ross, David, 1923, *Aristotle*, 6th edition, London: Routledge, 1995.

Shand, John, 2014, *Philosophy and Philosophers: An Introduction to Philosophy*, London: Routledge.

Shields, Christopher, 2014, *Aristotle*, 2nd edition, London: Routledge.

Studtmann, Paul, 'Aristotle's Categories', http://plato.stanford.edu/contents.html

Early Modern Philosophy and Scientific Method

Ayer, A. J., 1956, *The Problem of Knowledge*, London: Pelican.

Balthasar, Hans Urs von, 1991, *The Glory of the Lord: A Theological Aesthetics V: The Realm of Metaphysics in the Modern Age*, tr. O. Davies, Edinburgh: T & T Clark.

Banner, Michael, 2009, *Christian Ethics: A Brief History*, Oxford: Wiley.

Beer, Peter, 2010, *An Introduction to Bernard Lonergan: Exploring Lonergan's Approach to the Great Philosophical Questions*, Glen Waverley, Australia: Sid Harta.

Bentham, Jeremy, 1789, *The Principles of Morals and Legislation*, Darrien, CT: Hafner, 1949.

Bhaskar, Roy, 2016, *Enlightened Common Sense: The Philosophy of Critical Realism*, London: Routledge.

Bonhoeffer, Dietrich, 1937, *Creation and Fall: A Theological Exposition of Genesis 1–3*, in *Dietrich Bonhoeffer Works* Vol. 3. Minneapolis, MN: Fortress, 1997.

Brailsford, H. N. 1963, *Voltaire*, Oxford: Oxford University Press.

Brown, Colin, 1969, *Philosophy and the Christian Faith*. London: Tyndale.

Cottingham, John (ed.), 1996, *Descartes. Meditations on First Philosophy: With Selections from the Objections and Replies*, Cambridge: Cambridge University Press.

Descartes, René, 2000, *Meditations and Other Metaphysical Writings*, tr. Desmond Clarke. London: Penguin.

Galton, Francis, 'Eugenics: Its Definition, Scope and Aims', *The American Journal of Sociology* 10:1 (1904), 1–25.

Harris, John, 2004, *On Cloning*, London: Routledge.

Hogan, Edward, 'Divine Action and Divine Transcendence: John Polkinghorne and Bernard Lonergan on the Scientific Status of Theology', *Zygon* 44:3 (Sep 2009), 558–82.

John Paul II, *Evangelium Vitae* (25 March 1995). Available online at https://w2.vatican.va/content/john-paul-ii/en/encyclicals/documents/hf_jp-ii_enc_25031995_evangelium-vitae.html.

Lee, E. (ed.), 2002, *Designer Babies: Where Should We Draw the Line?* London: Hodder & Stoughton.

Lonergan, Bernard, 1957, *Insight: A Study of Human Understanding*, London: Longmans, Green & Co.

Lonergan, Bernard, 1972, *Method in Theology*, London: Darton, Longman & Todd.

McGrath, Alister, 'Profile: Thomas F. Torrance', *Epworth Review* 27:3 (July 2000), 11–15.

McGrath, Alister, 2001, *Scientific Theology 1: Nature*, Oxford: Blackwell.

McGrath, Alister, 2002, *Scientific Theology 2: Reality*, Oxford: Blackwell.

McGrath, Alister, 2006, *The Order of Things: Explorations in Scientific Theology*, Oxford: Blackwell.

McGrath, Alister, 2009, *A Fine-Tuned Universe: The Quest for God in Science and Theology*, Louisville, KY: Westminster John Knox.

Messer, Neil, 2011, *Respecting Life: Theology and Bioethics*, London: SCM.

Mill, John Stuart, 1863, *Utilitarianism*, Indianapolis: Hackett, 1979.

Nagel, Thomas, 1986, *The View from Nowhere*, Oxford: Oxford University Press.

National Commission for the Protection of Human Subjects of Biomedical and Behavioral Research, 1978, *The Belmont Report: Ethical Principles for the Protection of Human Subjects of Research*, Washington: US Printing Office. Available online at https://ia600404.us.archive.org/30/items/belmontreporteth00unit/belmontreporteth00unit.pdf [accessed 16 May 2018].

Peacocke, Arthur, 1984, *Intimations of Reality: Critical Realism in Science and Religion*, Notre Dame, IN: University of Notre Dame Press.

Peacocke, Arthur, 1990, *Theology for a Scientific Age*, Oxford: Blackwell.

Peat, Michael, 2013, *Answering Mendel's Dwarf: Thinking Theologically About Human Genetic Selection*, Oxford: Whitley Publications.

Peters, Ted, 1994, 'Genes, Theology and Social Ethics: Are we Playing God?' in Ted Peters (ed.) *Genetics: Issues of Social Justice*, Cleveland, OH: Crossroad.

Polanyi, Michael, 1958, *Personal Knowledge: Towards a Post-Critical Philosophy*, Chicago, IL: University of Chicago Press.

Sacred Congregation for the Doctrine of the Faith, 1974, *Declaration on Procured Abortion*. Available online at http://www.vatican.va/roman_curia/congregations/cfaith/documents/rc_con_cfaith_doc_19741118_declaration-abortion_en.html.

Sandel, Michael, 2007, *The Case Against Perfection: Ethics in the Age of Genetic Engineering*, Cambridge, MA: Harvard University Press.

Skene, L. and J. Thompson (eds), 2008, *The Sorting Society: The Ethics of Genetic Screening and Therapy*, Cambridge: Cambridge University Press.

Song, Robert, 2003, 'To be Willing to Kill What for all One Knows is a Person is to be Willing to Kill a Person', in Brent Waters and Ronald Cole-Turner (eds) *God and the Embryo: Religious Voices on Stem Cells and Cloning*, Washington, DC: Georgetown University Press.

Stump, J. B. and Alan G. Padgett (eds), 2012, *The Blackwell Companion to Science and Christianity*, Oxford: Blackwell.

Sutton, Agneta, 2008, *Christian Bioethics: A Guide for the Perplexed*, London: T & T Clark.

Torrance, T. F., 1969, *Theological Science*, Oxford: Oxford University Press.

Waters, Brent and Ronald Cole-Turner (eds), 2003, *God and the Embryo: Religious Voices on Stem Cells and Cloning*, Washington, DC: Georgetown University Press

Webster, J., 2005, *Confessing God*, London: T & T Clark.

Wollaston, Arthur (tr. & ed.), 1960, *Descartes Discourse on Method and other Writings*, London: Penguin.

Wright, Andrew, 2013, *Christianity and Critical Realism: Ambiguity, Truth and Theological Literacy*, London: Routledge.

Wright, N. T., 1992, *The New Testament and the People of God*, London: SPCK.

Kant and Idealism

Berkeley, George, 1901, *The Works of George Berkeley*, vol. 1, ed. A. C. Fraser, Oxford: Clarendon Press.

Braden, C. S., 1963, *Spirits in Rebellion: The Rise and Development of New Thought*, Dallas, TX: Southern Methodist University Press.

Buell, Lawrence (ed.), 2006, *The American Transcendentalists: Essential Writings*, New York: The Modern Library.

Critchley, Simon and William Schroeder (eds), 1999, *A Companion to Continental Philosophy*, Oxford: Blackwell.

DeArteaga, William, 1992, *Quenching the Spirit: Examining Centuries of Opposition to the Moving of the Holy Spirit*, Altamonte Springs, FL: Creation House.

Dresser, H. W. (ed.), 1921, *The Quimby Manuscripts*, New York: Thomas Y. Crowell.

Edwards, Jonathan, 1737, 'A Faithful Narrative of the Surprising Work of God', in Ola Winslow (ed.), 1966, *Jonathan Edwards: Basic Writings*, New York: New American Library.

Edwards, Jonathan, *The Works of Jonathan Edwards*, New Haven, CT: Yale University Press, 1957–2008.

Ellwood, R. S., 1988, *Religious and Spiritual Groups in North America*, Englewood Cliffs, NJ: Prentice Hall.

Farris, Joshua and S. Mark Hamilton (eds), 2017, *Idealism and Christian Philosophy: Idealism and Christianity*, 2 vols, London: Bloomsbury.

Fillmore, C., 1936, *Prosperity*, Kansas City, MO: Unity School of Christianity.

Foster, John, 1982, *The Case for Idealism*, London: Routledge & Kegan Paul.

Foster, John, 2000, *The Nature of Perception*, Oxford: Oxford University Press.

Foster, John, 2008, *A World for Us: The Case for Phenomenological Idealism*, Oxford: Oxford University Press.

Gura, Philip, 2008, *American Transcendentalism: A History*, New York: Hill and Wang.

Hegel, G. W. F., 1807, *The Phenomenology of Mind*, tr. J. B. Baillie, Digireads, 2009.

Kant, Immanuel, 1781, *Critique of Pure Reason*, tr. J. Meiklejohn, London: Dent, 1934.

Kant, Immanuel, 1785, *Foundations for the Metaphysics of Morals*, tr. Lewis Beck, Indianapolis, IN: Bobbs-Merrill, 1959.

Kant, Immanuel, 1790, *Critique of Judgment*, tr. Werner S. Pluhar, Indianapolis, IN: Hackett, 1987.

Marsobian, Armen and John Ryder (eds), 2003, *The Blackwell Guide to American Philosophy*, Oxford: Blackwell.

Mitchell, Robert, 2011, *The Awakening Word*, Bloomington, IN; Author House.

Neuman, H. T., 'Cultic Origins of the Word-Faith Theology within the Charismatic Movement', *Pneuma* 12:1 (1990), 32–55.

Pugh, Ben, 2017, *Bold Faith: A Closer Look at the Five Key Ideas of Charismatic Christianity*, Eugene, OR: Wipf & Stock.

Trine, Ralph Waldo, 1970, *In Tune with the Infinite*, New York: Bobbs-Merrill.

Existentialism

Allen, E. L.,1953, *Existentialism from Within*, London: Routledge.

Barth, Karl, 1962, 'Rudolf Bultmann: An Attempt to Understand Him', in Hans-Werner Bartsch (ed.), *Kerygma and Myth: A Theological Debate*, Vol. 2, tr. Reginald Fuller, London: SPCK, pp. 83–132.

Bultmann, Rudolf, 2007, *Theology of the New Testament*, Vol. 1, tr. Kendrick Grobel, Waco, TX: Baylor University Press.

Camus, Albert, 1942, *The Myth of Sisyphus*, tr. Justin O'Brien, London: Penguin.

Congdon, David, 'Is There a Kerygma in this Text? A Review Article', *Journal of Theological Interpretation* 9:2 (2015), 299–311.

Congdon, David, 2015, *The Mission of Demythologizing: Rudolf Bultmann's Dialectical Theology*, Minneapolis, MN: Fortress.

Cook, 1997, David, *Blind Alley Beliefs*, Leicester: IVP.

Cox, Claude, 'R. Bultmann: Theology of the New Testament', *Restoration Quarterly* 17 (1974), 144–61.

Fletcher, Joseph, 1966, *Situation Ethics: The New Morality*, London: SCM.

Greenway, Roger, 'Ethics of Evangelism', *Calvin Theological Journal* 28 (1993), 147–54.

Heick, Otto, 'Rudolf Bultmann Revisited', *Concordia Theological Monthly*, 41:5 (May 1970), 259–78.

Heidegger, Martin, 1927, *Being and Time*, tr. J. Macquarrie, New York: Harper & Row, 1962.

Longenecker, Bruce and Mikeal Parsons (eds), 2014, *Beyond Bultmann: Reckoning a New Testament Theology*, Waco, TX: Baylor University Press.

Magee, Bryan, 1987, *The Great Philosophers*, London: BBC Books.

Pugh, Ben, 2017, *Theology in the Contemporary World*, London: SCM.

Robinson, John A. T., 1964, *Christian Morals Today*, London: SCM.

Sartre, Jean-Paul, 1943, *Being and Nothingness*, tr. Hazel Barnes, London: Methuen, 1957.

Sartre, Jean-Paul, 1946, *Existentialism and Humanism*, tr. Philip Mairet, London: Methuen, 1948.

Schroeder, Roger 'Proclamation and Interreligious Dialogue as Prophetic Dialogue', *Missiology* 41:1 (January 2013), 50–61.

Secretariat for Non-Christians, 'The Attitude of the Church Toward the Followers of Other Religions: Reflections and Orientations on Dialogue and Mission', *Bulletin Secretariatus pro Non Christianis* 56:2 (1984), No. 29. Available online at www.shinmeizan.com/images/PDF/DialMiss.en.pdf [accessed 17 May 2018].

Shepherd, Nick and Sally Nash, 'Solid Steps on Shifting Sand: Theological Education for Work with Children, Young People and Young Adults', *Journal of Adult Theological Education* 11:1 (2014), 5–19.

Standhartinger, Angela, 2014, 'Bultmann's Theology of the New Testament in Context', in Longenecker and Parsons (eds), *Beyond Bultmann: Reckoning a New Testament Theology*, Waco, TX: Baylor University Press, pp. 235–55.

Taylor, Mark Kline, 1987, *Paul Tillich: Theologian of the Boundaries*, London: Collins.

Thiessen, Elmer, 2011, *The Ethics of Evangelism*, Downers Grove, IL: IVP Academic.

Thomas, J. Heywood, 2000, *Paul Tillich*, London: Continuum, 2000.

Tillich, Paul, 'The Problem of Theological Method', *Journal of Religion* 27:1 (January 1947), 16–26.

Tillich, Paul, 1957, *Systematic Theology*, Vol. 2, London: SCM.

Tillson, John, 'Elmer Thiessen and the Ethics of Evangelism', *Journal of Education and Christian Belief* 17:2 (2013), 243–58.

Troxel, A. Craig, '"All Things to All People": Justin Martyr's Apologetical Method', *Fides et Historia* 27:2 (1995), 23–43.

Wartenberg, Thomas, 2010, *Existentialism*, London: Oneworld.

Analytic Philosophy

Ashford, Bruce, 'Wittgenstein's Theologians? A Survey of Ludwig Wittgenstein's Impact on Theology', *Journal of the Evangelical Theological Society* 50:2 (June 2007), 357–75.

Austin, J. L.,1962, *How to Do Things With Words*, Cambridge, MA: Harvard University Press.

Ayer, A. J., 1946, *Language, Truth and Logic*, 2nd edition, London: Penguin.

Brown, David, 2008, *God and Mystery in Words: Experience through Metaphor and Drama*, Oxford: Oxford University Press.

Crisp, Oliver and Michael Rea (eds), 2009, *Analytic Theology: New Essays in the Philosophy of Theology*, Oxford: Oxford University Press.

Hauerwas, Stanley, 1981, *Community of Character*, Notre Dame, IN: University of Notre Dame Press.

Hauerwas, Stanley, 1983, *The Peaceable Kingdom: A Primer in Christian Ethics*, Notre Dame, IN: University of Notre Dame Press.

Hornle, R. F. Alfred 'The Religious Aspect of Bertrand Russell's Philosophy', *Harvard Theological Review* 9:2 (April 1916), 157–89.

Johnson, Eric, 'Rewording the Justification/Sanctification Relation with Some Help from Speech Act Theory', *Journal of the Evangelical Theological Society* 54:4 (December 2011), 767–85.

Jones, W. T., 1969, *A History of Western Philosophy: Kant to Wittgenstein and Sartre*, 2nd edition, New York: Harcourt, Brace & World.

Nielsen, Kai, 'Wittgensteinian Fideism', *Philosophy* 42 (1967), 191–209.

Lindbeck, George, 1984, *The Nature of Doctrine: Religion and Theology in a Postliberal Age*, London: SPCK.

Macquarrie, John, 1967, *God-Talk: An Examination of the Language and Logic of Theology*, London: SCM.

McGuinness, Brian (ed.), 1979, *Wittgenstein and the Vienna Circle: Conversations Recorded by Friedrich Waismann*, Oxford: Blackwell.

Monk, Ray, 1990, *Ludwig Wittgenstein: The Duty of Genius*, New York: Penguin.

Moore, G. E., 'The Refutation of Idealism', *Mind* 12 (1903), 433–53.

Nygren, Anders, 1972, *Meaning and Method: Prolegomena to a Scientific Philosophy of Religion and a Scientific Theology*, tr. Philip Watson, Philadelphia, PA: Fortress.

Ott, Craig, 'The Power of Biblical Metaphors for the Contextualized Communication of the Gospel', *Missiology* 42:4 (2014), 357–74.

Plantinga, Alvin, 1967, *God and Other Minds*, Ithaca, NY: Cornell University Press.

Popper, Karl, 1959, *The Logic of Scientific Discovery*, New York: Basic Books.

Quine, W. V. O., 1953, *From a Logical Point of View: Nine Logico-Philosophical Essays*, Cambridge, MA: Harvard University Press.

Ramsey, Ian, 1957, *Religious Language*, London: SCM.

Ricoeur, Paul 'The Metaphorical Process', *Semeia* 4 (1975), 75–106.

Russell, Bertrand, 1945, *A History of Western Philosophy*, London: Allen & Unwin.

Russell, Bertrand, 1959, *My Philosophical Development*, London: Unwin, 1959.

Russell, Bertrand, 1967, *The Autobiography of Bertrand Russell, 1872–1916*, London: Allen and Unwin.

Searle, John, 1998, *Mind, Language, and Society: Philosophy in a Real World*, New York: Basic Books.

Soskice, Janet Martin, 1985, *Metaphor and Religious Language*, Oxford: Clarendon.

Swinburne, Richard, 1977, *The Coherence of Theism*, Oxford: Clarendon.

Weigel, Arnold, 'A Critique of Bertrand Russell's Position', *Bulletin of the Evangelical Theological Society* 8:4 (January 1965), 139–58.

Williams-Tinajero, Lace Marie, 2011, *The Reshaped Mind: Searle, the Biblical Writers, and Christ's Blood*, Leiden: Brill.

Wittgenstein, Ludwig, 1922, *Tractatus Logico-Philosophicus*, London: Kegan Paul.

Wittgenstein, Ludwig, 1960, *The Blue and Brown Books*, New York: Harper & Row.

Wittgenstein, Ludwig, 1966, 'Lecture on Religious Belief', in Cyril Barrett (ed.) *Wittgenstein: Lectures and Conversations on Aesthetics, Psychology and religious Belief*, Berkeley, CA: University of California Press, pp. 53–72.

Wittgenstein, Ludwig, 1998, *Culture and Value*, revised edition, Oxford: Blackwell.

Wood, William, 'On the New Analytic Theology, or: The Road Less Traveled', *Journal of the American Academy of Religion* 77:4 (December 2009), 941–60.

Postmodernism

Bartholomew, Craig and Thorsten Moritz (eds), 2000, *Christ and Consumerism*, Carlisle: Paternoster, 2000.

Cook, David, 1996, *Blind Alley Beliefs*, Leicester: IVP.

Coupland, Douglas, 1991, *Generation X: Tales for an Accelerated Culture*, London: Abacus.

Delanty, Gerard, 2000, *Modernity and Postmodernity: Knowledge, Power and the Self*, London: Sage.

Derrida, Jacques, 1967, *Of Grammatology*, tr. Gayatri Spivak, Baltimore, MD: Johns Hopkins Press, 1976.

Derrida, Jacques, 1984, 'Deconstruction and the Other', in Richard Kearney (ed.), *Dialogues with Contemporary Thinkers*, Manchester: Manchester University Press, pp. 105–26.

Derrida, Jacques, 1992, 'Force of Law: The Mystical Foundation of Authority', in Drucilla Cornell, Michel Rosenfeld and David Gray Carlson (eds), *Deconstruction and the Possibility of Justice*, New York: Routledge, pp. 3–67.

Drane, John, 2000, *Cultural Change and Biblical Faith: The Future of the Church – Biblical and Missiological Essays for the New Century*, Milton Keynes: Authentic.

Foucault, Michel, 1975, *Discipline and Punish: The Birth of the Prison*, tr. Alan Sheridan, New York: Vintage, 1977.

Gibbs, Eddie and Ryan Bolger, 2006, *Emerging Churches: Creating Christian Community in Postmodern Cultures*, Grand Rapids, MI: Baker.

Grenz, Stanley, 1996, *A Primer on Postmodernism*, Grand Rapids, MI: Eerdmans.

Guinness, Os, 2000, *Time for Truth*, Grand Rapids, MI: Baker.

Hart, Kevin, 2004, *Postmodernism*, London: One World.

Hauerwas, Stanley, 1983, *The Peaceable Kingdom: A Primer in Christian Ethics*, Notre Dame, IN: University of Notre Dame Press.

James, William, 1907, *Pragmatism*, London: Longmans, Green & Co.

Jencks, C. (ed.), 1992, *The Post-Modern Reader*, New York: St Martin's Press.

Kaufman (ed. & tr.), 1976, *The Portable Nietzsche*, New York: Penguin.

Lyotard, Jean-François, 1979, *The Postmodern Condition: A Report on Knowledge*, tr. Geoffrey Bennington and Brian Massumi, Manchester: Manchester University Press, 1984.

Lyotard, Jean-François, 1983, *The Differend: Phrases in Dispute*, tr. Georges Van Den Abbeele, Manchester: Manchester University Press, 1988.

Lyotard, Jean-François, 1985, *Just Gaming*, tr. Wlad Godzich, Manchester: Manchester University Press.

MacIntyre, Alasdair, 2007, *After Virtue: A Study in Moral Theory*, 3rd edition, Notre Dame, IN: University of Notre Dame Press.

McKnight, Scot, 'Five Streams of the Emerging Church', *Christianity Today* (19 January 2007). Available online at www.christianitytoday.com/ct/2007/february/11.35.html.

McLaren, Brian, 2001, *A New Kind of Christian: A Tale of Two Friends on a Journey*, San Francisco, CA: Jossey-Bass.

McLaren, Brian, 2011, *A New Kind of Christianity: Ten Questions that are Transforming the Faith*, London: Hodder & Stoughton.

Milbank, John, 1990, *Theology and Social Theory: Beyond Secular Reason*, Oxford: Blackwell.

Milbank, John, 2004, 'Foreword' to James K. A. Smith, *Introducing Radical Orthodoxy: Mapping a Post-Secular Theology*, Grand Rapids, MI: Baker.

Miles, Steven, 1998, *Consumerism as a Way of Life*, London: Sage.

Murray, Paul, 2004, *Reason, Truth and Theology in Pragmatist Perspective*, Leuven: Peeters.

Nietzsche, Friedrich, 1882, *The Gay Science*, tr. Walter Kaufman, New York: Random House, 1974.

Nietzsche, Friedrich, 1901, *The Will to Power*, tr. Walter Kaufmann, New York: Random House, 1968.

Peirce, C. S. 1992–99, *The Essential Peirce* (2 vols), Bloomington, IN: Indiana University Press.

Rorty, Richard, 1989, *Contingency, Irony, and Solidarity*, Cambridge: Cambridge University Press.

Rorty, Richard, 1999, *Philosophy and Social Hope*, London: Penguin.

Smith, James K. A., 2006, *Who's Afraid of Postmodernism?* Grand Rapids, MI: Baker.

Starkey, Mike, 1997, *God, Sex and Generation X*, London: Triangle SPCK.

Stott, John, 'Conflicting Gospels', *Church of England Newspaper* (8 December 1989), 6.

Taylor, Charles, 2007, *A Secular Age*, Cambridge, MA: Harvard University Press.

Thacker, Justin, 'Lyotard and the Christian Metanarrative', *Faith and Philosophy* 22:3 (July 2005), 301–15.

Thacker, Justin, 2007, *Postmodernism and the Ethics of Knowledge*, Aldershot: Ashgate.

Tomlinson, Dave, 1995, *The Post-Evangelical*, London: Triangle.

Walker, Andrew, 1996, *Telling the Story: Gospel, Mission and Culture*, London: SPCK.

Ward, Graham, 2003, *True Religion*, Oxford: Blackwell.

West, Cornel, 2000, *The Cornel West Reader*, New York: Basic Civitas.

Westphal, Merold, 2001, *Overcoming Onto-Theology: Toward a Postmodern Christian Faith*, New York: Fordham University Press.

Index of Names and Subjects